Double Crossed

DOUBLEDAY

New York · London · Toronto · Sydney · Auckland

Double Crossed

Uncovering the
Catholic Church's Betrayal
of American Nuns

KENNETH A.
BRIGGS

PUBLISHED BY DOUBLEDAY

Copyright © 2006 by Kenneth A. Briggs

All Rights Reserved

Published in the United States by Doubleday, an imprint of The Doubleday Broadway
Publishing Group, a division of Random House, Inc., New York.
www.doubleday.com

DOUBLEDAY and the portrayal of an anchor with a dolphin are registered trademarks
of Random House, Inc.

Book design by Maria Carella

Title page photo: Sami Sarkis/Photodisc/Getty Images

Cataloging-in-Publication Data is on file with the Library of Congress.

ISBN-13: 978-0-385-51636-5
ISBN-10: 0-385-51636-3

PRINTED IN THE UNITED STATES OF AMERICA

1   3   5   7   9   10   8   6   4   2

First Edition

To Matthew and Joanna
In Memoriam
Jonah, Jesse, Kleone, and Isabelle

Contents

NO FIGURE HAS etched a more indelible impression on the nation's psyche than the nun. A vivid picture of the sister wrapped in a mysterious bundle of wool, with only a cameo of her face showing through, remains deeply embedded in the mind's eye of Catholics and non-Catholics alike. Sisters are the stuff of legend, fixtures in a cascade of plays, movies, television shows, Xerox commercials, and endless kitsch. Businesses crank out dolls, hand puppets, jewelry, T-shirts, and other products in their image. Some of these items evoke fond memories; others invite ridicule. Meanwhile, most nuns these days have moved so far from that portrayal that connections between the past and the present are often difficult to trace. Nearly everything from the old days—housing, work, prayer, dress—has been drastically altered.

But the specter of most sisters in street clothes these days does not easily displace the old larger-than-life picture of Sister Benedict swathed in a graceful uniform—itself modeled on the street clothes of eighteenth-century widows of eastern Europe. The fact that most Catholic sisters now work largely outside Church institutions has done little to curb the old-fashioned, in-house depictions such as are found in the films *Sister Act* and *Agnes of God*, in which nuns remain in fanciful, antiquated convents of yesteryear. An updated version occasionally does get through, notably the movie based on Sister Helen Prejean's book *Dead Man Walking*, the story of her ministry to a death-row inmate. It was by far the best profile yet of the contemporary sister.

Image, of course, is crucial in the sisters' struggle to stay alive. Only half a century ago, nuns were clearly set apart from the world behind walls, committed to a monastic schedule from sunup to sundown, combining prayer with a rigorous day of teaching or ministering to the sick. That image has been swept away by immense changes seemingly approved by the Church and enthusiastically embraced by the sisters. Communities cannot live off the nostalgia, nor do they want to. A new image has yet to replace the old one and time is running out.

Though the terms "nun" and "sister" are now used interchangeably (along with the more outdated and confusing word "religious"), until the last few decades these terms held sharply distinct meanings. Nuns were the insiders, those who lived in canonical cloisters practicing contemplation and rarely if ever venturing outside. Their lives were carefully orchestrated and always under the authority of a superior. Pope Boniface VIII way back in 1298 had issued a bull insisting that true nuns be confined to cloisters, though the same restriction was never imposed on male orders.

"Sisters" were defined as those who weren't bound by strict cloister, who left their convents to work in Church institutions such as schools and hospitals. Without the sisters, the American Catholic Church would never have been built and the world's largest private school system would never have taken root. Until early in the twentieth century, the existence of these "noncanonical" women was tolerated but they were not equal to the orders of nuns.

Over time, nuns have been revered, feared, and sometimes loathed by Catholics with long and sometimes hyperbolic memories. Nearly every Catholic school graduate taught by "the sisters" loved and admired some and steered clear of others. The "mean nun" story has become a genre, featuring the ruler-wielding, ear-yanking sisters in whom the mercy of God was undetectable. As a variety of urban legends, these tales are sometimes gross exaggerations and often told secondhand, or further down the line, as if they had been suffered by the tellers themselves. While inexcusable meanness certainly existed, it existed in a context in which parents expected nuns to both infuse and enforce a Catholic culture that nuns had not, for the most part, designed.

It was a tall order. Classes were often bursting at the seams and resources were thin. Most of the sisters appear to have managed well, even admirably, but there were misfits, some of them emotionally unstable, who were harsh and punishing. Given the otherworldly cast of their role, when violence erupted it was all the more memorable.

A shocking picture of another kind emerged in 1985 when the *Wall Street Journal* reported that legions of retired nuns were suffering because their communities (also known as congregations) were too short of funds to provide adequate support. Some nuns, the *Wall Street Journal* said, were actually living in poverty, on food stamps. The newspaper set the amount needed to meet the deficit in retirement needs at $2 billion. That total has since swollen to $6 billion. For centuries, communities had been financially independent of dioceses and other Church structures, scraping by because there were enough sisters contributing the token wages they earned mainly as teachers and nurses. But something had changed since Vatican II: there were fewer women entering convents, and of those who remained fewer were bringing in income; at the same time, more and more nuns were retired.

The system had worked only so long as the active workers could carry the retirees. But now the system had collapsed. Some relief arrived in 1971 when the U.S. Congress allowed nuns to apply for Social Security for the first time. Communities were required to make initial copayments in order to trigger the flow of government checks. For some, that demand became a severe financial hardship. Even then, Social Security didn't solve the problem. A nun retired after a lifetime of service to the Church needed more than a Social Security check to live on. National drives to aid the retirees receive overwhelming support, most notably the bishops' appeal, which nets more than twice as much as any other collection in the U.S. Church, but even with this generosity the funds put only a tiny dent in the deficit.

Though I have written about American religion for decades, I have paid too little attention to the Catholic sisterhood, an omission that reflects a larger and longer tradition of bypassing women's history. While the nuns were central to the story of American Catholicism and were key in showing the nation's women the possibilities of assuming leadership positions in society, they have been largely overlooked or ignored by historians and journalists. In part, this neglect has been the result of the nuns' exclusion from positions of power within the Church. Their subjugation to a male clerical order, I believe, not only kept them out of the public eye but also ultimately crushed their efforts to refashion themselves boldly and creatively. Much of the demise of religious orders at the dawn of the twenty-first century can be traced to the hierarchy's refusal to make good on the promise of renewal made by the Vatican forty years before. My purpose in this book is to examine those four decades to see what happened. To say that the period has been topsy-turvy—the most turbulent since nuns reached these shores—would be an understatement. During this span of time religious life has been turned on its head. In these pages I try to explain what has happened.

A word about terminology. Though, as will be noted, "sister" and "nun" have precise and distinct meanings in Catholic history, they are used interchangeably here, in accord with common practice in recent times. The same applies to the terms "congregation," "community," and "order," which have discrete origins but will refer uniformly in this book to groups of sisters living within a certain tradition inspired by a particular founder or founders.

Double Crossed

Introduction

Forty-five years ago, nuns covered the U.S. Catholic landscape like black-eyed Susans in a summer meadow. They taught the three R's under the canopy of a fourth—Religion—nursed the sick, guided the troubled, housed the disabled, ran hospitals and colleges, and performed countless other services for the burgeoning Church. They were garbed in wool serge habits bearing the style and color of the various orders, from somber blacks, grays, and browns to arresting purples and whites. Their heads were encased in wrappings and veils, their bodies draped in long, flowing capes. From their cloisters they alighted into the daylight and vanished again behind those walls by nightfall.

Today this remarkable cohort of American women has become nearly invisible day or night, and not just because most nuns no longer wear the habit. The species as a whole is fast disappearing, on the verge of extinction. In 1965, at the peak of membership, sisters numbered 185,000 in more than five hundred orders. By 2005, the total had dropped by more than half, to 69,963. Nearly 60 percent of those were over seventy years old; fewer than 6,000 were under fifty.

Only a handful of women have entered religious communities in recent years. From a high-water mark in 1962, when 32,000 candidates passed through the convent gates, the applicant pool has nearly dried up. A few hundred still come knocking each year—most of them at least twice as old as

the teenage girls who once joined—but many of them leave before taking final vows. A visitor to a convent these days is more likely to meet a nun in her
nineties than one in her twenties. Clearly, a culture rich in prayer, learning,
wisdom, and service is rapidly passing out of existence with no obvious
means of survival. With demise on the horizon, the sisters themselves differ
in what they believe the downward trend means. Some see it as a natural
death, the final stage in a ministry of service that is no longer tenable. Others
see it as a fallow time that will usher in new forms of religious life; they believe that death will precede a rebirth.

Two attributes have set U.S. nuns apart from their sisters in other parts
of the world. One is that America has had far more nuns than has any other
country. In 1850, at the outset of the huge migration of Irish and other European Catholics to U.S. shores, a tiny contingent of 1,344 nuns belonged to
nineteen orders in all of America. By 1900, that total had risen to 40,340
nuns in forty-five orders. Six decades later, that number had multiplied by
more than four. The other distinct feature of the U.S. sisters stems from the
unusual conditions in which they have existed. American democracy and the
spirit of freedom it engendered, especially in terms of personal choice and
mobility, have placed pressures on the American convent that are unsurpassed anywhere in the world. Maintaining stability in religious life presents
daunting challenges in a robust culture that offers so many alternatives and
practices and displays such disrupting social and technological change. The
story of American sisters on the frontier of modernity is, then, a lesson or a
cautionary tale for sisters in other advancing societies in Africa and Latin
America, where the numbers of nuns are increasing.

Because sisters were separated from the American mainstream—indeed
from the world—until the 1960s, they were often seen as peripheral at best
to the lives of Catholic women in general. But, in fact, nuns quietly set a
striking example for young girls by assuming leadership in fields that were at
the time monopolized by men. For decades, sisters attained what was otherwise restricted to a few upper-class women: a college education, professional
work, and a role in running major institutions. While they had enlisted in
the greater cause of God's church mostly for religious reasons and did not set
out to become crusaders for women's rights, they nonetheless became models of competence and intelligence for those women who would later press

for women's rights. Thus emerged the paradox of sisters in habits, living a medieval lifestyle, staunchly upholding a premodern (even antimodern) institution, while pursuing careers that in secular culture would have marked them as liberated. Their pursuits rubbed off. Little wonder, then, that a survey of women members of Congress not long ago showed that a majority of them had graduated from small Catholic women's colleges run by nuns. For a long stretch of U.S. history, nuns were, as a group, the best educated women in the nation and even the best educated among all its Catholics.

The story of the glories and agonies of the sisters, then, belongs squarely within the history of American women. Catholic nuns pioneered areas of learning and doing, usually by default because there was no one else to carry out the work, and they influenced, often implicitly, generations of Catholic girls to aspire to doing more with their lives than most women had ever dreamed of doing.

Yet, as noted earlier, the sisters' contribution has been largely written off or trivialized. As communities have teetered on the verge of disappearing in recent decades, little attention has been paid in the Church or the nation to the magnitude of the loss. One reason, it seems, is that history's neglect of the sisters falls within the larger neglect of women's history. Another cause is the sisters' refusal to promote themselves, since most of them were trained as novices to subordinate themselves to their superiors and their mission. Over the years, many sisters have increasingly found themselves torn between their sense of dignity as women and their abiding allegiance to a male-governed church.

Simultaneously, a growing voice among the sisters protested that they had long been second-class citizens in their own church. When sisters in the late 1960s and early 1970s became more assertive, inspired in part by a new wave of feminism, their discontent over their treatment by the Church resulted in clashes with bishops and the seat of supreme male power in Rome. Some priests and bishops supported the nuns; many others, however, were irritated and perplexed as the vast army of women, always perceived as being obedient and "selfless" servants, were challenging clerical authority. In the eyes of many clerics, these agitators was overstepping their "feminine" boundaries of passivity and self-abnegation. Vatican II had helped spark this awakening, though many bishops were appalled at its reformist consequences. A backlash against it from the hierarchy damaged many sisterhoods beyond repair.

Another reason to look at the recent history of sisters is that women are, in a larger sense, the Church's biggest problem. Nothing pointed to the seriousness of that problem more than the futile effort by the U.S. bishops starting in the late 1980s to draft a basic pastoral letter, or position paper, on women. Many bishops, following the Vatican's lead, sought to affirm the equality of the sexes while making clear why certain Church functions, such as the priesthood, are forbidden to women. After nearly a decade of hearings, negotiations, drafts, and Vatican vetoes of those drafts, the bishops finally gave up. The pastoral letter is for the moment a dead letter. Meanwhile, there are various signs of disaffection among Catholic women who complain that teachings aimed at them are formulated exclusively by a male hierarchy. The Vatican's absolute ban on artificial birth control, abortion, artificial insemination, in vitro fertilization, divorce, and ordination are only the most prominent points of conflict that are keeping increasing numbers of women away from the Church. A Gallup poll conducted for the *National Catholic Reporter* in 1999 indicated the scope of the loss. In 1987, 68 percent of Catholic women said they would never leave the Church; in 1999 the portion had dropped to 56 percent. Over the same period, those who said they attended Mass weekly declined from 52 to 43 percent. Among women age twenty-five to fifty-four, the figure for weekly attendance was lower, 35 percent, suggesting to many analysts an increasing level of dissatisfaction.

Such disaffection, of course, underscores the wide gap between men and women in an institution in which there exists no forum in which men and women can make major decisions as equals. The stories of nuns provide, therefore, a look at how men and women working for the Church have related to one another. The fact that priests, bishops, and nuns compose an unusual subculture (ordained male clergy versus lay, consecrated nuns) with particular patterns of thinking and acting tends to invest their interactions with a specific Catholic content and dynamic, but their encounters also indicate how Catholic men and women have generally viewed one another.

This book recounts what has happened to nuns since the Second Vatican Council set off the wholesale revamping of religious communities. To help make clear the tremendous shift that took place, some attention is given to the period just before the Council (also known as Vatican II) when nuns were strictly regulated in a climate suffused with stability. The Council, called by Pope John XXIII, was the most monumental event of the Roman Catholic century. Its grandest effect was to end more than 150 years of official Church hostility to the modern age, including its aversion to democracy and religious freedom. The 2,500 bishops of the Catholic world met from 1962 to 1965 and basically rewrote the Church's constitution in such a way as to redefine it as a fellowship of equals that accepted the wider world rather than rejecting it in isolation. One of the Council's sixteen major quasi-legislative documents was addressed to nuns. Although it was widely considered tame and uninspired at the time, there were elements in it that many nuns came to interpret as a mandate to make choices that had never before been allowed to them, choices that would shake up their personal and collective lives irrevocably.

The term most often used by sisters to describe the Council-inspired transformation that reshaped their religious communities is "renewal." In this context, the term means rediscovering the vitality that originally gave birth to those communities. Making them "as new" again meant, among other things, freeing them from layers of rules and regulations that Church bureaucracy had imposed on them for many years. The rules—covering everything from eating a banana to dressing for bed—had increasingly regimented their lives and insulated them from the outside world. Renewal was intended as a means of reviving congregations by giving them the opportunity to reach back to their founding sources of inspiration. This exercise was regarded as a means of establishing continuity with a living past that may have become obscured in one way or another. In theory, renewal was the hope of making something better, not something wholly new.

In subsequent years, some critics of the sisters' efforts to implement this idea believed that renewal often went too far, turning instead into an attempt to *reform* Catholic tradition by breaking with the past instead of distilling the best from it. It was often difficult to distinguish between renewal and reformation. Sisters generally embraced a remaking of their daily routines and a greater infusion of democracy because these changes were consistent with the best in their own traditions; they did not commit themselves to renewal in the spirit of rebellion. But some among them also resisted, even rejected, certain ways of thinking and behaving which they believed to be unacceptable (particularly with regard to the Church's views of women) and detrimental to the fulfillment of their congregation's calling. This stance seemed to classify them as reformers. Many Church authorities, meanwhile, saw the effects of renewal as dangerously reformist.

Was the outcome mainly renewal or reform? Much of the debate over the challenges sisters have encountered over the past forty years has been fueled in one way or another, directly or indirectly, by that question. It signifies an extraordinary moment in the Church's life, one marked by both uncertainty and promise. With the number of sisters falling like a rock, the question acquires further poignancy. What precipitated the plunge? Is it an accident of history that the forces of secular culture simply dried up the applicant pool? Did sisters bring the decline on themselves by doffing habits and moving into apartments, thereby scuttling their divine vocation? Or does Providence require that congregations as they have existed must pass away, having finished their good works, before rebirth in yet unforeseen forms can take place? These questions shadow this account at every point because they are the backdrop of the discussion. Answers are hard to come by.

The corollary conundrum is whether the loss of so many sisters was inevitable. Did the stunning shifts brought about by renewal to bring the Church into the contemporary world create the unintended effect of placing congregations even further out of touch with parish Catholics from whom they had drawn recruits in the past? Did the sisters rush toward change too quickly, creating too much conflict and disillusion? Did they succumb to tenets of feminism that placed them so much at odds with the institutional Church that they unwittingly lost enthusiasm and support for building up their own communities? Some sisters would say yes to one or more of these questions. There was turmoil and jarring change, confusion and anger, grief and defiance during a period of enormous dislocation. Some would say too much happened too soon. But many of the nuns would make a distinction between sorrow for the conflicts of renewal versus regret. Most do not regret the outcome of the greatest upheaval of their lives as nuns. Nor do they apologize for it. They are much more likely, with some exceptions, to see renewal as a saving grace than as an agent of decline, while they acknowledge that mistakes were made along the way. Perhaps the most telling criticism is that renewal took place before adequate thinking had been done.

Though sisters largely decided on their own how to revamp their communities under the new mandate from Rome, they were doing so, as noted, within the framework of the hierarchical Church. Though the Vatican Council had, inadvertently perhaps, left the sisters lots of room to determine these matters for themselves, many bishops and parish priests were accustomed to exerting considerable control over congregations and they saw no reason why their authority should be curtailed. This made for trouble on several fronts—sisters with their newfound burst of freedom ran headlong into clerics facing the unwelcome prospect of losing power. Not long into the renewal, the Vatican got into the act by raising objections to some actions taken by American nuns, and blocking others. Eventually it seemed that Rome had changed its mind and wanted to turn back the whole process, leaving only a few outward changes. To put the matter indelicately, the sisters had been double-crossed.

Harassment and pressure from the hierarchy, much of it coming directly from Rome, became such an obstacle and a distraction for the American sisters that, in my opinion, it seriously hampered the congregations from following their instincts in fulfillment of their visions and goals. Had they, who had been the soul of Catholic loyalty and dedication, been permitted to cultivate the promise of Vatican II as they understood it, the decline in their numbers might not have been so steep or so fast. Of all the factors that figure into the disappearance of sisters, none would seem to loom as large as the effort of the Church establishment to renege on a project given the sisters, ironically, by the men of Vatican II. If the hierarchy in particular had stayed out of it (admittedly not something hierarchies are wont to do), had trusted and encouraged these women to follow their own lights, perhaps sisters would have been better able to emerge with sufficient creativity, direction, and morale to survive on their own terms. For Church authorities, such independent thinking was foreign. If the powers that be stood in the way, it was because most believed they were doing what was right to preserve tradition, even though their resistance undermined their pledge to allow the nuns greater autonomy.

Before Vatican II, at the first stirrings of the nuns' quest for regeneration in the form of the Sister Formation Movement in the 1950s, a carrot-and-stick approach emerged. The pattern was set. A carrot from the hierarchy raised hopes; the stick was then applied when Church officials decided on their own authority—arbitrarily, some said—that things had gone too far.

Outside forces also intruded, drawing young Catholics into campaigns for human rights, thereby siphoning off many idealistic young women who once might have "gone into the Church." The civil rights crusade and the anti–Vietnam War protest, in particular, drew many of these young Catholics away from traditional, institutional religion into a movement that rejected the old constraints. They joined forces with some of the traditional sisters at places like Selma, Alabama, and the Mall in Washington, D.C., to support the rights of African Americans and an end to the war, but afterward the two groups went their separate ways. Legions of other Catholic students distanced themselves from the Church as they responded to the freedom drumbeat of the 1960s and 1970s without taking part in the campaigns for social justice.

Within this panoply of cultural forces, none was more important yet more ambiguous to sisters than the new wave of feminism that was cresting in the 1970s. Though sisters by example had modeled certain professional roles that feminists could respect, nuns had never, collectively, espoused a self-conscious movement for women's rights. Before the Second Vatican Council, a campaign for women's equality would have been unthinkable in the vast majority of sister congregations; it would have been seen as a revolt against the ethos of submission to authority that had long suffused the convent. After the Council, the hierarchy generally eyed the women's movement warily. As its influence permeated the sisterhoods, some prelates openly blamed what they called "radical feminism" for causing sisters to place their own desires ahead of the needs of the Church, steering them toward selfishness and wanton individualism. For many young Catholic women, the fruits of feminism were greater career choices, lessening the likelihood that they would enter religious congregations.

In the decade after the Vatican Council, as the banners of feminism coincidentally unfurled, the exodus from the convent gushed; tens of thousands of sisters went out into the world (more than 4,300 left in 1970 alone) to begin anew without the security or support of religious communities. The many reasons for this exodus will be explored. Some attribute it to the inability of many convents to pursue renewal rigorously enough, because they lacked the stamina and drive to complete what they had started so well. The motives propelling so many sisters to leave their orders included this element and many more.

Inadvertently, perhaps, when the Vatican Council declared that all Catholics were expected, equally, to "pursue holiness"—to seek a life of total conformity to Jesus Christ—it knocked the slats out from under the pedestal onto which nuns had been elevated above everyday Catholics in the pew. Until that time, sisters had been, religiously speaking, a cut above, officially occupying a "state of perfection" beyond the reach of ordinary laypeople. Rightly or wrongly, this elite status had been one of the convent's chief attractions for young women, not unlike the way the Marine Corps targeted young men. Now holiness was a calling no longer reserved for those who had, as nuns, taken the vows of poverty, chastity, and obedience. When the convent, often with the blessing of the nuns, ceased to have a corner on that special status, some sisters, sensing that the playing field had been leveled and that the "difference" had been erased, decided they could seek their special relationship to God as wives, mothers, or single professionals.

Over the past quarter century, as the preponderance of sisters moved into retirement halls and nursing homes, American religious communities seem destined to remain only as a remnant at best. Having done what they felt called to do, these sisterhoods are leaving the stage. Many do so with grace and thankfulness for having kept the faith. Some communities have already died with dignity.

But two survival strategies have emerged in theory if not widely in practice. They represent dissimilar approaches and interpretations of God's will for the sisterhood, yet they share an urgent concern for the recovery of galvanizing purpose that many sisters believe has been lost. Each approach might be seen as reflecting aspects of the order founded by Mother Teresa, the Missionaries of Charity, although perhaps unwittingly. That order has shown rapid growth and high morale, centered in the Third World, where conditions seem more favorable to religious orders.

One survival strategy mirrors Mother Teresa's focus on a common ministry, in this case to the dying. Sisters and resources are concentrated in a single effort, the way American orders once gave all their energies to their hospitals, schools, and orphanages. Most U.S. congregations have long ago given up such ministries for a variety of reasons. Most sisters choose their own work these days. But some would like to revive the concentrated ministry with a very special agenda, the cause of the poor. This alternative, which appeals mainly to progressives, advocates that communities adopt a common call to social justice.

The other strategy, favored by conservatives, is based on Mother Teresa's love of the traditional convent life that most American nuns abandoned in the process of renewal: habits, living together, community prayer, cooperative ministries, deference to Church authority, and so forth. The appeal is to turn back, in large measure, to the uniformity of the convent before Vatican II. It is an appeal made every day by Mother Angelica, in full brown habit, on her national cable outlet, the Eternal Word Television Network. Someone's paying attention, it seems. Congregations that did the least "renewal," such as the Carmelites, are showing modest signs of vitality and several tiny communities with a traditional outlook have sprung up in various parts of the country.

The aim of this book is to explore why matters have come to such a pass; why the exuberance of a revival turned into hard times; why the promise of the first days of a new springtime became such a struggle; why sisters stay the course in seemingly hopeless circumstances with surprising hope, even joy. To set the stage for the great causative event, the Vatican Council, and the upheavals that ensued, Chapter 2 looks at the culture of the convent before the Council. Chapter 3 is given to that primary force for change in the United States before the Council, the Sister Formation Movement. Chapter 4 looks at what the Council said about the customs and routines of sisters.

We begin with an account of a storied community of Ursuline nuns in the flatlands of Kansas who are grappling, like so many other American sisters, with the specter of endgame: how to remain faithful to their mission in the throes of loss.

✦

Chapter One

Making Waves in Kansas

---

oting a small hoe and pruning sheers, Sister Agatha Grosdidier crept her way along the flower beds straddling the massive stone Ursuline convent in Paola, Kansas, bending to paw the earth and clip a useless twig. She was lean and large boned with a broad, handsome face. A plain black head covering that fell back to the nape of her neck—a veil—was the only outward sign that she was a nun. The profusion of roses, irises, tulips, jonquils, wild sweet Williams, poppies, bluebells, and tiger lilies, among others, was her doing. Her love of tending flowers dated back to her childhood spent on a Kansas farm. It was a passion that she later saw as helping her to nurture children in the classroom.

When she wasn't digging in the dirt, Sister Grosdidier answered the convent phone or sewed aprons. In 1995, she was ninety-five years old, the eldest of the sisters. For nearly seventy-five of those years, she had been an Ursuline sister in Paola, a farming town forty miles south of Kansas City. Her chronology coincided remarkably with the history of the sisters' community. She was born five years after the Paola community's founding by thirteen nuns and three postulants, or trainees, and had lived to celebrate its hundredth anniversary in 1995.

Sister Grosdidier was the kind of sturdy survivor who attracts accolades such as "remarkable" or "awesome." She was astonishingly robust, with a sparkle still dancing in her eyes. Her health had been so resilient that an insurance man, noting that no claims had been filed under her name, called the convent to ask if Sister Agatha was still alive. She loved tacos, spicy foods, and chocolate milk shakes. Lighthearted and quiet, she adored her flowers and her sisters, and her sisters adored her. She was special, but she did not see herself that way; rather she was a sister among sisters doing the ordinary things. It had been for her the best life she could imagine.

Longevity and constancy had been hallmarks of Ursulines for nearly five hundred years. St. Angela Merici (1474–1540) began the community in sixteenth-century Italy, forsaking riches to feed the poor. She took the name of the order from the ancient German saint Ursula. Two centuries later, in 1727, the Ursulines became the first order to reach North America when French nuns from Rouen planted a convent in New Orleans seventy-five years before the city became absorbed into the United States. The Ursuline migration to Kansas had been by way of Louisville and St. Louis. Over that inclusive span of history, the sisters had endured waves of plenty and scarcity in both numbers and resources. Various branches had waxed and waned. By the dawn of the twenty-first century, the Ursulines still carried a distinct heritage but generally fit the profile of most other orders. Their story has become the familiar story of scores of communities from Sinsinawa Dominicans to Sisters of Mercy to Blessed Sacrament nuns. The circumstances differ, as do the particulars of their community arrangements, but they are much more alike than dissimilar. Sister Grosdidier and her fellow Paola Ursulines, therefore, reflected a much wider picture of the recent struggles and triumphs of American nuns in the mid-1990s.

Sister Grosdidier joined the Paola sisters in 1924 when they numbered more than fifty. She had shopped around before making a decision. The Ursulines won her allegiance because, unlike the nearby Benedictines, they had somewhat less stringent rules. They allowed sisters to go home if a parent died, for example; the Benedictines did not.

The majestic stone 1920s convent where she had moved as an excited young postulant had evolved into a three-story hub-and-spoke structure. At the ground-floor center stood a hand-carved solid walnut statue of Angela Merici bringing a basket of bread to peasants in a field.

Over the decades, the Ursulines had become a fixture in the Archdiocese of Kansas City and, like so many orders, an absolute necessity. Sister Grosdidier stepped into line to do her duty: she taught the children, instilling in them as best she could the Catholic faith. The Archdiocese of Kansas City had relied upon the Ursulines to do this work with special competence; the sisters were renowned for their energetic and spirited teaching. Even now with the order in steady decline, half a dozen sisters served as principals of archdiocesan schools and several others were teaching in them.

From the beginning, the community had been, in practice, under the authority of the archdiocese rather than under the direct rule of the Vatican (whether an order was "diocesan" or "pontifical" has many complex implications in terms of Church politics. Most orders prefer to be overseen by the Vatican so as to avoid meddling from local bishops closer to the scene). The Ursulines had therefore always allied themselves closely to the archdiocese.

Twenty years after taking final vows of poverty, chastity, and obedience— in the aftermath of World War II—Sister Grosdidier was happily teaching typing and other commercial skills to high school students. The community had swollen to nearly one hundred. Like those in every order, the Ursulines were women living on their own, having to raise their own funds to pay their own bills. The diocese paid sisters a token amount to teach (far below prevailing teacher salaries) but otherwise bore no responsibility for the sisters' financial welfare. The combined stipends from many nuns working as teachers made subsistence possible, although when the number of teachers declined there was a serious shortfall. In addition, in the early decades of the twentieth century the sisters owned two hundred acres on which they planted corn and vegetables and herded cattle to supply the convent kitchen. On another section of the spread, oil wells pumped a shallow pool of low-grade petroleum. Since then, the unprofitable wells have been capped and large chunks of the property sold off to a Wal-Mart and to the developers of a strip mall to pay the bills for retired sisters such as Sister Grosdidier. Thirty-four acres were donated for a special education center for mentally disabled children.

The nerve center for the Paola Ursulines' industry and creativity, the mother-house convent, is medieval and monastic, hollow and ghostly. The halls, prongs radiating from the center, are mysteriously dark, spare, and tomblike. A cozy chapel, where the sisters gather each day for Mass celebrated by a priest who serves as their official chaplain, features a marble altar, Austrian stained-glass windows, and a 1974 modernist mural titled *St. Ursula and the Ursulines of Paola,* which had stirred some debate.

By contrast, the public rooms, where family and guests are received and social events staged, are filled with light and creature comforts. Two parlors serve as elegant galleries for outsized paintings of bishops who were counted among the founders of the community. Two busts symbolize the sisters' commitments: one of Pope Benedict XV, representing the Church; the other, William Shakespeare, who stands for their dedication to learning.

The most stunning contrast to the convent's darkness is the mellow pastel "wicker room." It is chockablock with the kind of furniture that gives the room its name, high-back chairs, sofas, footrests, and rockers, some bearing a blue embroidered *U* on the seat pad, not unlike the sitting room of a *Titanic*-like ocean liner from the early decades of the century. It is a space where girls from the adjoining Ursuline Academy, which closed a quarter century ago, had danced with and romanced their male guests at receptions and proms. Scattered throughout the social rooms, glass cases display collectors' items. One shows bells of porcelain, glass, brass, and silver; another features crosses from all over the world, many of them encrusted with gems. The most unusual case contains five hundred toy mice.

Such displays were, of course, for the benefit of the stream of outsiders who gained limited access to the convent during the years when the community flourished. Paola was a healthy branch of the Ursuline tree for many decades, though it never grew to the size of some branches in more populated areas.

In its centennial year, 1995, a total of forty-five nuns belonged to the community. Nobody, young or otherwise, was preparing to join. Three years later, the number had dropped to thirty-six, all but two of the departures through death. The average age was in the sixties. The last to enter, in 1980, was Sister Karen Klaffenbach, at age thirty-six, but she died tragically in her forties five years after my visit. A young woman who entered at the same time soon left.

In the dining room, Sister Grosdidier and the remaining nuns took their simple meals cafeteria-style. Some wore pantsuits, others dresses with or without a veil, still others tops and pants; two very old nuns appeared in full, modified habit. Their numbers included an authority on American ballet who had recently retired from the faculty of Loyola University of New Orleans, a massage therapist who still practiced in Paola, and a former high school principal. Meals were among the remaining rituals. The noontime meal, for example, began promptly at twelve o'clock and food was collected and consumed with hushed dispatch. Dirty dishes were unloaded from the trays to the stainless-steel counters to bring matters to a close.

The customs of the dining room conveyed the values of mutual respect, simplicity, routine, and devotion to community that continue to characterize Ursuline tradition. The sisters remained powerfully drawn to the example of St. Angela. More than a wooden statue of one who has receded into the mists of history, the saint is a constant reference point, a continuing source of inspiration, very much among them still.

The order to which St. Angela had given rise was anchored in the mainstream of American sister communities, neither as liberal as some nor as conservative as others. While there was little talk of women's ordination or reading of feminist literature, there was, at the same time, much personal autonomy and little expected conformity. Mass was conducted by traditional standards, though somewhat unusually, the prayers were rendered in inclusive language. The sisters' work was still located mostly in Church institutions, but those who were still able to work had more choices.

But the order had already weathered big changes. The Ursuline community that Sister Grosdidier entered in 1924 was a far cry from what the founder had intended. St. Angela's aim was to serve the poor by avoiding the Church's insistence that nuns be shut away in cloisters. She therefore sought a new way of religious life that spurned the wearing of habits, the taking of vows, and living in cloistered community. She created a distinct kind of sisterhood that was free to move about to do its work. It became a model for hundreds of communities that straddled the line between strict adherence to a cloistered regimen and an ad hoc arrangement that combined service to the world with enclosed religious discipline. This type of serving community came to dominate religious life in the United States during the great nineteenth-century Catholic immigration. But gaining acceptance for it from the Church hierarchy was difficult, as the early Ursuline experience showed.

So long as St. Angela remained alive, her concept of the Ursuline difference held together and the community was free to follow its own lights. When she died, however, Church officials stepped in, forcing the sisters to take vows, to put on habits, and to be cloistered. Her experiment had ended; her example lived on. Ursulines had become a fixture in Catholicism, among the most prominent of religious orders.

The decrees of Vatican II spurred the order to yet another turning point, requiring the sisters to revise their constitution to reform both their living patterns and the way community decisions were made. By the late sixties and early seventies, the Ursulines were faithfully fulfilling their assignments and they, like hundreds of other orders, had taken sharp turns.

Confusion and conflict accompanied these shifts. Sisters dropped out, some to marry, others disenchanted or drawn to other vocations opening to women. The year 1968 marked the greatest exodus. Strange twists of fate illustrated the volatility. A sister living at a diocesan high school, for example, said she fell in love with a police officer when he rushed to her high school convent to investigate a break-in. The couple soon married. The nun who had done the most to pioneer the new habit in 1964 suddenly left. In a stiff blow to the community's identity, Ursuline Academy, which had taught girls since 1898, closed in 1971 because of a shortage of teaching sisters and money. The order's two-year junior college had folded long before.

In writing a new constitution with the prompting of Vatican II, the sisters had, collectively, completely revamped the way the order was run. The kind of single-handed authority wielded by Paola's legendary superior, Mother M. Charles McGrath, came to an end. In its place, a system of power sharing gave an executive committee and the community as a whole decisive control over most matters. The obligatory prayer and worship schedule was dropped. Sisters no longer simply took work assignments defined by the superior; they could negotiate or propose their own work situations. Greater flexibility was granted in where a sister lived.

While the movement toward democracy found much favor among the sisters, the job of translating the theory into practice, in the midst of so much other tension and confusion, proved difficult. That task fell to Raymond Dieckman, a slight, soft-spoken nun who, when I visited in 1995, still preferred a simple black veil with a vest and skirt and, in the absence of an obligation, rose at 4 a.m. to pray. Raised in Kansas City, she entered the convent with seven others in 1952 (two of whom remained in the community) and was educated at Creighton University. In an unusual twist, her father (whose letters to her had been read by sisters in authority as part of the normal practice of the old days) spent the last years of his life at the convent, driving sisters to and fro and doing odd jobs.

In 1974, at age thirty-six, Sister Dieckman became the youngest superior ever elected by the Paola Ursulines. After two four-year terms, she returned to the ministry she holds dearest, chaplain to a hospice. Her experience as superior was difficult, she said, because there were no guidelines for how to lead in the new era. Nuns had always been dependent on the superior for nearly everything. Permission was required to do anything of significance and full obedience was expected. When the rules changed the lines of authority became murky. There was insecurity on both sides.

"I spent a lot of time trying to decide what my role of superior was," Sister Dieckman said. "Even the sisters didn't know where to go to get a final word. What was I supposed to be as a superior when all these other matters of decision were being parceled out to others? Should they get approval or not? What were they supposed to be talking to me about? Sisters were coming to me full of struggle." Out of the view of other sisters, she met with the archbishop for advice. Amid all the tension and perplexity, she said, some sisters felt their religious world had caved in on them and wondered if the community might fall apart.

The congregation didn't collapse, she noted, but neither could it return to the past or write a script for the future. Though she was no outspoken feminist, she believed the women's movement had prevented the sisters from looking backward by inoculating them against the "positions of servitude" to which they had been relegated. "We were always cheap labor," Sister Dieckman said. "The Church has to realize it has to meet our needs."

The Church had shown little intention of serving their needs. To the contrary, Rome had for nearly three decades fought to keep convent change within strict boundaries it believed appropriate, far short of the aspirations and expectations held by many sisters.

Without any sisters, of course, the point about subservience would be moot. If the clock ran out on Paola, any alternative would meet a dead end. Little wonder that destiny haunted the mind of the community at the time of my visit. How long could they keep the magnificent fortress of a convent, this monument to the glory days? How would the big medical bills get paid? Who would care for the old ones?

In the early 1990s, Sister Klaffenbach was the only thirty-something in the group. A handful of sisters in their forties and fifties made up most of the remaining preretirement-age nuns, though many continued to work well beyond age sixty-five. About half of the Paola Ursulines worked full-time in one profession or another. Most were educators and parish assistants.

For Sister Klaffenbach, a cheerful, outgoing woman who ministered to college students at the Newman Center of the University of Kansas, the destiny of the community was nothing like an abstract exercise. Chronologically speaking, at least, she was the end of the line. Her love for the sisters overflowed. As a teenager, she had visited the convent to do chores and provide rides. To her, the sisters were "fabulous people, even the kookiest of them, who laughed a lot." She had joined their company at age twenty-one, after graduating from college with a degree in biology and chemistry. The day of her first vows, she remembered happily, "was perfect, just the way everyone says weddings should be."

As a nun she taught in a diocesan high school and a junior high school, obtained a master's degree in theology, and served as a member of a parish staff, specializing in adult education. The experience was good, she recalled, except that women on the parish staff with more experience and more education were likely to be outranked by less qualified priests. She had qualms about a hierarchical church in which, she said, men rose faster and further in responsibility than did women and women religious. Women's ordination should be looked at more, she thought, but "you have to set it aside or it will drive you nuts."

At Kansas University, where she was interviewed five years before her untimely death, she organized a small community of students who lived together. Some had visited Paola, perhaps with some interest in becoming sisters, but it was still too soon to tell. It was obvious that Sister Klaffenbach, who preferred blue jumpsuits and white blouses, would spearhead whatever efforts were made to attract candidates. But she had a fallback position in case none of it worked out. It was based in a theology of community purpose and God's will. "If it's in the plan for us to peter out, then we will," Sister Klaffenbach said pensively. "If we do so knowing who we're supposed to be, then it doesn't matter to me."

She continued: "Do I get lonely? Oh yes. Older sisters sometimes say, 'We had companionship, you don't.' I treasure these old people. They have the key to the future. I'd like to have somebody to share the dream with. Many of those I do share it with won't be here."

Already many more nuns were resting in the beautiful grassy cemetery behind the convent than lived in the existing community.

In the hundredth-anniversary brochure, Sister Klaffenbach and Sister Grosdidier were featured on the opposing last two pages, community bookends, separated by six decades, bound by a hope for the future of the Ursulines of Paola that seemed, on its face, nonsensical. But both were confident that the way ahead would be more challenging than anything the community had confronted during its first hundred years.

Neither would go far down that road. Sister Grosdidier lived just two more years and died painfully as the result of a scalding accident in bathwater. Three years later, Sister Klaffenbach succumbed to illness. Much of the shock of the deaths was derived from the loss of the community's "bookends." Symbolically the deaths were crushing.

The election of Sister Pat Lynch as superior in 1994 was a vote of confidence in some kind of future. Sister Lynch was able to absorb all the worries, fears, and anxieties about the community without losing her faith in a new day. From her own life, she had learned to face tragedy. A brother had died when she was three; her mother when she was five. Her childhood had been spent largely with relatives in Philadelphia. Her sister, Peggy, had left the Ursulines in 1968 to become a nurse; she had married a doctor.

Sister Lynch's strength and demonstrated versatility would be tested again. In her years as an Ursuline, she had been a teacher, speech therapist, and a member of a special education team. She was a personable, good-humored, candid woman of about fifty at the time of her election whose passion for the community often intersected with the recognition of hard realities. With the convent slowly going to ruin—rugs wearing thin, wallpaper flaking—and the sisterhood shrinking, she and her executive council were under a mandate to find solutions. Leasing space to other agencies and renovating the convent to permit occupancy by senior citizens, along with the sale of more land, were high on the list of alternatives. Consultants were brought in.

Finding adequate tenants in the social service field proved difficult, because of both Paola's relatively remote location and the need to fit the building's peculiar contours to the needs of agencies. The best option seemed to be the renovation of the third floor, where the novices had once prayed and sometimes cried themselves to sleep from homesickness, into a facility for assisted living. That choice both fulfilled the sisters' sense of public service and provided them, on paper at least, with regular income. Other than that, the retreat business was fairly brisk and, in the summer of 1998, the convent welcomed teams of Southern Baptists who arrived for one-week stays to help build new churches in the area. To Sister Lynch, the Baptists were "a blessing"; they had taught the sisters that they could happily share their building with religious outsiders. Sharing their space with total strangers was another possibility. A tourist agency wanted to run bus trips from Kansas City to the convent. The sisters were pondering the implications of tourism.

Sister Lynch worked the various ideas through her trusted council in the late 1990s, which included Sister Klaffenbach, and with the full meeting of sisters, the general chapter, which took place every four years. The result was a plan to reconstruct the second-floor living quarters to house the nuns who lived on the premises (it would include a new dining room and redesigned apartments) and to renovate the top floor for assisted living, which included the installation of two new elevators.

The price tag for this project was $3 million. Paola Ursulines had never conducted public fund-raising before, but under Sister Lynch's guidance, a campaign was launched, complete with the hiring of a development director, a young woman who was a grandniece of Sister Grosdidier. Almost overnight, a Web site appeared. A newsletter also sprang up in an effort to assist both recruitment and fund-raising by strengthening the network of sisters, former sisters, former students of the sisters, and friends of the sisters. A section of the newsletter was devoted to alumni, detailing the activities of women who had left the community some thirty years ago or more. These women had formed a kind of diaspora and many had kept in close touch with Paola's affairs. A "former member day" recently had attracted scores of women from all over the country.

Fund-raising was an untried and risky venture, an effort to get the Ursuline constituency to support what might seem like a lost cause. But as sociologists have indicated, orders are not organizations in the normal sense. The laws of defeat, disillusionment, and self-protection that seem typical of other failing ventures don't apply to declining sisterhoods, at least not to the same degree. The Ursulines of Paola had little to promise contributors except their assurance that God would provide a way for them to keep going. Judging by the enormous goodwill the public felt toward the sisters based on market surveys, Kansas Catholics thought God certainly should provide for them.

On a daily basis, Sister Lynch said, the two toughest problems at the community were the "aging and death of sisters" and "who's going to do the work that needs to be done? We've got people in their eighties keeping us alive." She refused to accept death for the community. "We could decide to take no new members," she said, "but I'd like to see us live into the future. We are at a pivotal point now. Prayer is at the core of it. Everything we do makes a difference. I think Ursulines will prevail."

From the reports she received, Sister Lynch believed as the decade of the 1990s ended that interest in religious life was on the rise. The decision by the sisters to forge ahead meant that they continued to believe the community has a future, she said. "They want to stay the course, be faithful to their vows, to their commitment to their vocation as Ursulines, and to the archdiocese. They are saying we must do something; we can't do nothing."

THE PAOLA URSULINES posed the question of why religious orders found themselves in such straits. Perhaps the most commonly held assumption among Catholics was simply that young women would no longer choose a way of life that ruled out marriage and children. But there were problems with that explanation. Becoming a nun has never been the dream of every Catholic girl. The convent has always appealed to the few. To restore vitality to communities, it would take only a few of the millions of young Catholic women to take vows. The pull toward marriage and family surely remains powerful, but to many women, Catholic and otherwise, the ideal of marriage has suffered the disillusioning realities of failure and divorce. It would be hard to argue that wedding bells sound better now than they had in the 1950s when television exhibited the flawless *Ozzie and Harriet,* at the very same time that convent recruitment peaked. Likewise, the opening of so many fields of work to women could explain why most young Catholic women don't consider convent life, but in those earlier days the preponderance of women became housewives and still there were numbers of women who joined convents.

Moreover, despite the wholesale alterations, since Vatican II communities retained the core ideals and dedication that had always drawn young women. One of the enduring attractions was community life, the opportunity to participate in a shared purpose and to become a valued member of a group. Though most sisters no longer lived all together, they usually kept in close touch. For the Catholic woman, community life offered a way out of isolation and a means to connect to others both personally and spiritually. The hunger for that kind of community seemed, if anything, to be growing. The sisters also preserved a sense of vocation, dedicated to equipping each woman to do her ministry. Education had been made available, from college to Ph.D. programs to specialized degrees in law, medicine, theology, and other disciplines. The convent had become a center for fostering intellectual and professional opportunity. Why wouldn't that factor, taken in combination with the other facets of community life, make for a strong inducement?

Then there was the sisters' commitment to community service and, to a significant degree, to the cause of social justice. No group in the church has identified itself more with these altruistic human rights endeavors than nuns. Young people, meanwhile, have shown growing interest in volunteerism and social outreach. Such circumstances would seem to favor recruitment, but they have not so far. Idealistic, activist Catholic women are staying away.

Why should an institution with so much apparently going for it suffer so? No single explanation suffices. While conservatives like to blame the decline on abandonment of the old ways, liberals often claim that the sisterhood is a movement whose time has passed. But a fuller explanation probably would be more complex, more mysterious, factoring in cultural shifts and the broader web of Church politics. Women are not coming. Perhaps some have turned away out of dismay that a somewhat mythological past could not be repeated; others because the expanding lures of a secular culture seem far preferable. But what of that minority who were drawn to the convent's purposes that had, after all, remained at the center of its life?

The following chapter presents some idea of what the convent was like before its foundations were shaken after the Second Vatican Council. From all appearances, it had esprit; it had coherence; it had focus. Is its memory, after all, worthy of fond nostalgia?

Chapter Two

Living by the Rule: The Way It Was

B ack in the 1950s, the problem convents faced was feast, not famine. Young women, most of them still in their teens, flocked to the sisterhoods in record numbers, raising the total number of nuns in the United States to the highest level ever. From 1951 to 1952, for example, the number of sisters jumped by nearly 5,000 to 156,696 and would peak by adding another 10,000 in the next decade. The question was not attracting recruits but finding places to put them. Once they entered, young women embarked on a daily routine of prayer, work, meals, and recreation, spelled out in precise detail, from sunup to sundown. The structure seemed unshakable.

Most Catholics probably assumed this regimen had been handed down untouched for centuries, but such was not the case. Communal living and praying had existed in one form or other through the ages, but only during the past century had religious orders been expected to submit to a common set of standards. Growing uniformity was a reflection of the Church's growing centralization after the First Vatican Council (1869–70). For nuns, standardization of convent life meant that the convent rule book suddenly became much fatter, crammed with regulations ranging from rituals for donning the habit in the morning to proper use of the eyes. By 1917, this body of guidelines was incorporated into Roman Catholicism's first general law book, the code of canon law, which regulated all areas of the Church's practice. It contained a staggering two thousand separate rules and regulations that effectively governed every aspect of a nun's life. No such unified code had ever existed for nuns.

Many sisters describe religious life in the 1950s as a sort of Gulliver rendered immobile by myriad Lilliputian cords. It was for them a protected, even comfortable, existence, but the restrictions in their view often thwarted the stated purposes of the community.

This culture was sorely tested and largely rejected by the upheaval that was to come. Any effort to grasp the magnitude of that departure begins, therefore, with a picture of what that earlier culture was about. Some nuns recall it, especially in lengthening hindsight, as an idyllic time; many look back at it as nightmarish. The story of what has happened to nuns like the Ursulines of Paola begins, therefore, with a look at the 1950s as a benchmark, the final act in the drama of the old nun culture. Paradoxically, of course, the old culture, often seen by some sisters as retarding progress, celebrated its last hallelujah during the biggest boom that the orders had ever known. Against this backdrop of apparent success and stability, the sharp decline in orders after the Vatican II shakeup only proved to other sisters that the old ways should have been left alone.

During that post–World War II heyday, the currents delivering new blood to religious orders were surging. Support for a girl's decision to "take the veil" came from many directions. A Sister of St. Joseph remembered "the great fanfare" with which she and her twenty-four companions were sent off to the convent in 1958 by hundreds of parents, brothers, sisters, and other relatives, and the rousing welcome they received from their fellow sisters upon their arrival. "The day was momentous," the sister recalled, "like a college graduation. And yet I can't remember the day of my college graduation. There was mystery and awe and a looming sense of being on the brink of holiness. I thought if I died that night I would go right to heaven."

Convents were bursting at the seams. New buildings were sprouting up all over the nation to house this throng of postulants (newcomers who tested their calling for at least six months) and novices (those who were accepted, received the habit, and began training in preparation for first, or temporary, vows). With potential recruits so plentiful, many orders tempered their robust advertisements for themselves with a dose of caution, both beckoning

Catholic girls with glimpses of the rousing spirit within the convent and reminding them that the sisters' difficult vocation was not for everyone.

Catholic girls by the thousands in those years devoured books such as *Bernie Becomes a Nun,* the story of a Brooklyn girl, Bernadette Lynch, who strived toward her goal of becoming a Maryknoll sister. The text, by Sister Maria Del Rey, was supplemented by two hundred striking photographs of the candidate's progression, from the moment she informed her adoring parents that she had decided to enter the convent to the taking of permanent vows of poverty, chastity, and obedience. The autobiographical tale was heroic and inspiring, radiating and epitomizing the strength, exuberance, optimism, and idealism that animated communities of U.S. sisters.

Though the various congregations all shared the Latin Mass, a common body of Catholic teaching, and similar types of work in Catholic institutions, they rarely cooperated on projects or had contact with one another. By the fifties, rivalry for recruits and prestige was often keen, though for the most part the competition was unacknowledged or muted. There had long been jousting among the orders, but under the spur of the American competitive spirit, the intensity had perhaps unwittingly been sharpened.

Religious orders could actually afford to be selective in those days, contingent on the wishes of the Great Recruiter Who alone, it was assumed, planted a burning desire for this life in the hearts of particular Catholic girls.

The fresh faces at the convent belonged mostly to girls just out of high school (Bernie was somewhat atypical in her time, having worked briefly as a Wall Street secretary after graduation), while some entered before finishing high school. A nun, even many a former nun, tends to know precisely how many were in her "class" or "band" and how many remain in the order, and can recite that data at a moment's notice.

The atmosphere described by Sister Del Rey reflected the upbeat climate of the post–World War II era that spurred growth in the nation's churches and synagogues. This spurt in American religion was accompanied by dramatic shifts in Catholic demographics, thanks in large measure to two factors that raised levels of education: expanded parish schooling provided by the nuns, and the G.I. Bill of Rights bestowed by a grateful U.S. government on war veterans, allowing them to pay for a college education. Hundreds of thousands of eligible Catholics, many of them children of poor immigrants, seized the government's offer. Thus began the massive infusion of Catholic families with baby-boom children into the middle and upper classes and the consequent revitalizing of U.S. Catholicism. This, in turn, fostered a spirit of Catholic pride that was conducive to the recruitment of priests and nuns.

Looking back, Bernie's world of "fitting in" with the Maryknolls seemed quite natural at a time when conformity was generally extolled throughout American society. If nuns stressed sameness, so did corporations, schools, and social clubs. The man in the gray flannel suit was in his own way analogous to the woman in a black habit. Indeed, as sociologist Will Herberg argued in *Protestant, Catholic, Jew,* the most trenchant analysis of the religion of that decade, the three faiths had increasingly melded around a common set of convictions Herberg called "the American way of life."

Aptly, Bernie's story both exulted in the everyday routines of religious life and exposed her readers to its possible pitfalls.

"If you cannot find good companions among your own group of postulants," Sister Del Rey tells her readers early on, alluding to a possible stumbling block, "then religious life will indeed be bleak for you. During all your life, you will be put in small convents with, say, three to twelve Sisters. You must learn to be happy with any group, contributing your share of the good humor and kindly familiar spirit." The rewards to be reaped were understood to come from the nun's ties to the whole group and a common cause rather than from one-to-one friendships. Being a Maryknoll nun was a "joyful," experience, Sister Del Rey writes, because of "the warm family spirit that knits together a group of women serving God wholeheartedly." Bernie's sisters "laugh easily," Sister Del Rey said, because "[t]hey have everything to gain in this world and nothing to lose."

The unabashed confidence of this appeal resembled the "few good men" theme later used by the U.S. Marine Corps—religious life was a great life for the relatively few who could cut it. The romance and sublimated eroticism was captured in the widespread image of the nun as the "Bride of Christ" who took Jesus in spiritual marriage for the sake of perfecting the soul. A promotional pamphlet from that time, entitled "Brides of Christ," refers to the "ecstasy that comes from following just such a shining loveliness. Her Lover is a soul-Lover in all the strength of that great word. He leads her along to wind-swept places and fills her being with a great white peace. As her Lord, he might coerce her service; but He prefers to win her pledge. In countless ways Christ drew His bride to Himself."

Over the next thirty or forty years, departures and deaths shrank those numbers drastically, especially among those who entered before Vatican II. Three examples: one sister said she had begun with fifty-five other postulants and eight were left; for another, the figures were, respectively, forty-two and three; for still another sixty-seven and twelve. For most of the remaining sisters, the exuberance of abundance had given way to the mournfulness of scarcity. The consensus among the sisters seemed to be that numerical strength such as they had known would likely never return, but with a certain resilient hopefulness they were still holding out hope against the odds.

Though customs differed from one congregation to another, the pattern of induction went something like this in those pre–Vatican II days. A candidate, most likely still a teenager, entered a community as a postulant and was isolated with her class or "band" for at least six months, during which time she learned the community's traditions and practiced a fixed daily schedule of prayer, study, worship, work, and mealtime rituals. From postulant, she became a novice for another two years or so, entering more fully into the flow and dynamic of the community and deepening her spiritual life. Successfully completing the novitiate qualified her to take first or "temporary" vows of poverty, chastity, and obedience. Depending on the community, she might stay in that final formation period of first vows for from five to ten years before reaching the end of the process, permanent vows, after which, for institutional purposes at least, she would be considered "formed."

Obviously, formation entailed much more than being drilled in the basics. It was the means by which a young woman took on an identity and accepted the order's conception of what should matter to her and what shouldn't. For the first half of the last century, what counted most was the good of the community, expressed in a life of compliance with an orderly routine that embraced the practices of prayer and penance and work assignments in schools, hospitals, and other Church settings. The sister was expected to observe most of protocols of the professional teacher or nurse. She lived for the community; the community did not live for her.

Formation, then, involved seeing oneself as a communal being, and "self" meant little. Any significant alteration of that understanding could have immense repercussions.

WHEN BERNIE and her entering group became postulants, they were, typical for the age, exhorted to seek holiness by submitting wholly and unquestioningly to the guidance and direction of their superiors. In the church's theology, superiors were imbued with the "grace of office," that is, God spoke from the top of the hierarchical pipeline, the pope, and downward through the ranks. All members of the community were obliged to follow the wishes of the superior as if her commands were handed down by God Himself. The voice of mother superior was the voice of God, plain and simple. The flow of power was purely vertical and pyramidal. "The individual had no standing or dignity," as a Daughter of Charity remembered the days before the sweeping changes. "There was no such thing as consultation. Someone else took charge of your life. Anyone who got a slip in the mail [a message from mother superior in her convent mailbox] knew her life was about to change."

The religious culture the nuns of the 1950s entered had been shaped in Europe over many hundreds of years. Its values generally reflected the subordinate—some say inferior—status of women throughout the Christian world. Emphasis was placed on humility, self-forgetfulness, and subservience. Self-promotion and pride were the besetting sins. Superiors sought to combat such attitudes through meting out various disciplines and penances. Men's orders also stressed forms of self-abnegation, to be sure, but generally far less. Only the sisterhoods made these observances an obsession, a defining characteristic.

During her brief postulancy, the candidate absorbed the discipline of the convent and examined her motives; arriving at the threshold of the novitiate, she may have, according to the practice of her order, approached the altar adorned in a wedding gown to offer herself as a symbolic Spouse of Christ, reemerging during the Mass in the habit of the order, the novice's distinctive headwear covering a shaved head. All this unfolded as proud parents and relatives wept.

After achieving this milestone she was given a new name to signify a radically new identity, a new life in Christ. The Bible contained precedents for this custom. The patriarch Abram became Abraham, Sarai became Sarah, Jacob became Israel, Simon became Peter, and Saul turned into Paul after his conversion on the road to Damascus. Candidates in some communities lay prostrate, covered by a black funeral pall and surrounded by candles to symbolize the death of the old self. The new name was first made known by the superior. Often the order imposed the name of a male saint (for examples, Sister Ignatius or Sister Ambrose). A novice might be allowed to submit preferred names to the superior but there was no guarantees any would be chosen. Her surname was removed, a practice that had been in force only since the French Revolution. One reason given for eliminating the surname was that it prevented entrants from wealthy, powerful families from trading on their names for advantages or becoming targets of revolutionaries.

After at least two years in the novitiate, the aspirant would take her final vows before the bishop: poverty (surrendering her personal goods in order to rely entirely on the community), chastity (forswearing marriage and sexual intercourse), obedience (the willingness to do the bidding of her superiors).

The stories of battles and hardship, fought out largely behind the scenes, often contrast starkly with the folklore that emerged from the enigmatic, secretive lives of the nuns. By the time Bernie entered Maryknoll, highly stylized depictions of this rigorous religious existence were ingrained in the public consciousness, and they have remained there ever since. One of them, conveyed mostly by books and movies, typically portrayed the mousy, girlish nun in tightly wrapped headgear and habit, wreathed in sweet innocence and exuding a naive, improbable faith that moved mountains. A sterner adaptation was a more commanding figure whose faith led her to attempt the impossible, always in strict obedience to her superiors.

Sister Ann Patrick Ware, a Sister of Loretto, wrote in the foreword to the book *Midwives of the Future,* "In novels and movies sisters generally appeared as gentle, naive, well-meaning but somewhat dimwitted folk who were forever making preposterous demands, often of thugs or steely business tycoons, demands which somehow tugged at a forgotten heartstring and enabled the grace of God to move a stony heart. Not a bad image, all in all, but not the story we would tell."

The image of the convent world Bernie entered in the 1950s was, therefore, deeply entrenched, seemingly indestructible, though, as Sister Ware notes, one outstanding movie of that decade, *The Nun's Story,* poked a hole in the pristine picture by telling the story of a sister (played by Audrey Hepburn) who walks away from the convent after finding it unbearable. For most nuns in the congregations of women on American soil, however, the external, vital signs of institutional health were robust in the 1950s.

In key respects, of course, the sisters were still far from the mainstream in which Catholics were increasingly swimming. The chief distinction was that the sisters clung to a nineteenth-century identity that had largely been imposed upon them by the First Vatican Council. That conclave of cardinals and bishops reacted with masculine thunder to the threats to the Church from European revolutions. Seeking to elevate the otherworldly image of the Church in order to blunt Continental egalitarian ideals, the bishops and cardinals formally invested the pope with infallible power over faith and morals; the vertical, hierarchical nature of Catholicism was understood (the Church was essentially equated with the hierarchy); and the Church was further defined as the idyllic "perfect society." Under this conception, with Roman Catholicism defining itself as "the one true church," nuns were to resist worldliness and to aspire to a spiritual ideal that required a degree of discipline that was more restrictive and exacting than that expected of anyone else in the Catholic religion. Theirs was a "state of perfection" whose daily customs included virtually nothing that the sisters chose freely for themselves. These expectations for nuns were part of Rome's claim to supernatural authority, a parry to the revolutionaries' worldly thrust, and as such it was a sublimated war strategy with male combativeness stamped all over it. Religious life was to be dominated by cardinals and bishops as perhaps never before in Church history.

Early in the twentieth century, as this wave of macho control spread through the Church, strictures on nuns' daily existence steadily tightened, culminating in the procrustean 1917 code of canon law that epitomized the legalistic mentality of embattled popes. All the rules together were commonly called the Rule. "Keep the Rule," candidates were told, "and the Rule will keep you." Among its hundreds of provisions were those banning "particular friendships," the insistence that hands be kept folded under the scapular, and, one of many strictures against immodesty, a "custody of the eyes" commandment intended to prevent provocative or indulgent gazes.

The effect of this tight control over all sisterhoods was to rob congregations of distinctiveness by pressing them into the same mold and removing them further from the society at large. Although there were general proscriptions against listening to the radio; corresponding with friends; being alone with men, including fathers; driving a car or using the telephone, the orders had developed so independently that not all differences could be erased. On a secondary level, apart from canonical law, communities followed their own customs in such matters as the details of dress (wimples, coifs, veils, scapulars, and so forth), how they initiated newcomers into the novitiate, the celebration of major holidays, and policies toward visits with outsiders. Anyone with a practiced eye could spot the difference between a Benedictine and a Sister of Charity as readily as a baseball fan could distinguish a Brooklyn Dodger from a St. Louis Cardinal.

While each congregation had been subjected to varying amounts of Church involvement and interference, each had been independent of other ecclesiastical structures and totally on its own financially. In the case of teaching orders, income came mostly from the pittance each sister received as a stipend for her work, which went directly to the congregation (in 1940 the average was $40 per month for a teaching sister of the Erie, Pennsylvania, Benedictines; by 1978, the payment had increased to $400). Vegetables, sides of beef, and other staples were often donated by parishioners and parents of the Catholic students to supplement the meager cash flow. In some of the parish schools, pupils would roll canned goods down the aisles to help replenish the sisters' pantry. A sister stationed in a rural school recalled that the yield one year included pheasants, chickens, and half a hog. Especially in the early decades of the twentieth century, money was scarce in nearly every community and educational opportunities were in short supply. There were exceptions, but budgets were bare minimum. Sister Mary Agnes O'Donnell, ninety years old, of the Blessed Virgin Mary Sisters of Des Moines, Iowa, spoke recently of being one of five in her 1927 class of novices who were selected to go to graduate school. In her case, it was for a master's degree in history at Columbia University, a strange and intimidating place for a nun who had never been to a big city. She was given $10 for her first semester expenses and remembers exactly how it was spent: "$4.85 for a history book entitled *The History of Nationalities and Naturalization,* $5.00 for a book on Renaissance poetry, and 15 cents for shoe polish."

In an effort to instill humility, each nun in the convent of the 1950s was normally required to ask permission of a superior for virtually every little thing from a pair of shoes to a pen or a dose of aspirin. In an attempt to focus each woman's life within the community, sisters were not allowed to speak with outsiders except in the line of duty. Contact with family was limited by some orders to once a year and permitted scarcely more often by others. Cracks in the isolation were rare. Prioresses and mothers superior, normally elected by the community to speak for God, either allowed no radios or television sets in the recreation room or carefully picked the programs the nuns could hear or watch. Momentous events in the world could take days, even months, to penetrate the confines of the convent. Elderly sisters from an apostolic community told a nun-sociologist recently, for example, that news of the atomic bombs dropped on Japan reached them weeks after the attacks took place. Both outgoing and incoming mail was subject to be read by superiors. Defense against lesbianism was a chief motive behind the prohibition of "particular" friendships. Silence was the norm usually except for recreation and certain other specified times. During meals, excerpts from holy books were read aloud. Although strong loyalties bound sisters within a common life, a Sister of Charity in New Jersey expressed the sentiments of sisters engaged in a recent round-table discussion when she noted that all the formalism and distance and silence kept them from learning much about one another personally.

Subjugation of self was also behind the thick code of penances required for the smallest infractions such as misplacing a book or breaking a drinking glass. Not only was pride the great foe at the head of the list of deadly sins; it was the fountainhead of all other sins. In the "cause of stamping out 'pride' by instilling 'humility,' " explained Sister B., a member of a Sister of the Sacred Heart congregation, pausing over a cup of tea, the postulants and novices were told "to fail a test so that someone else would feel successful . . . and not to play [French composer] Debussy because the music was too sexy and shouldn't be heard in convent walls. And this was supposedly a modern congregation." Another longtime nun said, "I am reminded of asking permission for soap and other necessities—and kneeling to do so—never using the word 'mine' but rather 'ours,' looking alike, doing the same things at the same time, and on and on." College graduates, relatively few in number at that time, were especially suspected of bearing excess pride; therefore they were sometimes harshly treated.

In her book *Grace Before Meals,* Patricia Curran, a Sister of Notre Dame de Namur, outlined the elaborate web of dining rituals and penances in two communities, the Dominicans and the Notre Dame de Namur, before Vatican II. Among the mealtime penances for various infractions were kneeling during the meal, kissing the feet of other sisters, and lying on the floor of the entryway for sisters to step over on their way in. These measures were not seen as punishment for its own sake but as an aid to sanctification, to bring the sister or aspiring sister to a greater degree of purification. This was the higher way, the way bounded by the vows, the way of perfection.

In recent decades, movies and television have relentlessly caricatured that enclosed system of unquestioned authority. The figure of the mother superior has become Attila the Nun, commanding total obedience. *Sister Mary Ignatius Explains It All for You* was but one of the depictions. In these plays and films, each little rule, each of those two thousand canon laws, could become the excuse for pettiness and atrocity. These depictions are, in large measure, hyperbole, but there are real-life parallels. At a conference in 1995, for example, Sister Thomas Roach, a Sister of St. Joseph, told how, when she was a novice, the mother superior called her on the carpet for walking too fast. "Finally," she said slowly and darkly, her eyes fixed on the floor, "Mother superior made me drag a quacking toy duck behind me for a week." She seemed not yet to have recovered fully from the embarrassment.

Sister Roach also retained a vivid example of how isolated her Illinois community was from the rest of the world. "Every year, because we worked in hospitals, we went to the annual meeting of the regional hospital association," she said. "We would be driven to the meeting in a big chauffeured limousine and hear the speakers and discussions. But at lunchtime, instead of eating with the others in the hotel, we filed out of the hotel, climbed into the limo and ate the sandwiches we had brought with us, while the driver kept circling the parking lot so he wouldn't block traffic. That was to help us stay away from talking to strangers."

For active nuns—the vast majority of sisters who worked in the Church's schools and other institutions—the demands of the code were especially taxing. Religiously, they were to follow the rubrics of monastics, rising at dawn for prayers and Mass, keeping silence in the convent, filing by rank into the refectory, listening to selected pious readings while they ate, seldom permitted to visit their families (in one order, sisters were not even allowed inside the homes of their families). But while they lived much like monks or cloistered nuns, they also worked a full day outside the convent in a school, hospital, or agency of Church welfare. In addition, most teachers attended summer school from the end of the spring session to the start of fall classes within the same ritual framework.

Though many sisters before the great changeover took control of their communities, schools, and service centers to a degree that no other group of American women had done before them, they were still under the thumb of male authorities who could and did act, at times, erratically and arbitrarily. Male hierarchical control, of course, was nothing new. When a nineteenth-century bishop of New York, John Hughes, took issue with some Sisters of Charity who were operating homes for poor boys in his city under the direction from the mother house in Emmitsburg, Maryland, for example, he insisted that the sisters break away to form a separate community under his jurisdiction. The sisters were torn between their order and their boys. The bishop refused to allow a sister sent from Maryland to check the facts, though negotiation or mediation seemed out of the question from the start. In the end, about half of the sixty sisters returned to Maryland; the other half obeyed the bishop, establishing a new community in 1846, the Sisters of Charity of St. Vincent de Paul.

More than a century later, frictions still marred relations between Charity sisters in New Jersey and male authorities. At one Catholic school run by the sisters, the parish pastor entered an eighth-grade classroom demanding to know how many students had missed Mass on the previous Sunday and how many attended every week. The sister resisted the question on grounds that it was a matter of personal conscience. The principal, a sister, defended the teacher while the bishop pleaded with the principal to side with the pastor in order "to uphold his [the pastor's] manhood." In the end, the sisters broke the stalemate by reluctantly withdrawing from a school they had served longer than they had any other school in the diocese.

Over their long histories, religious congregations have naturally lived through good and bad times, periods of repression and periods of enlightened leadership. Some orders started out as outsiders, even renegades, and eventually became accepted. Perhaps the chief cause of the trouble and confusion that regularly marred relations between nuns and the Church hierarchy was a sweeping decree that went back to the thirteenth century. Pope Boniface VIII, seeking to keep nuns under control, ruled in 1298 that all women under vows must be confined within the walls of a cloister. Only nuns in such an enclosure were to be considered "religious." The problem arose when, in ensuing centuries, inspired women felt compelled to start new religious communities to serve the needs of the poor and needy in the world, but their ministry made it impossible for them to keep strict confinement to a cloister. They therefore sought exemption from the rule, but to little avail. The sisters of these communities took the common three vows of poverty, chastity, and obedience, wore distinct clothing in the custom of habits, and returned from their ministries to a walled-off community life, silent and prayerful. But these measures obviously fell short of the requirement of total isolation from society.

Such hybrid communities—those with one foot in worldly service and the other in the cloister—sprouted for centuries, existing outside Rome's formal recognition as official congregations yet winning a place in the affections of ordinary Catholics. Sometimes popes forced communities into enclosure, as has been noted in the cases of the Ursulines after the death of their founder, Angela Merici; the Congregation of Notre Dame in the sixteenth century; the "English Ladies" founded by Mary Ward; and the Visitation Sisters in the seventeenth century. (Men's communities were far freer. Jesuits, for instance, were permitted wide latitude in where they went and how the lived.) Other communities such as St. Vincent de Paul's Daughters of Charity finagled their way out of confrontations. For the Daughters, it was simply a matter of refusing to call themselves a religious community. The saga of women religious who felt a divine spark in the face of a male hierarchy manuevering to control them is a tale of anguish and gritty, sometimes heroic courage. And shrewdness. When the Jesuit president of Fordham University rebuffed a request by the superior of the Immaculate Heart of Mary Sisters of Scranton, Pennsylvania, to enroll twenty of her sisters in university courses, she bided her time, then sent him a box of fine cigars. When the next semester came around, her students were admitted, no questions asked.

Back in 1869, Pope Pius IX had finally granted active sisters recognition so long as they wore habits and lived in communities. Thousands of teachers, nurses, and child care workers were urgently needed across the array of U.S. dioceses to provide for the influx of new Catholics. Sisters could do this work dirt cheap *if* they were allowed to leave the convent for portions of the day. Total enclosure was obviously impossible. Desperate bishops, seeing the value of such semi-cloistered orders, either begged European congregations to send sisters or founded new groups themselves. Of the 261 religious communities existing in the United States before 1900, 58 were founded by bishops or priests to fulfill this purpose.

The concession Church leaders made to these "active" communities, by 1900 the mainstays of the vast Catholic health, education, and welfare system, was to ask sisters to take the same three vows in a "simple" sense, on a year-to-year basis. Their communities, however, were still denied formal approval as religious congregations; only cloistered nuns retained the designation "religious." The "actives" were like the volunteer fire department, long on service, short on benefits.

Orders such as the Ursulines and the Daughters of Charity had long lived in this twilight zone in which they were often both taken for granted and looked down on. Some, such as the Franciscans and Dominicans, were among the oldest of the old traditions, but the vast majority of the orders—an astonishing 80 percent—had existed for less than two hundred years. Well-known communities such as the Sisters of Charity, founded by Elizabeth Seton (the first U.S. sister to be made a saint), and the Sisters of Mercy, founded by Catherine McAuley, the daughter of a prosperous Irish family, were among those that were established relatively recently, in the nineteenth century.

The irony inherent in the perpetuation of this double standard between cloistered and active congregations—first class versus second class—still pained many sisters. The later waves of sisters were arguably most responsible for teaching and showing the immigrants and their descendants what Catholicism was all about. Some scholars would contend that active sisters, more than any other element in the Church, gave early American Catholicism its distinctive flavor. Professor Margaret Susan Thompson, a Syracuse University historian who has focused on nineteenth-century congregations, says active sisters conveyed "an implicit understanding of what it meant to be Catholic" by exhibiting "a sacramentalism not tied to the sacraments," through doing acts of mercy and illustrating that "being Catholic always means serving the poor and the immigrants and reaching out to non-Catholics." But while active sisters were purveyors of Church doctrine on the ground and in the trenches of immigrant America, they received little respect from Rome.

Pope Leo XIII provided some relief when, in 1900, he granted the active communities of "working nuns" official status as congregations. The Church's most numerous and most dedicated laborers at last had Rome's favor. The one proviso was that Rome reserved the right to approve every jot and tittle of a congregation's constitution before granting such recognition. Much later in the century, with the 1983 revision of the code of canon law, the distinction between solemn and simple vows would be erased. All permanent vows (those taken after temporary vows) are now considered solemn.

By the 1950s, when bright-eye Bernie found her way to Maryknoll, the active sisters coexisted at a distance from the contemplative sisters and all congregations were governed by their own Rome-approved constitution. Convents were loaded. The chain of authority was clear. Things ran smoothly. But cracks had appeared in the fortress.

The Reverend Bernard Haering, the moral theologian and noted author who was Pope John XXIII's personal confessor, has said, "After Auschwitz, we can never look at absolute obedience the same way again." Most nuns seem to agree reflexively. The old way was too hard, too unforgiving, too conducive to being taken over completely by petty tyrants who appeared in congregations with probably the same frequency as they do everywhere else.

Despite such excesses and abuses, however, the old way had internal coherence and a seamless rationale that made sense to those who understood it (the nun who was forced to drag a toy duck behind her said she was "always in trouble" and thought her penance "perfectly normal" at the time). In the order and stateliness of the old way was design and a kind of beauty that went with the horaria, the precisely segmented schedule of daily worship, prayer, work, and replenishment. However outmoded it might have been, the routine had an enviable clarity and focus that has yet to be replaced. In the earlier decades of this century, rank-and-file Catholics understood it, too, because it was closer to the sacrifice and discipline of their own restricted lives. As Catholics moved onward and upward, however, they joined an up-scale milieu of individualism and self-expression that was less enamored of self-denial and strict obedience. The gap began to yawn soon after Bernie donned the habit. And, of course, the nuns coming into the convent at that time, having been affected by the same culture, brought it with them into the sisterhood, making it significantly more difficult for younger sisters to hold on to the tradition of the past.

Contemporary sisters showed scarcely a trace of desire to return to such a past, but many expressed a degree of nostalgia for a time when orders were flourishing and they knew exactly what they were supposed to do. As a means of mobilizing large numbers of essential personnel, the old convent had performed with remarkable efficiency. Elderly and not-so-elderly nuns who had lived through the revolution refrained, for the most part, from disparaging the old way, seeing it as perhaps befitting a time and place and, for all of the now apparent troubles in it, having served the honorable purpose of lifting the fortunes of the immigrant masses of another time. To continue to minister to the mainstream Catholic population of today—middle-class, upper-middle-class, and upper-class Catholics—no longer seems as appropriate to the mission and ministry of many nuns as serving the poor. But to these veterans who endured for many years the rigors of convent boot camp, it was something to remember with fondness mingled with a feeling of good riddance.

Sister Patricia Curran's study of the dining rituals of two congregations has led her to conclude that the year 1960 marked a radical turning point in the way nuns thought about their daily rituals. Before then, she found, sisters tended to believe that the elaborate system of penances acted out in the dining room was essentially beneficial. According to Sister Curran, sisters coming into orders in the early decades of the century were largely motivated toward religious life by their own need for penance. Those entering after 1960 saw no inherent value in such practices. "My own research and that of Joan Chittister, a Benedictine," Sister Curran asserts, "designates 1960 as the definitive year when convent culture lost its hold on the religious aspirant." And what does she cite as the chief cause? A "questioning spirit" that began as a whisper in the fifties and gradually grew into a loud protest against "perfectionism, privatism and formalism."

As the crosswinds gained force in the next decade, the facade of security and harmoniousness blew off religious life, revealing all the diversity and restlessness within the convent walls. The upheaval likewise revealed starkly how much that life depended on the sufferance of male clerics. Though the degree of bishops' interference into the affairs of the convent varied greatly from place to place, the potential for meddling has always existed. For all of their considerable autonomy, often earned at great price, forty years later the sisters were vulnerable in ways they had not yet experienced in 1960.

The fact that the old way fell apart, or was broken apart on purpose, for a purpose, has taken a long time to resonate fully within communities of women religious. What was lost was a powerful, attractive, inspiring world of neatness and rigor and good, collective works.

A sister tells the story of a member of her order who suddenly saw where the loss of members and traditions might lead. "We went to our general chapter (legislative) meeting together," she said deliberately. "She was overwhelmed by the realization that this could all end and may be ending. She cried most of the day and, I suppose, it was cathartic in many ways. She died shortly thereafter—at age fifty-four."

Looking back, a Sister of Notre Dame said ruefully, "We were striving for perfection so maybe God would love us."

To seven elderly nuns gathered around me at the table at the Sisters of Charity mother house in Convent Station, New Jersey, on a spring afternoon, the convent of the 1950s enshrined a higher calling, one that was embraced by some and doubted by others. They remembered being placed on that higher plane, above the mass of Catholics, elevated on that pyramid whose pinnacle was Rome, assigned a lofty perch on the bean stalk. It was a place not everyone was comfortable with. "To be holy," said one nun, "we had to be apart from the world. It was drummed into us that every time I went into the world I returned less a nun." Another said, "We used the word 'higher.' We were making vows, we gave up certain goods of the world and our own will. We were reminded by our own parents how much holier we were than they were." Still another commented, "You took it all for granted. All nuns sat in the front pew at Mass, took Communion first. It was our place."

They also remembered uneasiness at being consigned the role of the higher female being in a vertical, hierarchical, rigorous rendition of the Church, one in which they felt alien. Some said they never bought the idea. Others came to a sharp awakening at one point. "I went home with my mom to shop," said a sister who is now a college professor, "and I was in my habit, of course. As we were getting off the bus, an old lady who was at the swinging door stood back to let me off ahead of her. I was never so humiliated. For the first time I said, 'O God, this is wrong.' "

Chapter Three

Improving by Degrees

A t the head of the column plodding cautiously from a sure past toward an unformatted future were two sisters of uncommon talents, Sister Mary Emil Penet and Sister Ritamary Bradley.

The two sisters collaborated on an endeavor called the Sister Formation Conference, which became the most powerful movement to sweep the American sisterhood before the dawn of the Second Vatican Council. Its vitality lasted only about a decade—starting in the mid-1950s—but thousands of sisters still look back at this brief interlude as an incandescent period that transformed how they thought and lived as nothing ever had before. "Formation," the traditional process of molding the candidate for the spiritual and practical requirements of a life under religious vows, had remained quite constant for nearly two centuries. The Sister Formation Conference began to shake up that process.

The conference, which existed at first under the wing of the National Catholic Educational Association (NCEA), the U.S. bishops' agency in Washington that coordinated the activities of Catholic schools, needed the blessing of the male Church leaders before it could sink roots. That permission was obtained. But when many bishops came to see the conference as an instrument of independence and experimentation among nuns, they moved to tighten a grip on it and eventually undermine it.

Despite the setbacks, the afterglow of Sister Formation is still vivid almost five decades later in the drama and excitement that suffused sisters' testimonies about it. Sister Mary Lea Schneider, president of Cardinal Stritch College in Milwaukee, for example, recalled fondly how the conference first led sisters to question the way women were treated by the Church and the wider culture. In her 1994 essay, "Educating an Elite," Sister Schneider declared that the result was nothing less than "independent thinking and the development of a truly independent mind" that reached beyond religion into social and political issues. The pull toward a traditional view of nuns as "wedded to Christ" had never totally let up, she said, but a new, assertive image was gaining force. "The conference," she said, "led sisters from a narrow church-oriented identity to recognize service to the broader world and to perceive church-in-the-world."

At the heart of Sister Formation was an effort to refine a sister's identity from dependent child to thinking adult. The central aim was to strengthen her intellect and her professional competence by providing her a four-year college degree before she was sent out to work; in the mid-1950s only a handful of orders offered sisters higher education. The vast majority of teaching nuns were rushed into the classroom as teenage sisters, barely having taken their vows and with little or no college education. In general, higher education was subsumed under the community's routines of prayer and service rather than valued for its own sake. A sister's college credits would be crammed into a string of university summer sessions. Among nuns, the process was known, both sardonically and realistically, as the twenty-year plan.

In pressing an agenda to allow every sister a bachelor's degree at the outset, Sister Formation leaders mirrored a heightened emphasis on higher education across the country after World War II. In particular, leaders of this initiative for nuns stirred a new consciousness among sisters, sometimes unwittingly, that resulted in a new grasp of their vocation. Most significantly, the life of the mind gained respect of its own. Nuns would begin to see themselves as individuals instead of cogs in an anonymous machine, feeling, one sister remembered, "as if finally I, Theresa, had some dignity." The growth of critical thinking that often accompanied this rise in dignity was, of course, problematic for the old order. In effect, nuns began asking more unsettling questions. A surge of pride was palpable. Never before had a cause been by them, for them, and about them.

None of these developments would have been possible without the talents of the pair of sisters who became Sister Formation's driving, two-cylinder engine.

Sister Penet, a college professor at Marygrove College in Detroit, fired the opening salvo for this bold campaign in a 1954 speech to the National Catholic Educational Association. An Immaculate Heart of Mary sister and a recognized scholar, she had been invited as a last-minute substitute to a session devoted to the topic of sister education. Noting that there had never been such an emphasis, she stated bluntly: "We have never looked upon our Sisters as a human resource to be used to the utmost intellectual capacity of each one—perhaps because they are women, perhaps because things go slowly in the Church and teaching nuns are still a novelty, and perhaps because we have so many of them. Which is a little like saying that we have been thinking that Sisters are expendable."

In an effort to remedy that deficiency, the Sister Formation Conference was created as the first truly national organization that brought together nuns from different orders in a common cause. Sister Penet was its founding genius, lobbying timelessly for support of church leaders, orchestrating regional conferences to convince major superiors of its benefits, and fashioning its guiding concepts. She saw Sister Formation as a concept "that stood not only for the education of the Sister in a formal and academic sense, but for all the influences, spiritual and intellectual, formal and informal, pre-service and in-service, which go to make her a better religious and a better professional person."

The importance of congregations putting their heads together can scarcely be overestimated. Until then, nearly all sisters lived in hermetically sealed communities, discouraged from any contact with nuns from different orders, often suspicious of one another. For all the Church's "oneness" and universal practices such as the Latin Mass and the doctrines taught to children, most religious women and men existed in communities that were as distant from one another as if they were competing Protestant sects (and, in fact, the genius of the Catholic system was that spiritual visionaries and misfits could go off on their own without having to leave the Church or cross paths with others they might have quarrels with). Sister Formation broke down the walls, allowing a wide variety of nuns to get to know one another. They met, joined forces, and in reaching toward a common goal built consensus for pursuing a broader set of objectives in the years ahead. Sister Ritamary Bradley remembered the initial discomfort: "It was all just a little tense because up to this time communities didn't meet together." But they went ahead and did it without asking "permission."

In making the conference fly, Sisters Penet and Bradley openly acknowledged their debt to sister-educators who had been proposing an upgrading of training requirements for more than a decade. But the idea needed a vehicle. The two midwestern sisters provided that and much more.

Fitted out in full habits, their heads wrapped in black and white, Sisters Penet and Bradley were virtually indistinguishable from other members of their respective orders. Yet they were both anomalous as scholars having earned Ph.D.'s; both were well respected in their communities for their intellectual achievements. Sister Penet became the conference's first executive director. Sister Bradley was named the first editor of its official periodical, the *Sister Formation Bulletin,* which provided a forum for refining and testing the conference's goals. As a team, they complemented each other: Sister Penet was the theoretician and organizational whiz; Sister Bradley, the quieter, literary voice. Together, they resembled the partnership of Susan B. Anthony and Elizabeth Cady Stanton in the cause of woman suffrage, two complementary personalities converting principles into a practical campaign.

Sister Penet was catapulted to prominence while working as a philosophy professor at Marygrove, a women's school run by her order, the Sister Servants of the Immaculate Heart of Mary (IHM) in Monroe, Michigan. She was born in Detroit in 1916 (she later incorporated her father's name, Emil, into her religious name), and her devotion to higher education for sisters was rooted in her own past. She had entered the IHMs after finishing her B.A. at Marygrove in 1936 and trying a year of law school at the University of Detroit (1936–37). After joining the community, she undertook the long march to a doctorate while teaching high school in Akron, Monroe, and Detroit.

St. Louis University, a Jesuit institution, awarded Sister Penet a doctorate in philosophy in 1950. Though she thought of herself as a moral theologian—one who studies the nature of the Catholic moral life—she was forbidden by Church policy to study theology of any kind because she was a woman. Women were judged by the Church to be unsuited for this discipline—the formal exercise of thinking about God—which, ironically, was called the "queen of the sciences" in the Middle Ages. The ban was defended largely on grounds that women lacked sufficient reasoning power and that they were disqualified from the "Magisterium," the Church's teaching and theological authority, which consists exclusively of the male hierarchy. Sister Penet followed the example of a few other precocious graduate school sisters by pursuing the next best permissible discipline, philosophy, which ranked just a notch below theology and was considered the stepping-stone to it. And like other graduate school sisters, she availed herself of whatever classes in theology she could.

By all accounts, Sister Penet was a gifted teacher with a probing, penetrating mind. Normally reserved, she could roar like a lion when the cause of the sisters was threatened. Arguing for a separate sister conference, for example, she assailed a gathering mostly of Catholic school superintendents who took a dim view of her efforts to weaken their control over the teaching sisters and to raise the sisters' pay. "Sisters are afraid," she declared. "They do not wish to be mercenary. They are trained to endure. They have been too timid to act in isolation and they have no institutionalized manner of acting together." Nuns rarely spoke with such candor in public. To the superintendents, all male, such declarations no doubt sounded like a call to arms, an echo of unionizing.

Sister Bradley was born the same year as her partner and although she came from a very different background, her path had covered some of the same ground. Raised in the small Iowa farming town of Stuart, she had entered the Sisters of Humility of Ottumwa, Iowa, at age seventeen in 1933. Given the low levels of sister education and the Great Depression, she had been one of the lucky ones; her intellectual gifts were recognized and she was sent to college, first to Ottumwa Heights Junior College then to Marygrove, where she graduated with a bachelor's degree, two years behind Sister Penet. Like her cohort, Sister Bradley earned a Ph.D., from St. Louis University, persevering part-time for fourteen years while teaching full-time at her order's college, Marycrest, in Davenport, Iowa, and attending to the mundane duties assigned by her community (at one point she was a housekeeper for the bishop of Davenport). Her field was medieval writing; her dissertation was on Chaucer. Literature was another means of covertly tapping into the forbidden fruit of theology. She was an aesthete as well as a scholar, turning out a steady stream of finely wrought, meditative poems in addition to crafting meticulous academic articles. She seemed well on her way to a quiet life in academia.

Sister Penet fiercely admired Sister Bradley's talents, lauding her at the time of the Sister Formation Conference as "the most promising young scholar in any of our women's colleges," and eagerly sought her out to edit the conference's official publication, the *Sister Formation Bulletin*. Its initial edition, in the fall of 1954, was an eight-page, no-frills mimeographed production made possible by the $100 Sister Bradley wheedled out of the National Catholic Educational Association. The *Bulletin* soon became widely circulated among religious communities; it was the first publication edited by nuns themselves and covering a range of topics from sisters' education to strikingly new concepts of religious life. The unifying theme was feminist in substance if not in name: the worth and dignity of women.

From the first, the *Bulletin* established a format that ensured variety. It always included one article about the training, or formation, of sisters, educationally and otherwise, by an expert on the subject; reviews of books and other writings that examined formation; features on communities trying new methods of preparing sisters; and reports on Sister Formation Conference activities both nationally and regionally. The publication's astonishing popularity was attributable to fine writing and hot topics, and the message was often subtle. There were accounts of sisters taking charge of their own lives for the first time. New ideas were put forth about the nature of religious life; there were even discussions of theology. Provocative thoughts streamed from a procession of effective writers, among them scholars, cardinals, sisters from a wide assortment of orders and professional practices, priests, and religious superiors. Ideas traveled and were copied. The system creaked and shook as entirely new forms of education and inculcation took shape.

"A high quality of spiritual and intellectual reading was being given to sisters," writes Marjorie Noterman Beane, author of *From Framework to Freedom,* which traces the history of Sister Formation. "No longer were priest-authors directing what sisters would be reading, but sisters were determining what up-to-date material would be given to their fellow sisters."

Sister Penet, a woman of exacting standards who was sparing in her praise, credited Sister Bradley for making "the most noteworthy contribution to the theory of the movement" when the *Bulletin* was just three years old: "There is an emerging philosophy of Sister Formation—and it owes more to Sister Ritamary than to anyone else. Furthermore, she has made this theory understandable and actually understood by the leaders in our communities of women." The new ideal was to develop vowed women intellectually, psychologically, and spiritually in a setting of service.

The very elements that spawned enthusiasm for Sister Formation and its voice, the *Bulletin,* namely freedom and opportunity, caused Church authorities, including many mothers superior, to shudder. As officials who believed in a divinely ordered flow of power from top to bottom, they feared that the conference was creating a disruption in the line of command. Many authorities therefore believed that the sisters' gains would be their loss. In the end, the struggle would be over who had the right to make decisions about many of the most crucial areas of sisterhood. Sisters Penet and Bradley, somewhat unwittingly, had been heading straight for that confrontation since the beginning.

The extraordinary pair worked in close cooperation until outside opposition and Sister Penet's dismay at the prospect of broad-based renewal helped bring the conference down. Collapse though it did, the democratic impulse had invaded the convent for good.

By the mid-1990s, Sister Penet was infirm and unable to talk about her experiences. Sister Bradley, who in 1975 helped found the *Mystics Quarterly,* a continuation of her medieval passions, was living near St. Ambrose University in Davenport, Iowa, where she had taught English for decades. She remained engaged in many of the issues that had gripped Sister Formation in its early stages.

As she looked back on events from the vantage point of her early eighties, she saw the trouble that crushed the conference as stemming from the refusal by her and other Sister Formation leaders to surrender the conference's independence and cave in to growing pressure from higher-ups.

The issue of control was paramount. Continued autonomy by the Sister Formation Conference would have hastened change. By containing it, Church authorities, including major superiors who weren't accustomed to having their nuns operate independently and cooperatively, blunted this drive toward greater self-determination. Sister Penet was staunchly opposed to outside control, but later relented. Sister Bradley never gave up; neither did Sister Annette Walters, a Sister of St. Joseph and a noted psychologist who replaced Sister Penet as executive director of the conference in 1960.

The core question from the beginning of the Sister Formation movement was what nuns needed, professionally and personally, to excel in their roles as teachers, nurses, and administrators. The consensus was that their training was alarmingly inadequate; Sister Formation was a response that had some important theoretical support.

A drumbeat for the educational upgrading of sisters had been gaining momentum years before Pope Pius himself weighed in on the subject. As early as 1941 Sister Bertrande Meyers, a Daughter of Charity, had published a doctoral dissertation, "The Education of Sisters," in which she advocated a new approach that would strengthen professional and academic training. Her work was based on a survey of how sixty orders educated their sisters. Sister Penet would later credit Sister Meyers for stimulating her own crucial thinking on the subject.

At issue was how much education a sister received before taking a teaching assignment. Some were sent out with thirty hours of course work or fewer and almost none started out with a bachelor's degree. The vast majority of the nearly 95,000 teaching nuns in 1950 plodded along, summer after summer, a few courses at a time, on that "twenty-year plan," as nuns had tagged it, for a B.A. or B.S. Meanwhile, states were raising their standards. By 1952, a total of thirty-three states required or would soon require teaching candidates to have a bachelor's degree (in 1950, only 45 percent of public school teachers had graduated from college). Meeting this new requirement was all well and good, except for one problem. How would the demand for better-educated women religious square with the need by bishops and pastors for teaching nuns? Tensions would grow around that question.

Before that friction arose, however, a prominent Holy Cross sister put the case for improving the education of sisters on the front burner. Sister

Madeleva Wolff, C.S.C., a distinguished poet and renowned president of St. Mary's College in South Bend, Indiana, chose the site of the 1949 National Catholic Educational Association to deliver a paper, "The Education of Sister Lucy," that became a centerpiece in the campaign to secure higher education for sisters. In her paper, she argued that the fictitious Sister Lucy would teach at a great disadvantage without full degree preparation, which she probably would have received if she hadn't entered religious life. Moreover, she said, lack of training as a professional would likely weaken Sister Lucy's commitment to her vocation.

If religious communities began at once to "complete the education of our young sisters before sending them out to teach," Sister Wolff said, "practically all of the immediate generation will have their degrees and licenses in two or three years." With her undergraduate degree in hand before teaching, Sister Wolff said, Sister Lucy could spend her summers attending graduate school and she would have the satisfaction of feeling competent as a teacher. Sister Wolff described the piecemeal undergraduate system as "shortsighted" and "stupidly extravagant" in its use of the young nuns' talents.

Implementing such a program was still a way off, but the rationale was taking shape, thanks to Sisters Meyers and Wolff. The chief obstacle was still the Catholic school establishment itself, which relied on ever-increasing numbers of bodies to fill positions, in some areas for as little as a few hundred dollars a year. Pastors were reluctant or hostile to the idea of hiring lay teachers in the interim while nuns were earning bachelor's degrees. While educating young sisters seemed like a great idea, many of those in charge of Catholic schools believed the makeshift "twenty-year plan" had worked well enough and was worth retaining, especially given the crush of rising enrollments. Push would soon come to shove.

The ideas behind Sister Formation sprouted, in fact, from calls from the Church's highest authority for a reexamination and amendment of religious life to fit it better to modern conditions. Pope Pius XII, who occupied the Chair of St. Peter from 1937 to 1959, was usually remembered for flashing red stoplights of moral and ecclesiastical restraint, yet in this instance he flashed green go-ahead signals. In fact, Catholics who decried the vast revisions that came after Vatican II were sometimes surprised or nonplussed to discover that the major instigator of revision had been none other than Pope Pius XII, the last of the monarchical popes in the steeply hierarchical nineteenth-century mode encoded by Vatican I (1869–70) in the doctrine of papal infallibility. Further, they were surprised to learn that the pope had set "renewal" in motion some twelve years before the Second Vatican Council was convened. In the following years, nuns were to take much initiative on their own, to be sure, but the process had been set in motion largely by a pope whose name was not normally spoken in the same breath with the word "reformer."

As an astute observer of modernity's effects on the Church, Pope Pius XII had become concerned that vocations to the religious life had declined steeply in Europe, and he attributed the slump in part to convents' remoteness from the world of daily life. In particular, he was alarmed that nuns were less well trained as teachers than were their secular counterparts.

Acting on these concerns, the pope summoned the leaders of both male and female religious communities to Rome in 1950. He challenged the assembly to revitalize their communities and, in so doing, to emphasize two objectives. The first was to enhance "theological education and professional credentials for those teaching and doing other professional work." The other was more surprising. The pope called for "the elimination of outdated customs and clothing that estranged them from those they [the sisters] served."

His directives found resonance most readily, of course, among those U.S. sisters who had given the matters some thought. By the early 1950s, the face of Catholic America was dramatically changing, prompting new questions of how the Church fit into the modern world. Simply put, Catholics were on the move. Catholic men who had served in the armed forces during World War II were using the G.I. Bill of Rights to pay their way through college or had already earned a degree. Catholic women were attending college and joining religious sisterhoods in record numbers. Catholic families, gaining in prosperity, were headed for the scores of new suburbs. Catholic baby boomers would soon be crowding parochial classrooms. Parish churches, rectories, schools, and social halls sprouted all over the landscape. As a support unit, sisters continued to prepare young Catholics for this new world while at the same time feeling pressures to equip themselves better for the task.

Three years later, in 1952, after Pope Pius had voiced his wishes on the subject, the NCEA invited four nuns to respond to the pope's admonitions at its annual convention. One of those respondents was Sister Penet, who, as noted earlier, outlined the problems as (1) carving out enough time for the young nun to receive proper education before becoming a teacher; (2) finding enough money to pay for that education; and (3) needing to better understand the difficulties and needs of nun-teachers. The answer to the first problem, she said, was hiring more lay teachers to fill in while nuns were finishing college. Regarding financing, she proposed a survey to find out what resources congregations had. And to learn more about the conditions of nuns in the classroom, she suggested some sort of new group that could coordinate information and ideas among mother houses.

Angry Catholic school superintendents rose at the convention to denounce the latter idea as utter nonsense, contrary to the interests of the Catholic schools, but the debate resulted in the naming of a survey committee to explore these areas, with Sister Penet as its head. A year after the first meeting opened the door, she was calling for the establishment of a separate organization for sisters within the National Catholic Educational Association.

By 1954, the association agreed, authorizing a distinct entity, the Sister Formation Conference, and naming Sister Penet as its executive director. Her platform was direct and unequivocal: a four-year degree for every nun before she enters the school setting as a professional teacher. In a speech to that founding convention, she noted that pressures from expanding Catholic schools had pushed sisters into the classroom prematurely, and that the reason, in part, was that too few lay teachers had been hired. Furthermore, she said, many nuns had taken so long to finish their degrees that they were "almost too old to make it economical." But her strongest plea was for greater dignity for nuns by recognizing and developing their intellectual talents.

This earthshaking moment in the history of the nation's sisters arrived under the rather bland, tidy rubric "formation." Ducks fly in formation; troops move according to it; high school bands demonstrate many varieties of it. In the language of sisters, "formation" has normally meant both the training needed to be a sister and the religious-behavioral mold of sameness into which the candidate is pressed once instruction is finished. It was intended largely as a cookie-cutter experience that would bind the candidate's thinking and acting to that of the community. There was little room for any concept like individualism. Young women were supposed to fit in; conformity was a cherished virtue.

Any departure from this pattern would have been unimaginable without the encouragement and sponsorship of the National Catholic Educational Association. Safe harbor was crucial, for the sisters could not, practically speaking, go off on their own. No other Church institution was a logical candidate for the task. Within the confines of the NCEA, Sister Formation had a degree of autonomy from major superiors and from the bishops. Whether it had too much leeway was an issue that would eventually split the conference ranks, but for a decade the NCEA maintained a decidedly hands-off policy toward the sisters. In the early days, the leaders of Sister Formation moved ahead with a marked degree of boldness and freedom; their enthusiasm for what was widely perceived as overdue innovation quickly spread. A new age of cooperation dawned as sisters began working together, planning strategies for achieving conference goals and designing a curriculum.

That did not mean that the conference had been cut loose to act on its own. Rome was watching; so were the bishops. Sister Penet attempted to keep the hierarchy apprised of Sister Formation's major initiatives and sought its approval. In addition, the conference's existence depended, in part, on the creation of a national consultative committee of priests to represent the larger order and to serve as a means of assuring Church authorities that all was in order. The idea of nuns running their own show made many bishops, priests, and school superintendents very nervous. The conference existed, finally, on the sufferance of an always tenuous permission.

In 1952, the National Catholic Educational Association provided the umbrella for the fledging organization by authorizing an exploratory committee of sisters to act as a springboard. The committee soon sent questionnaires to 377 major superiors of orders in the United States; an astounding 80 percent of them were completed and returned. The information they gleaned disturbed the committee members. Among the findings: 58 orders were sending out beginning elementary school teachers who had completed fewer than thirty college credits. Another 118 congregations had no college facilities of their own or no nearby church-related college or university with which they coordinated sister education. Already thirty-three states had plans for requiring a bachelor's degree for teaching certification, but only 13 of the congregations in those states had plans for addressing the new requirement.

Financial reality also began to peek its head from beneath decades of denial and burial. Almost half of the communities surveyed (45 percent) said that the costs of supporting a sister at a basic level exceeded the amount of her teaching stipend, which came to as little as a few hundred dollars a year (sisters from one community were paid $45 a month, for example). The fact that many orders were subsidizing Catholic school systems rather than the other way around suddenly became common knowledge among the communities, providing ammunition for future struggles over compensation.

Sister Penet and her advisors took the results from the questionnaires and wove them into the broader quest to find ways to restructure formation. With the benefit of this kind of research, the goals of Sister Formation became a great deal more than providing the young sister with a quality college education, important as that was.

In pursuit of the objective of getting sisters a quality college education, the conference pressed congregations either to establish their own colleges or to cooperate with one another to share facilities. Dozens of such institutions, commonly called "juniorates," sprang up to educate sisters who had completed their novitiate training and had taken their temporary vows. During their time in college, sisters would, according to the plan adopted by most communities, continue to pray and keep the congregation's religious routine. In theory, the sisters would become, in the words of Sister Penet, "psychologically mature, intellectually disciplined, broadly cultured and professionally competent."

Sister Formation leaders thought that achieving this lofty goal meant creating a college curriculum for sisters training to be teachers, nurses, and social workers. A team led by Sister Penet crisscrossed the country consulting orders and educators and, by 1956, had put together a recommended sequence of courses for the sister colleges, funded with a grant from the Ford Foundation. The curriculum, contained in the Everett report, named for the Washington State city where the first large-scale exploration had taken place, gave heavy emphasis to theology (which nuns had hitherto been officially barred from studying) and philosophy but also contained large helpings from the social sciences—sociology, psychology, and economics—as well as generous portions from the humanities.

Although the curriculum never received full acceptance from the orders (it was implemented in only a handful of sister colleges) and was soon criticized by some sister-educators as too rigid, the conference's more general aims of improving the sisters' education and promoting high ideals permanently revised assumptions about the training of a sister. She would never again be a faceless servant but, increasingly, a woman whose education would enhance her understanding of her responsibilities both to her community and to herself. Most significantly, she was being taught to think for herself.

Something of the effect of this shift is evident in one Sacred Heart sister's recollection. "The sisters in my entering group were the first to complete their degrees BEFORE going out to teach," she said. "I would also add that we were allowed to choose our field of study based on our abilities and in discussion with the dean of students at our college. I can recall in one summer session I attended, being in classes with much older sisters trying to finish their degrees who had considerable teaching experience, some smarter than the professor."

Another sister, an Ursuline, remembered her order's first theology courses. "Just at the time I entered," she said, "and under the impetus of the Sister Formation movement, our province contracted with the local Jesuits for a novitiate program in theology. Looking back, it must have been quite an experience for some of those professors, used to droning on in Latin [the language still taught to seminarians but not expected of others], to suddenly be expected to teach a room full of eighteen- to twenty-one-year-old women in English. Some of those women even questioned the material. How was I to know that Father X had never been questioned before? I know I could never have survived the day-to-day stuff of religious life without the strong sense of conviction and purpose that those studies gave me."

The threat posed to priests and bishops by this burst of free thought cannot be overstated. Three decades after the Sister Formation Conference, the hue and cry from critics of renewal was that sisters had succumbed to a variety of the self-centeredness that plagued the whole American culture. On the other hand, many sisters believed that while there had been excesses of individualism, to be sure, the overall move toward greater self-reliance was both necessary and sound.

The conference's intellectual vitality during its first decade was carried chiefly by the *Sister Formation Bulletin,* whose circulation had reached 11,000 around the world (demand for certain issues ran as high as 25,000) when Sister Bradley was forced out of the editorship position in 1964 (the publication continued to exist, as did the conference, as much tamer versions of their former selves).

Looking back at her decade at the helm, Sister Bradley wrote in the Summer 1964 issue that she had "scrupulously parried off efforts—sometimes vigorously pursued—to make it become an official voice, or to be a molder of a collective mind." A factor in her ability to withstand such pressures was that Sister Bradley mingled articles by sisters and theologians that raised prickly questions about Church teaching or practice with those written by high-ranking cardinals and bishops whose views carried the punch of the official Church. The words of the Reverend Bernard Haering, John XXIII's right-hand moral theologian and a sometime critic of the Church, could coexist with those of the craggy Richard Cardinal Cushing of Boston, the confessor to the Kennedys. The most influential Catholic thinkers appeared regularly in its plain printed pages, among them Augustin Cardinal Bea, another close friend of the pope's; Karl Rahner, the eminent German theologian whose ideas shaped the Second Vatican Council; and Thomas Merton, the American activist, writer, and Trappist monk. Contributions to this ongoing discussion provoked debate. None proved more provocative than an article with the seemingly innocuous title "The Local Superior as Spiritual Leader," written by Sister Annette Walters, the Sister of St. Joseph who had succeeded Sister Penet as executive director of the conference.

In her article, in the Spring 1963 issue, Sister Walters, a trained clinical psychologist, endeavored to apply the insights of the psychological discipline to the religious life. That process may sound entirely sensible to most Catholics today, but back then much of the Catholic community was still steeped in a pre–Vatican II mentality that firmly held that there was no truth outside the Church, social science or no social science.

The sister superior, Sister Walters said, must respect the individual personality, being careful to see each sister as a person of worth rather than a unit of production. "The continuing mental health of Sisters," she wrote, "requires that the superior see them and deal with them as unique and personally valued individuals—not just as more or less useful cogs in an apostolic machine. . . . When the work of the community takes precedence, in the mind of the superior, over the people doing the work, the sense of corporate mission and responsibility may be lost." Addressing an especially touchy issue, Sister Walters said that in her estimation a good leader "does not use her official position with a heavy hand in exacting obedience"—although sisters superior commonly misused their authority, according to anecdotal evidence. Authoritarian leadership was rebuked not only as an ineffective means of running a group but as indicative of a superior's own psychological problems. Superiors who acted in this "rigid, unyielding, and legalistic" manner were diagnosed by Sister Walters as victims of "unresolved psychological complexes and unconscious fears." She concluded, "The rigid, compulsive superior is not simply a person who is naturally strict, while remaining just and charitable." With regard to the well-being of sisters, Sister Walters said that psychology had shown that for "emotional, intellectual, or spiritual maturity, it is required that the individual make her own decisions." An overbearing, intrusive superior could, by implication, stifle maturity. What sisters needed was to be treated with dignity and given space to develop on their own.

The article touched off a firestorm. Scores of superiors read it as an indictment of their leadership (especially their right to intercede as a sister's conscience and, in some cases, her psyche) and protested Sister Walters's analysis to high Church officials. In 1964 she was forced to leave the Sister Formation Conference and hopes of the conference continuing as a progressive leader were dashed.

No other *Bulletin* submission touched such a central nerve, but many others, some of them by international figures who were part of the European reform movement, in the *Bulletin* and elsewhere delivered broad attacks on conventional thinking about the sisters' vocation and the whole character of Roman Catholicism. Father Haering, a trailblazer in moral thought, and Cardinal Leon Suenens, a remarkable combination of archbishop and theologian, stood out. Most notably, excerpts from Cardinal Suenens's then-forthcoming book, *The Nun in the World,* appeared in the *Bulletin*'s pages, causing a sensation. Those ideas would coalesce at the Second Vatican Council but were available for preview in the *Bulletin*.

Over the *Bulletin*'s first ten years, then, it walked a tightrope, asserting its intention to foster freedom of thought but always with the underlying awareness of the consequences of going too far. Sister Walters's article tested that freedom and may have hardened opposition against it.

The tension around the article was part of a larger reaction to the *Bulletin* and Sister Formation. A fissure opened by the late 1950s between Sister Penet and more reform-minded sisters. Sister Penet regarded Sister Formation mainly as a conservative curriculum for sisters that would better fit them for traditional roles. Sisters Walters and Bradley saw the conference as a much broader movement that would transform a nun's self-image.

Though Catholics were generally breathing the first whiffs of fresh air from the opening of the Second Vatican Council in 1962, American sisters had been exercising a council of their own for some twelve years under the auspices of the Sister Formation Conference. This despite the fact that they had nothing whatever to do with Vatican II itself. They had been thinking new thoughts, testing new ideas in that unusual laboratory, the likes of which had never been seen. But the specialness of this movement became its undoing.

The existence of a separate group of nuns who didn't clearly follow the usual lines of authority raised problems in Roman Catholic culture. By the approval of the NCEA, the Sister Formation Conference had a place to hang its hat that was not within the regular hierarchical order. To safeguard the conference's privileges, Sister Penet had set up consultant groups with priests, school superintendents, and major superiors to enlist their support. Rome was informed of the conference's every move, and when the conference's operating officers believed permission was necessary from a bishop or other churchman, it was secured. In short, the conference tried to cover its flanks in order to maintain itself as a think tank relatively free of clerical control, a movement that shaped its own agenda and published its own ideas. Through it all, Sister Bradley managed to keep the *Bulletin* in the good graces of the bishop whose permission was needed to publish it, and to satisfy supervisory eyes at the Vatican.

Yet from the start, some superiors and some clerics were uneasy about the conference's loose tethering to the hierarchy. Sister Bradley recalled, for example, that during her and Sister Penet's extensive travels to promote Sister Formation, they met with James Cardinal McIntyre of Los Angeles, who was known to believe that the NCEA was a dangerously leftist organization. "What is your relation to the NCEA?" the cardinal asked, to which Sister Penet replied wryly, "Tenuous, your excellency." Moreover, the job of deciding how sisters were to be formed had always belonged to each order's tradition and its leadership. With the advent of Sister Formation, the task had been given over largely to educators, sister intellectuals such as Sister Penet and Sister Bradley. As time passed, more superiors grew discontented with what seemed to them a diminution of their responsibilities and a loss of control over a new blueprint for sister formation, one they had not produced but were expected to implement.

The Conference of Major Superiors of Women (CMSW) in 1956 provided a focal point for much of this uneasiness. Ironically, the CMSW conference was established at Rome's insistence against the wishes of major superiors. Since 1950, Rome had proposed such a conference as a means of aiding progress in congregations and improving communications among them, but the U.S. superiors had initially turned down the suggestion. By 1956 they had relented because of Vatican pressure and the attraction of being able to work cooperatively. Two hundred thirty-five major superiors organized as the CMSW; more would join later.

Another threat to the Sister Formation Conference's autonomy arose mysteriously and darkly from Italian politics. In 1952, Pope Pius XII sponsored a small, broad-based group called the Better World Movement to oppose what he saw as a communist threat in the upcoming Italian elections. The movement's official founder was a fiery priest, the Reverend Ricardo Lombardi, and its principal public business was conducting religious retreats. By the late 1950s, the movement was faltering and in need of new blood, preferably in the United States. With that in mind, Father Lombardi chose Sister Mary Josetta, president of St. Xavier College in Chicago, as his surrogate to lead the Better World Movement in America. Her assignment was to link her organization, which worked with clergy and laypeople, with the CMSW and the Sister Formation movement. The objective was to consolidate control over nuns.

With allies among the major superiors and, more significantly, in Rome, the Sacred Congregation of Religious—the Vatican agency that governed women's orders—hoped to streamline authority over the hitherto scattered elements of women religious. Advocates of this plan hoped to move all three groups under one roof, thereby handcuffing Sister Formation. The plan would not succeed. Yet already, the elected chair of Sister Formation, Mother Mary Regina Cunningham, a highly respected Mercy Sister and superior, was actively working in favor of subordinating Sister Formation to the CMSW. Toward that end, she had collected dozens of supporting letters from major superiors. The kind of conference to which Sisters Walters and Bradley had devoted themselves was vanishing in the shroud of that dark night.

From the first, the ever politically astute Sister Penet saw a danger that the CMSW might move to take over the Sister Formation Conference and place it solely in the hands of the superiors. She quickly petitioned the NCEA to make the Sister Formation Conference a permanent part of its structure. "It seems to me," she wrote to Sister Formation officials in urging them to support her move with the NCEA, "that it is absolutely necessary that something like this be done now to ensure that we will go on, and to ensure that we can enter into some working relationship with the Higher Superiors Conference [aka the CMSW]." Relations with the CMSW might be necessary, but for Sister Penet they were best conducted from an organizational distance.

The hand of the Sacred Congregation of Religious was also moving behind the scenes to bring Sister Formation under the vertical authority of the CMSW, a move that was certain to stifle Sister Formation's ability to decide its own future. Vatican officials visited the United States in the late 1950s and said as much. Sister Penet steadfastly refused to surrender her group's independence. Her appeal to the NCEA was successful, and in early 1957 Sister Formation became a regular section of the organization. The NCEA affiliation would presumably ensure security for Sister Formation and give it a base from which it could relate to the major superiors and to the rest of the hierarchy, for the most part on its own terms. Ironically, the CMSW itself had had to fend off a ploy by the Vatican in 1958 to place it under the control of the Conference of Major Superiors of Men, the organization of the heads of men's religious orders.

The arrangement with NCEA brought no peace. By the early 1960s, the Sacred Congregation of Religious was insisting that Sister Formation be turned over to the CMSW. Sister Walters, who had been elected executive director when Sister Penet decided to step down after three years, wrote to the Sacred Congregation of Religious in 1962 complaining that "legalistic questions" and "petty harassment" by the CMSW had prevented Sister Formation from getting the cooperation and support it needed from the major superiors' group. Such obstacles and noncooperation, suspected as tactics to force Sister Formation to give in to the CMSW, "strike us as fundamentally evil," Sister Walters said.

As a result of the strife between the two groups, the Sacred Congregation of Religious sent two lieutenants, Archbishop Paul Philippe and the Reverend Bernard Ransing, both high-ranking officials in that office, to investigate the conflict. Father Ransing handled the bulk of the day-to-day traffic from U.S. religious orders and was known to believe that Sisters Walters and Bradley were recalcitrants who were keeping the Sister Formation movement from conforming to the Congregation of Religious's desire for control. He wanted these troublemakers removed.

The two Vatican officials summoned the two sisters to a late-evening interrogation on the eve of the 1963 CMSW executive committee meeting. Sister Bradley remembered that night in Cincinnati as "an inquisition." She and Sister Walters were in Minnesota when the archbishop called. They were whisked away by car in the middle of the night. Arriving in Cincinnati, they were told the archbishop would meet them at 9 P.M. that evening. The meeting lasted for three hours. Lurking behind all other technicalities and issues of canon law was an implicit loyalty test by which the sisters would be measured. The officials reserved the right to define what loyalty and obedience meant so far as Rome was concerned, although the sisters had their own interpretations. At this emergency grilling, the Vatican men asked the two sisters a lot of questions about their activities with Sister Formation and reviewed the contents of the *Bulletin,* but the probe finally boiled down to the question of whether the sisters would defer to Rome's wishes. Bradley and Walters refused to approve placing Sister Formation under the command of the CMSW.

The repartee was always lively, sometimes salty, Sister Bradley recalled.

After she had responded to one of the archbishop's questions, she said he pointed his index finger at her and proclaimed, "I pronounce you competent," to which she replied, "Thank you, your excellency, I never doubted that." He also mentioned sending them both to Rome for three years so that the sisters could, in his words, "learn the truth." Sister Bradley asked him if that was an invitation or an order. "Nobody ever refuses Rome," he assured her. "Your excellency," she said, "somebody just did."

By the end of the session, the archbishop had generally praised Sister Formation and said he found nothing disloyal or unorthodox in the *Bulletin* (including Sister Walters's hotly debated article, "Local Superior as Spiritual Leader," which had recently been published). To the contrary, he commended the publication. But for the two sisters who sat through the three-hour ordeal, defeat of their effort to keep Sister Formation independent was at hand.

Most superiors seemed to agree that the matter was simply one of exercising proper authority by placing Sister Formation more surely within their oversight. The formation of nuns did, after all, fall within their jurisdiction even though they had allowed Sister Formation a measure of freedom. There was much gratitude for what the Sister Formation Conference had done to improve the sisterhoods. But in the view of many superiors the experiment had crossed an invisible line and moved toward establishing itself free of superiors and should, therefore, be brought properly within their control.

The morning after the late-night meeting, with Archbishop Philippe presiding at the CMSW executive committee meeting, the vote in favor of absorbing Sister Formation with the CMSW was one shy of being unanimous. Because the superiors could derail Sister Formation by restricting the participation of their subordinate sisters within the movement, their vote was tantamount to destiny. Key support for Sister Formation from progressives was missing. Respected leaders such as Mercy Sister Elizabeth Carroll extolled the conference but thought it had done its job and was a spent force. The lone dissenting vote was cast by a Benedictine superior, Mother Gemma Piennett, prioress of Mount Angel Convent in Mount Angel, Oregon, who had worked with Sister Formation. Her act of defiance was later cited by Sister Bradley and others as among the chief motives behind the Vatican's decision to summarily remove Mother Piennett as prioress without stated cause.

For Sister Walters and Sister Bradley, allies and close friends, the final blow was the defection of Sister Penet a few months later. In March 1964, Sister Penet wrote to Mother Cunningham that in her opinion there was now "no present conflict or conflict of interest between the Sister Formation Conference and the Conference of Major Superiors of Women." She added that "the two organizations are acting in loyalty and good faith and deserve our gratitude and cooperation."

Sister Penet had been the chief gladiator in the cause of independence for Sister Formation. With her keen mind and deft leadership, she had won many a tactical battle against stronger forces. But she had been cautious about allowing sisters to be educated with non-sisters and had become deeply distressed by the changes in religious life, including the changes in dress that Vatican II ushered in. The Sister Formation Conference had gone too far for her. For a few shining years, she had been an extraordinary voice of innovation and renewal, but when Sister Formation teetered on the brink of absorption, Penet threw in her lot with those who would render it putty in the hands of major superiors. Her agreement with the decision to collapse the conference into the CMSW drove a wedge between her and the two sister-victims of the inquisition. More than a trace of betrayal hung in the air. "I regret the circumstances that separated us," Sister Penet wrote many years later to Sister Walters, who lay dying. "I never ceased loving you."

Sister Penet had displayed a vision and an organizational wizardry without which the Sister Formation Conference would have been unthinkable. She later became the president of her alma mater, Marygrove. By then, she had become disillusioned by renewal. At heart, her preservationist convictions gave way only for the radical cause of the education of nuns, a concern born of her love of the life of the mind. Sister Formation was for her a curriculum that served hierarchical ends. Therefore, she opposed much of the rest of what sister communities were becoming, finding them too humanistic and secular. Or perhaps it was a matter of conserving energy for the thing that mattered most. She had fought one battle with bishops who resented young nuns being sent to college before staffing schools and may have longed for a peaceful convent without further controversy.

The subsuming of Sister Formation under the control of the major superiors meant the end of the line for Sister Formation's executive director and *Bulletin* editor.

In the aftermath of the move, a key figure in the hierarchy's policy toward nuns, Bishop Philip Hannan of Washington, labeled the women "troublemakers" and "contentious people" in discussing them with the Reverend Luis Dolan, the American head of the Better World Movement. Bishop Hannan singled out Sister Bradley as a "crazy woman."

The two women were summarily cut adrift.

But their enemies weren't content with just forcing them out. In the view of their adversaries, the two sisters had threatened authority with unconscionable brashness and audacity. Rumors circulated that the two sisters were crazy, and charges of reckless leadership were leveled in letters written by some major superiors. Sister Walters suffered what Sister Bradley called "character assassination" from these assaults, attacks that hampered her ability to practice as a clinical psychologist. Among the indignities was the cancellation of a lecture she was to give at Catholic University. She remained in her community, however. By contrast, Sister Bradley was shunned by her own order, the Congregation of the Humility of Mary, forbidden to live in the community or to receive an assignment from it. After drifting for a few months, studying on her own, she was awarded a fellowship in literature at the University of Minnesota through the intervention of the poet Allen Tate. She was also encouraged through correspondence by David Riesman, a Harvard sociologist whose study of higher education acquainted him with her work in Sister Formation. She was then invited to teach at St. Ambrose University in Davenport, Iowa, where she shared a house with Sister Walters. She remained there as a distinguished scholar long after her official retirement as an English professor, conducting occasional seminars in her field of medieval mystics, until her death.

Her order, the Sisters of Humility of Ottumwa, never spoke to her about its reasons for ostracizing her after she was forced out of the Sister Formation Conference. But the widespread assumption was that she had violated the supreme commandment of obedience to superior authority. No matter how profound and vital the Sister Formation Conference was, no matter how admired the *Bulletin,* the two sisters most closely identified with the leadership of the movement had chosen to challenge the wishes of the superiors of the orders who wanted to clip the conference's wings. Dismayed by her order's attitude, Sister Bradley finally left it in 1972 to join the Sisters for Christian Charity, a relatively new community of a few hundred members that was noncanonical; that is, it did not seek official Church approval under canon law. The shift had no effect on her teaching at St. Ambrose or her living arrangements. She and Sister Walters continued sharing a house on a quiet street in Davenport.

Eventually Sisters Bradley and Penet would part company over the direction of the movement. Sister Penet, at heart a traditionalist, objected when she saw the conference's aims turning into decisions to abandon or modify the habit and allow young novices to enroll with regular students outside religious communities. Sister Bradley, by contrast, continued to champion the more extensive spin-offs. Her advocacy eventually cost her dearly: ostracism from her order, shunning by the Catholic Church. The two sisters went forty years without seeing each other. But in the beginning of their partnership, the skies were bright and promising.

The Sister Formation Conference continued under the auspices of the CMSW but lost steam. Its very success had diminished somewhat its reason for existence. The influence it had exerted on the breadth and depth of the sister's education and on her self-image was extraordinary. At the end of the conference's first decade, it could take credit for establishing a four-year college education for most sister novitiates. The number of all sisters with at least a bachelor's degree rose from a small fraction before the conference was founded to more than half (over 90,000 of about 174,000 nuns) in 1966. The number of sisters with doctorate degrees also climbed sharply. During the 1950s, 73 more sisters earned doctorates than had done so during the previous decade (302 versus 229). With Sister Formation in high gear, that figure shot up by nearly 200 to 484 during the 1960s.

The movement's emphasis on integrating mind and spirit had helped bolster each sister's confidence and enhance her ability to trust in her own gifts. There was a ripple effect. Sister Margaret Cafferty, for example, remembered being inspired in the late 1950s to make "my life count for something" by the example of two teachers, one studying for her Ph.D. in sociology at Berkeley, the other getting a master's in philosophy. At age seventeen, Sister Cafferty entered the Sisters of the Presentation of the Blessed Virgin Mary in San Francisco and went on to become a much-admired executive secretary of the Leadership Conference of Women Religious before her premature death. Sister Marie Joan Harris's first years as a Sister of St. Joseph of Carondolet typified an increasingly common pattern. She began her college studies full-time at once and, after teaching for a year, was sent to Kansas University to complete a Ph.D. program in chemistry before beginning her profession as a college teacher and administrator. The choice of work for a sister, once confined mostly to teacher and health care worker, expanded rapidly, thanks in no small part to the Sister Formation Conference. A group of Sisters of Loretto seated around a table in their Denver, Colorado, home in the fall of 1995 illustrated the diversity. Among them was a bereavement counselor in a hospice, a school nurse, a distance-learning advisor for the state, the director of a tutoring center, a political activist who was a secretary at a Lutheran church, and a lawyer. Each had switched ministries several times.

Because of the advances encouraged by the Sister Formation movement, sisters would increasingly ease away from a convent system where their lives were regimented to a more open arrangement wherein they would take a large measure of control over their God-given lives, moving from a passive style of behavior to an active one. No wonder, indeed, that sisters who had come under this influence embraced the further renewal of Vatican II with such fervor. The impact of Sister Formation was summed up by Sister Ann Patrick Ware, a Sister of Loretto: "Sister Formation challenged mediocrity in religious life and service, and, at the same time, introduced a humanizing self-respect, respect for the God-given talents of others, and a concern for loving relationships." Sister Schneider of Cardinal Stritch College put it more formally, calling the conference "the most formidable self-conscious exercise of self-transformation in the history of women religious."

No amount of subsequent pressure could entirely contain or reverse that liberation. Young nuns had been exposed to contemporary culture and scholarship; they had been acclimated to reform. By 1956 a survey found that 86 percent of local superiors believed the *Bulletin* to be essential reading, a sign that the wall between the convent and the outside world had been irrevocably breached. Sister Penet's ideal had been to educate sisters as "Renaissance women." In the end, she accomplished perhaps more than she had set out to do. The stumbling block to further progress was the allegation that Sister Formation activities verged on disobedience.

Not long ago, Sister Bradley traveled to Sister Penet's bedside in the retirement center of her community in Michigan. The two women had been separated for thirty years. The old warmth was rekindled. The differences were forgotten. The glory of the movement was for a brief moment alive again. "Do you think the Sister Formation Conference did more harm than good?" asked Sister Penet, who had turned against many aspects of renewal, including the alteration of the habit. Sister Bradley replied, "Lots of good."

As the visit was ending, Sister Bradley gently took Sister Penet's face in her hands. "We're both old ladies now," she said quietly, smiling warmly. "A lot of time has passed."

Sister Formation's energies were dwindling as the Second Vatican Council swung into full gear. For nuns, the first movement made possible a second in the aftermath of Vatican II. The two acts belonged within a single drama. Like all Catholics, the sisters were caught unawares by much that transpired at the Council that transformed Catholicism. But by another token, their participation in Sister Formation had anticipated it. "Most of all," Sister Ware wrote, "Sister Formation lives in the fact that it developed a biblically and theologically literate population, ready for the new teachings of the Second Vatican Council."

Chapter Four

Vatican II: Unforeseen Consequences

he idea of a Second Vatican Council had gestated for decades before it hatched. In the early decades of the century, the writings of Europe's leading Catholic thinkers, among them Karl Rahner, Hans Küng, and Yves Congar, had proposed a decisive shift toward a more open and outgoing Catholicism. Most of these "progressives" had been branded as dissidents by Rome for their boat-rocking teachings and had been silenced or otherwise disciplined at one time or another by Vatican superiors. It took the charm, the goodwill, and the boldness of Pope John XXIII to overrule entrenched attitudes and bring the dissidents in from the cold. It took the pope with a smiling embrace of the world to fill the nave of St. Peter's Basilica with the first Council in a century, the twenty-first in all of the history of Western Christianity. (John himself died after the Council's first session; he was succeeded by Pope Paul VI, who finished it.) The seats were filled with the 2,500 world bishops, among whom cardinals and archbishops generally wielded the greatest personal authority. A select number of non-Catholics were also invited as observers with limited speaking privileges. Some of the same theologians who had been under Rome's censure were on hand as "periti," special theological advisors. No nuns were invited to the great hall during these first sessions. A few were admitted at the end just to listen, after a struggle.

As auspicious as the opening was in the fall of 1962, scarcely anyone could have imagined the monumental scope of the Council's achievements by the time it ended three years later. A huge institution with the trappings of medieval culture still dominant had been thoroughly revamped; it was the last major component of Western culture to undergo such time-warp transformation. Through the work of the Council the Church became considerably demystified and more attuned to the modern world. Laypeople would be expected to be more actively involved in Mass and other liturgies and be encouraged to look favorably on non-Catholic faiths. For nuns, the fresh wind swept briskly through the convent, affecting how they prayed, lived, and worked. If the Second Vatican Council did not exactly make all things new, it made nearly everything *look* new.

Great fanfare attended Pope John's call for what is, by tradition, the closest thing to a legislative session at the Church's highest level. Full-scale Church Councils are rare and spectacular events. Ecumenical Synods, as they are also called, decide where the Church stands on matters ranging from the most philosophical to the most mundane, from the nature of Jesus Christ to the rubrics of confession. Councils have usually coincided with great cultural and religious ruptures. The last one, convened by Pope Pius IX in 1869, had been a rally against the European political and intellectual revolutions that had overthrown monarchies and would soon deprive the pope of his territories outside Vatican City. The nearest Council to that had met three centuries earlier, when the sixteenth-century Reformation split the Church. Given their rarity, when a Council speaks, the Church listens.

The crisis Vatican II was addressing was the widening gulf between Catholicism and modernity. The Enlightenment—mostly science—had challenged both the Church's philosophy and its morality, leaving the papacy increasingly isolated. Pope John XXIII grasped the problem and shocked the Church by calling the Council in 1959. He had been supposed too old and lacking in astuteness, but this man with a radiant heart and stout conviction fooled nearly everyone by ordering the patient to the hospital for a full examination. Born to poor parents as Angelo Giuseppe Roncalli, he had served in diplomatic posts for the Vatican in Turkey, Greece, and France before becoming cardinal-patriarch of Venice. When Pope Pius XII died in 1958, after a nineteen-year papacy marked by stern authority, Roncalli, a relatively laid-back pastor, was elected his successor, largely on the assumption that he would serve as little more than a jovial interim caretaker while the cardinals decided on a longer-term candidate. But Roncalli turned out to be the pope who summoned bishops from their scattered dioceses around the world to Rome to deliberate and legislate about how Catholicism should bridge the divide. (Given his surprising performance, he should be made the patron saint of the underestimated.)

From the first, the Church fathers—as the bishop-participants were called—signaled that they would follow the pope's daring by indicating that they desired a thorough examination of the Church following no prescribed blueprint. At the outset, they flatly rejected a plan by a group of powerful Roman cardinals to short-circuit the process by pushing through a few superficial reforms that would leave the system basically untouched. The strategy to preserve the status quo was led by Alfredo Cardinal Ottaviani, head of the Holy Office—the Vatican department in charge of conformity to Church doctrine. By rejecting that plan in favor of starting with a clean slate, the bishops challenged the dominant image of the Church Cardinal Ottaviani had sought to preserve: perfect and otherworldly.

A major source of optimism for the progressives among U.S. sisters was the effort by a cardinal who was a close friend of Pope John XXIII and whose beliefs could often be reasonably assumed to reflect the pope's own. Leon Joseph Cardinal Suenens, Archbishop of Malines-Brussels, published a groundbreaking little book, *The Nun in the World,* in 1962, the year the Council began. It was nothing less than a brief for sweeping change along the lines of Sister Formation. In his book the widely admired cardinal subjected religious life to blunt, even harsh, scrutiny using language that was both pointed and gentle. An advance excerpt had appeared in the *Sister Formation Bulletin;* its call for thorough overhaul had taken many Catholics by storm. Publication of the entire book only broadened and sharpened the debate.

Cardinal Suenens wrote that the contemporary nun "appears to the faithful to be out of touch with the world as it is, an anachronism." She was too isolated, too remote, too encased in a habit that estranged her from the very people she would serve, some of whom associated her with "a certain childishness, naivete." A contributing factor was sexism, he believed. "It is well known," he stated sardonically, "that what one can only call the antifeminist tradition has had a long inning." But in his opinion the sister had been too slow to claim her dignity. "As a nun," he said, "she will not allow herself to claim even a few of the rights that women have managed to obtain bit by bit from man in our modern society." Sisters had outpaced other laywomen in obtaining professional responsibilities in such fields as medicine and college teaching, to be sure, but their gains came in the context of the closed world of the sisterhood, where women were not accorded the rewards and opportunities available in secular society.

The cardinal offered his own platform to help remedy these ills: reforms in dress, living arrangements, and working conditions set up so as to free nuns from the minutiae of canon law to enable them to be better ministers. He also urged the orders to go back to their roots to rediscover their spirit. *The Nun in the World* brought those ideas to a wide audience. It could be read as the outline of a program to be advanced by the progressive element among the bishops as the Council approached, somewhere up the line, the question of nuns.

But the high expectations also met hard realities. Nuns stood at the periphery as the conclave was planned and started. Sisters, and women in general, were excluded from the commissions preparing the agenda and from the list of official invitees. Neither their views nor their counsel were solicited in any significant way. Wives of the representatives of other Christian churches were allowed into the sessions as observers. Officials from non-Christian religions were likewise invited, as were Catholic laymen. But no women, no nuns, were involved. Only after the Council was half over did Cardinal Suenens successfully plead the cause of women. He reminded his brethren that Vatican II wasn't representing "half of humanity." Rome responded by inviting twenty-three women to the third and fourth sessions as auditors, joining nearly three thousand men; that meant they could watch and listen but not speak on the floor. Small wonder, then, that many sisters were initially perplexed over what this ecumenical council had to do with them. Inclusion of nuns at the Council had been something of an afterthought. The invitation had been rather late in arriving, and it was conditional.

Two Council sessions had ended, in fact, before the first Catholic sisters were officially seated in St. Peter's Basilica for continuation of the conclave. Some of the most important business had already been concluded, including the Dogmatic Constitution on the Church, but the Council had a long way to go before finishing the Pastoral Constitution on the Church in the Modern World (Gaudium et Spes) and other items including the document on religious.

Among the women present were ten nuns including Sister Mary Luke Tobin from the United States. As president of the Conference of Major Superiors of Women and superior of the Sisters of Loretto, she was highly respected and a natural choice. As it happened, Sister Tobin was already en route to Rome on the U.S.S. *Constitution* when she heard of her invitation. She had set sail at the request of the CMSW to undertake a reconnaissance mission aimed at learning more about what the Council might be doing about religious life. She intended to stay a short time. The news of her appointment reached her in the mid-Atlantic when reporters called from the United States to ask for her reaction. As a result, Sister Tobin stayed through the third session and returned for the fourth.

She was in many respects an embodiment of the Sister Formation movement and a precursor of what so many sisters would become after Vatican II: well educated, assertive, articulate, candid, self-assured, alert to issues of justice, and devoted to the vision of a renewed church that was emanating from the Council. She counted among her good friends the noted Trappist monk Thomas Merton and read theologians who were transforming the Church's thinking, principally the great German Jesuit Karl Rahner, whose writing, Sister Tobin says, turned her life around. She was both a tough critic of the Church and a believer in its ultimate redemption. She could more than hold her own with seasoned, sometimes imperious, hierarchs. While at the Council, she encountered Ildebrando Cardinal Antoniutti, head of the Vatican department in charge of religious orders. On one occasion, the cardinal summoned her after seeing her picture in a newspaper. She showed him a picture of a Sister of Loretto in a Hartt Shaffner & Marx suit that the community had chosen to replace the traditional habit. "He never looked me straight in the eye," she remembered recently in her Denver, Colorado, home, her oblong face radiating warmth while her eyes shone with intelligence and good humor. "He took the picture, took a pen, and drew the skirt down, the sleeves down, then added a little veil."

Sister Tobin's grit and sagacity made her a natural leader among the sisters at the Council; her perseverance was essential to enduring a climate decidedly inhospitable to them. In Sister Carmel McEnroy's engaging, full account of what the sisters experienced at Vatican II, *Guests in Their Own House,* Sister Tobin said that she and other nuns were either "ignored or trivialized." Referring to the bishops, Sister Tobin surmised that a few approved of the women's presence, some did not, and the majority "acted indifferently," some looking "scared." An Italian auditor, Sister Gladys Parentelli, has written (*Mujer Iglesia Liberacion*) that Archbishop Pericle Felici, who occupied the key post as secretary of the Council, never acknowledged the women or even gazed in their direction although he sat in close proximity to where they were. During breaks, when the schmoozing and lobbying took place, the sisters were forbidden to mingle with the men but rather were directed to a coffee station set aside just for them.

(Sister McEnroy, the chronicler of the sisters' view of Vatican II, faced severe difficulties of her own in dealing with Rome. In 1995 she was ousted from her tenured faculty position at St. Meinrad's Theological Seminary in Indiana after more than twenty years as a respected theology professor. She had run afoul of the Vatican by signing a petition in favor of women's ordination, a position Rome forbade clergy and sisters from even discussing publicly.)

With the women installed as auditors, the question was whether they would be included in the commissions that worked the documents into shape for presentation on the floor of the Council. Among sisters, great interest was obviously focused on the preparation of the Council's statement on religious life. That document was still being crafted by a commission overseen by Cardinal Antoniutti when the sisters arrived. Allies of the nuns approached the cardinal with a proposal to admit nuns to the commission proceedings. The cardinal flatly dismissed the suggestion, according to the Reverend Bernard Haering, the prominent moral theologian who pleaded the nuns' cause for greater inclusion at the Council. Moreover, Father Haering recalled, the cardinal remarked facetiously that the nuns might "try again at the Fourth Vatican Council."

A woman's voice was never heard on the floor of the Council in St. Peter's. Among the missing was famed British economist Barbara Ward, who was asked to prepare a paper on poverty and hunger, only to be barred from delivering it at a Council session. A layman read the speech in Latin. Other laymen also made interventions but the women, both sisters and other laywomen, were nowhere to be heard during a conclave called to speak for the universal church.

One door did open. The commission in charge of the Pastoral Constitution on the Church in the Modern World (Gaudium et Spes) asked six women auditors to be seated at the business sessions. The six, with full vote, joined thirty bishops, forty-nine theological experts, and ten laymen. Acceptance of the document came after long debate and a stack of drafts. It became one of the landmarks of the Council, promoting human rights and social justice and urging the Church to overcome its alienation from the world by working diligently for its betterment. Involvement in the development of this document, at 23,335 words the longest produced at the Council, had a lasting effect on the participating sisters. Among the document's most important legacies has been its commitment to racial equality.

Sister Tobin, now in her late eighties, readily quotes word for word a passage from that document that encapsulates for her the most powerful message she derived from her Council experience. It is a passage that was influenced by the women who were there. She still repeats it as a call to arms: "With respect to the fundamental rights of the person, every type of discrimination, whether social or cultural, whether based on sex, race, color, social condition, language or religion, is to be overcome and eradicated as contrary to God's intent."

Over four autumn sessions, from 1962 to 1965, the Church in Vatican II reformulated many of the basic images by which it now understood itself—not so much as a flawless masterpiece but as an imperfect work in progress. On another plane, the Church changed such everyday basics as the language in which Mass was celebrated (from Latin to the vernacular) and regulations for marriages between Catholics and non-Catholics (mixed weddings were now sanctioned). Debates among the bishops on these guiding concepts were often protracted. In the end, they expressed their conclusions, sometimes settled by close and contentious vote, in sixteen major documents.

Four constitutions—on the Church (Lumen Gentium), divine revelation (Dei Verbum), sacred liturgy (Sacrosanctum Concilium), and the Church in the world (Gaudium et Spes)—wielded the greatest authority as doctrinal definitions of the Church's fundamental character. The decrees and declarations addressed pragmatic and pastoral topics from education and training of priests to religious freedom and relations with non-Catholics. The most comprehensive was the Dogmatic Constitution on the Church (Lumen Gentium) because, as the U.S. Constitution did for the United States, it provided Catholics a basic understanding of how the Church defined itself. Among its stunning conclusions: Roman Catholicism no longer insisted that it was the "one true church," and clergy and hierarchy ceased ranking above the laity. Baptism was the ticket that admitted all Catholics equally to the Church as the "people of God"; it was similar to the rights conferred by citizenship in democracies. Other distinctions in the Church, such as ordination, important as they might be, were to be considered secondary to that godly peoplehood. Of most significance to nuns was the startling claim about what it meant to be holy. The bishops scuttled the idea that some (primarily nuns, priests, and bishops) should aim to be holy while most laity need not bother. In its place, they insisted that holiness is the responsibility of *every Catholic*. Precisely this pursuit of holiness had elevated nuns and priests to a level above that of the laity. Now the mystique was threatened. A single phrase had ended a virtual monopoly.

The switch undermined the foundation on which the nun's identity had stood. Technically, nuns had always been *lay* by virtue of not being ordained, but their elevated lives in pursuit of holiness had given them an honorary station between lay and clerical. Lumen Gentium evened the playing field: nuns were laypeople seeking holiness in a way that was equal to, not better than, that of other laypeople and clerics. This loss of identity was made more difficult by the fact that the sisters' vocation, unlike ordination to the priesthood and the taking of marriage vows, was not defined and buttressed by a sacrament. Sisters had already drifted in ambiguity; now it seemed to many that the only sure distinction they had was being taken away.

What else would the Council mean in particular to life within religious communities? Many sisters hoped it would encourage the momentum toward greater personal freedom and dignity that had been generated by the Sister Formation Conference. But they had also seen the conference crippled by Church authorities—including their own superiors as well as male clerics in America and Rome—who believed that Sister Formation had stretched its wings too far. While it was doubtful that the sisters, having breathed fresh air, could ever again be as fully restrained as before, the question was what the Council might do to help or hurt what many saw as the progress that had already been made.

What the nuns eventually received was a statement directed at those under vows to religious communities. Nuns were by far the most numerous of those who were affected, and their communities were most in need of updating, but the statement was also meant for the "religious" brothers and priests who belonged to orders such as the Dominicans and Jesuits. The document was a mixed signal, a hurriedly prepared text called Perfectae Caritatis (Decree on the Renewal of Religious Life). It had sailed through the conclave along with a rush of other last-minute items in the waning days of the Council's final session in the fall of 1965.

The pronouncements on the "people of God" and the inclusiveness of holiness broke molds and set sisters' spirits soaring. Most seemed ready, even eager, to shed special status, though some believed that it was the sine qua non of the sister's vocation and would be abandoned only at great peril; still others worried about what identity would replace it. By comparison, the Council's document on religious life, Perfectae Caritatis, landed with a thud. Fresh thought and bold faith, hallmarks of the two great constitutions of Vatican II on the Church (Lumen Gentium) and the Church in the world (Gaudium et Spes) were notably absent in the one document of Vatican II specifically intended for men and women under vows. As noted earlier, women religious had no part in writing the document. As Patricia Wittberg, a sociology professor and Sister of Charity at Indiana University at Indianapolis, explains, Perfectae Caritatis did none of the "groundbreaking theology" for religious that the constitution on the Church did for the laity; it exhorted religious in general terms to summon again "the original inspiration" that gave rise to their communities.

The very name of the document, Perfectae Caritatis, or "Perfect Love," was a throwback, bespeaking the pre–Vatican II image of perfection that the Council seemed otherwise eager to discard. On its face, the document lacked vigor, clarity, and any indication that religious life had, in fact, been reexamined in any depth. But its implications were profound, even revolutionary to the degree that they seemed to authorize a wholesale redesign of the sisterhood by, of all people, the sisters themselves.

Perfectae Caritatis prescribed two guidelines. One, that congregations "return to the sources of all Christian life," meaning principally the Gospels. Two, that they would seek "an adjustment of the community to the changed conditions of the time."

Calling for "a continuous return to the sources of all Christian life and to the original inspiration behind a given community," the instruction asserted that the Church profited by the "special character and purpose" of each community. It continued: "Therefore loyal recognition and safekeeping should be accorded to the spirit of the founders, as also to the particular goals and wholesome traditions which constitute the heritage of each community."

Like Rorschach inkblot tests, these guidelines were open to considerable interpretation. Returning to the Gospels sounded safe and secure, but anyone who has delved into the Scriptural accounts of Jesus knows they are loaded with spiritual and psychic dynamite, sometimes firing up a revolutionary prophet who brings loud and biting judgment on the institutions of the Church. In any event, this requirement carried potential surprises. Neither was the request to return to "the original inspiration" of the community (as Perfectae Caritatis had defined it) necessarily an innocuous exercise. Some orders had never really understood the torment out of which they were born; others had never even known their abused founders. In some cases, founders who were tinged with what the Church considered scandalous behavior had been shunned or expunged from the record, replaced by a male cleric considered more suitable. Among certain other orders, the origins had simply been lost or obscured. In the old days, nobody much asked such questions or sought to uncover the mysteries. Now sisters were being asked to examine exactly why their orders had come into existence in the first place and who was responsible. The search for answers did not always lead to a consoling ending.

As for the second instruction to adjust to "changed conditions," Pope Pius XII had a decade earlier alluded in a general way to the possibilities of altering such things as prayer schedules, customs books, even the habit to some unspecified degree, and now the Council, under his successors, Popes

John XXIII and Paul VI, had flung open the door, however inadvertently. Expanding modestly on the theme, Perfectae Caritatis said: "In the work of appropriate renewal, it is the responsibility of competent authorities alone, especially of general chapters [the orders' highest governing bodies], to issue norms, to pass laws, and to allow for *a right amount* of experimentation, though in all such matters, according to the norm of law, the approval of the Holy See [the Vatican state] and of local Ordinaries [normally the bishop] must be given when required. In decisions which involve the future of an institute as a whole, superiors should in appropriate manner consult the members and give them a hearing" (italics added).

There was much of what politicians call "wiggle room" in many aspects of the Council's words, the most significant being how the modern sister ought to dress. A brief section set forth an ambiguous prescription that would allow hundreds of congregations to reach their own conclusions. "Since they are signs of a consecrated life," Perfectae Caritatis said, "religious habits should be simple and modest, at once poor and becoming. They should meet the requirements of health and be suited to the circumstances of time and place as well as to the services required by those who wear them. Habits of men and women which do not correspond to those norms are to be changed." To members of progressive congregations, in particular, this sounded like an invitation to a large measure of sister autonomy. Nothing would be more rancorous, however, than the struggle over the habit, which will be discussed in detail later in the book.

To a degree, at least, the Council fathers were dead serious about the need for renewal for religious orders. Like others in the Church, bishops wanted nuns to be freed of burdens that hindered their service so as to improve the Church's mission. Indeed, the decree on religious life warns against adaptations that are "merely superficial" and suggests that if some failed to grasp what modernity was all about they should be schooled in "the prevailing manners of contemporary social life, and in its characteristic ways of feeling and thinking." For American nuns, those lessons had been imparted some time ago or would be shortly. Ten years hence, many U.S. sisters had taken society's pulse and had adapted to it. In fact, they would sometimes be accused of being too immersed in it.

What was the "right amount" of experimentation, and under what circumstances were congregations supposed to seek approval from Rome or the local bishop? The vague formulation in Perfectae Caritatis sounded much like Roman classical law that made abstract pronouncements such as an absolute prohibition on divorce but kept an abundance of dispensations around to take care of those who failed to live up to Church teaching. For the next decade, congregations would joust with Rome over the "appropriate" boundaries between Rome's proper authority and their legitimate freedom.

As mundane, general, and non-radical as Perfectae Caritatis appeared to be, it became the one product of the Council that in hindsight the bishops perhaps most wished they could take back. Its open-endedness and the confusion it would generate could scarcely have been imagined by the Council fathers who framed it. These were the unintended consequences of refusing to take women religious seriously enough to involve them in the process of renewal at the highest levels and of grossly underestimating how far renewal had already gone among American nuns. The Americans took it as their duty to move ahead, to fill in the blanks in the vague directives, redesign their community lives, and find their own solutions. If the Council treated Perfectae Caritatis as a routine obligation and a pro forma contribution, a rationale for mild, acceptable reform (hadn't sisters always more or less done the hierarchy's bidding?), the sisters took it as a bold marching order.

Other documents of the Council, not directed specifically at nuns, had an enormous impact on sisters. One has been mentioned: the "universal call to holiness" from the Dogmatic Constitution on the Church that knocked nuns off their spiritual pedestal, inspiring some, demoralizing others. The second was the appeal from the Pastoral Constitution on the Church in the Modern World (Gaudium et Spes) document to cast the ministry of the Church beyond Catholic institutions to works of mercy and justice to people of all places and faiths. Ministries of nuns had been dedicated to the Church's own health and education programs; now their sights would start to shift to projects aimed at to eradicating poverty and racial bias. Perfectae Caritatis gave license to rearrange the community. Gaudium et Spes gave the nuns license to redirect their ministries. Mobilizing for social justice would add further tensions between sisters and bishops.

Prophetically, the Council endorsed a collaborative method of conducting Church business that U.S. nuns had modeled for some time, especially in the Sister Formation Conference. Shared decision making had taken root when sisters from a wide variety of congregations began consulting together. Its impact on education and nuns' self-identity had been incalculable. Shortly thereafter, the Conference of Major Superiors of Women adopted the same cooperative model and thereby broadened participation. For the first time in the history of religious orders, sisters were making decisions cooperatively on an intercommunity basis rather than by the dictates of mothers superior. Vatican II's promotion of "collegiality," a concept that also favored collaboration over strict hierarchical rule, was a step in the same direction. Those sisters attending Vatican II had that lesson reinforced, writes Sister McEnroy. It was at the Council, she concludes, that they learned to be "audacious" in terms of expecting dialogue as a way of life.

The resolve with which sisters proclaimed and practiced their imperative in the years following the Council fueled their incentive to fulfill the highest aims of Gaudium et Spes for justice and service to the world. Many congregations would turn their energies away from certain kinds of activities such as teaching in Catholic schools in favor of projects to combat racism, feed the hungry, and find shelter for the homeless. The challenge set forth in that Vatican II constitution was not easy to fulfill, however, and arguments over where best to devote the energies of congregations have continued from that day to this. But the concern for justice has turned back on the Church. The words imploring justice outside have been increasingly applied inside.

For Sister Tobin and other women religious at the Council, the immersion in the process of drafting a document as momentous as Gaudium et Spes touched off a passion for a renewed church that has never quit—despite all the disappointments and rejections. The nuns were outsiders in the great conclave, pressured into accepting only a limited advisory role on one of the major commissions. But, paradoxically, from their vantage point on the periphery they captured the Council's grand themes in an unfiltered, inspired manner, perhaps learning more than the bishops who were engaged in the debates and compromises. In any event, the outsider nuns saw clearly in that conclave the promise of a new day dawning and they brought that hope home with them. Indeed, Sister Tobin said her great letdown on returning from Vatican II was that the bishops were too lukewarm in passing the word about the Council to their people. To her, this omission signified that the bishops had failed to drink deeply enough of the Council's spirit. By contrast, nuns were excited, despite all the ambiguities of Perfectae Caritatis and the insecurities that awaited them.

Shifts in thought among U.S. sisters underlay much of that excitement. The First Vatican Council's prevailing image of the Church as a "perfect society"—eternal, unerring, and unworldly—had held nearly total sway over Catholicism. But the Sister Formation movement had helped popularize an image that had been revived from the ancient past: the Church as the "Mystical Body of Christ."

In a July 1993 issue of the *Catholic Historical Review,* Sister Angelyn Dries, O.S.F., explained the transition in thinking during the 1950s as a dramatic move away from the inherited notions of what a Catholic was supposed to be. The "perfect society" image, she wrote, stressed Christian idealism and a bent toward otherworldliness, legalities found in Church codes and teachings, obedience to ecclesiastical superiors, and a thinking process that began with fixed, unchanging truths taught by the hierarchy and from those deduced conclusions. By contrast, Sister Dries continued, the emerging Mystical Body imagery emphasized the value of the whole person over Church law, the search for Scriptural truth over passive absorption of biblical meaning from official Church interpreters, and a kind of thinking that began with insights drawn from personal experience rather than from ready-made truths handed down from on high. Among the values she found in the new imagery were "authority of expertise, collaboration and consensus, the virtues of creativity, originality, rationality, adaptability and proficiency." The "perfect society" model had done damage by always insisting that sisters compare themselves to an impossible ideal, Sister Dries wrote. By comparision, she said, Sister Formation's emphasis on education had helped introduce means by which the sister could appreciate her own worth—her person, her professional competence, and the value of theological learning.

Sister Dries, writing three decades after the Council, argues that the "Mystical Body" image itself served as a dynamic bridge to a more profound reshaping at Vatican II of the image of the Church as a "people of God," carrying out its mission as a "pilgrim people," on their way but not yet finished or perfect, gathered to serve the world rather than withdrawing from it, primarily a peoplehood marked by baptism who constituted an organism of mutual love and ministry rather than an institution ranked in hierarchical order. For nuns, being "people of God" meant the possibility of losing certain privileges associated with the old order. Some American sisters gleefully welcomed the shift as a liberation; others feared or denounced it as a betrayal of everything women religious had stood for.

Thus, among the nuns present at Vatican II there were mixed sentiments on renewal, but for Sister Tobin there was little but glorious gain. A conviction took shape in her. Nuns were part of that peoplehood, with a mission to bring faith and justice to the world as called for in the Council's Pastoral Constitution on the Church in the Modern World (Gaudium et Spes). The need for the Church, in general, and sisters, in particular, to minister to the poor and oppressed transformed her sense of vocation. "I saw the Church in this evolution," she recalled, "and I was in the swing of it. I remember saying 'this is our work.'"

On December 8, 1965, Pope Paul VI closed the Second Vatican Council and Roman Catholics around the world breathed a sigh of astonishment. Most had never imagined that their church could undergo such a thorough renovation. From the start, the Council's reformist intent had reverberated throughout Catholicism. As one after another result poured forth from St. Peter's, the faithful reacted with a mixture of jubilation and despair. The old face of the Church had been replaced by an untried visage whose features were not immediately apparent. Those who cheered this transformation as a liberation from the insular, authoritarian church were countered by those who saw this shift as a devastating loss of proper authority and as a pretext for robbing Catholicism of its precious mystery.

Pope John XXIII had opened the Council on October 11, 1962, by exhorting the Church to shun insularity and turn outward toward all humanity while preserving Catholic doctrine intact. The challenge, the pope said, was to make that teaching better practiced and understood. Those were two distinct matters. "The substance of the ancient doctrine of the deposit of faith is one thing," the pope said, "and the way it is presented is another." Doctrine must remain firm, Pope John said, "But at the same time [the Church] must ever look to the present, to the new conditions and new forms of life introduced into the modern world which have opened new avenues to the

Catholic apostolate [ministry of service]." The message was clear: the Church, in the pope's view, was badly out of touch with the modern world with regard to both evangelism and service.

The Council acted on that mandate by opening the Church to a review that was stunning, rethinking how the enduring teachings of the Church might apply to everything from the role of ordinary Catholics to the nature of the sacraments to the legitimacy of non-Christian religions. They took the fabric of Catholicism as it was handed to them, as if it were a piece of exclusive formal wear; then unweaving it thread by thread, they refashioned it into an everyday travel garment ready to be worn in a wide variety of circumstances.

The words of the Council, among other things, knocked down barriers between religious traditions, reduced the distance separating clergy and laypeople, and charged Catholics with the moral responsibility for the injustices existing among all people. A door was opened for parishioners to take part in the Mass *with* the priest; a door opened for bishops to *share* authority with the pope; a door opened for non-Catholics to receive *some* credit for possessing at least part of the truth; a door opened for nuns to reexamine the roots and customs of their vocation.

Putting those monumental words into concrete reforms has been difficult work and is still continuing. The Council's messages have run into resistance by those Catholics who believe that Vatican II gave up too much of the traditional church and those who think it didn't go far enough. That tension inflamed communities of sisters, causing protracted disputes over the content and scope of renewal. Beyond that strife was the struggle over who would direct that renewal—the nuns or the Vatican. From the start the sisters and the Roman authorities were on a collision course.

Chapter Five

Old Habits Sometimes Die Hard

O n the day Vatican II folded its tent, an august, worldwide assembly of nuns met in Rome for the first time in a climate of ripening potential. Called the International Union of Superiors General, the assembly had been set up as a forum to air ideas and tactics in an effort to coordinate the Council's designs.

Sister Tobin was there, still there. She had weathered the male disapproval that had greeted her arrival at the Council as one of the first women auditors. She had withstood failure in her effort to win over Lawrence Cardinal Sheehan of Baltimore in her campaign to seat sisters on the commission that was preparing the document on religious life (Perfectae Caritatis). Nevertheless, her enthusiasm for the purposes of Vatican II never waned, and her reputation for thoughtful, loving, courageous leadership had only deepened among the sisters at the Council. As the pope's grand conclave came to an end, Sister Tobin was rewarded by being elected to the board of this new international association of sisters.

At the superiors general inaugural session, Sister Tobin spoke about the need for reforms in the ways congregations were governed, drawing substantially on the work of Harvard-educated sociologist Sister Marie Augusta Neal, S.N.D. Sister Tobin's main point, which struck a sour note with some in her audience, was that superiors had too much power and that this relative autocracy should be replaced by a more democratic process.

Moderating a panel discussion on the talk was Archbishop Paul Philippe, O.P., the Vatican official in the Sacred Congregation of Religious who had headed the team that wrote Perfectae Caritatis and, before that, had played a key role in stifling the independence of the Sister Formation movement. The archbishop apparently objected to the governing issue and other features of Sister Tobin's talk that he believed were not in the best interests of nuns. He therefore called for a new election of board members with the obvious aim of showing Sister Tobin the door. She won again, by more votes than she had before. Something was stirring.

In the years right after Vatican II, Rome would issue six directives aimed at explaining how to implement Perfectae Caritatis, of which the first, the Apostolic Letter Ecclesiae Sanctae, remains the most memorable and significant. Writing nine months after the Council wrapped up, the pope endorsed "experiments that run counter to common [Church] law" with the murky proviso that they be "embarked upon with prudence." Congregations were to hold general chapters in order to decide how the renewal applied to them and, in so doing, revise their constitutions, subject to approval by Rome or a competent male authority. The only restriction was that the nuns were not supposed to change the "nature and purpose of the institute." The subsequent five directives issued from Rome during the period of experimentation were an effort to put the brakes on what American nuns in particular did with their window of opportunity.

Meanwhile, the sisterhood train was rolling in a new direction. At first, the most startling developments, so far as most Catholics were concerned, tended to be those that involved the most obvious matters. Nothing was more obvious or volatile than the change in habit, the very image of the sisterhood.

The Ursulines in that remote town of Paola, Kansas, became the first community to cause a sensation by tinkering with this tradition. When their two sister pioneers stepped out in Oklahoma City the week of Thanksgiving 1964 wearing strikingly simplified habits that they themselves had designed, with the blessing of their superior, the story made news all over the world.

Sisters in Paola in the mid-1990s still spoke with wide-eyed admiration and excitement of Sister M. Charles McGrath, the superior who brought about the crisis. Aware of the significance of that moment, Mother McGrath provided her own account of it in a book, *Yes Heard Round the World*, that covered the history of the community. In it, she recalled her decision concerning the habit and its impact. "For several years," Mother McGrath wrote,

> *Sister Stephen Miller, who was teaching in Bishop McGuiness high school in Oklahoma City, Okla., had been asking to experiment in habit changes and to adopt a more contemporary dress. I had put her off, saying the time was not here yet for such changes. But finally in October of that year, when I was visiting the sisters at McGuiness, she brought up the subject again and this time, it must have been the guidance of the Holy Spirit, that finger of God that daily traces pathways in our lives, pathways we see only in hindsight, I said yes. I had no more reason to think the time was here in 1964 than in 1962 and 1963, but I said yes, the "yes" heard round the world, for it precipitated the "habit revolution" in the lives of women religious.*

The sisters' new design discarded, among other things, the coif (the tight white cap), the guimpe (the white head binding), the wimple (front and shoulder covering), and the floor-length skirt. In its place, the two sisters wore a black skirt, white blouse, black weskit with the Ursuline insignia, and a white ribbon to tie back their hair. When they debuted their new outfits in public, the uproar began. Irate Catholics spotted them and immediately phoned Mother McGrath to complain. Newspapers and television played the story big. Pictures of the odd-looking sisters occupied the front pages of major daily newspapers in the United States and abroad. Video and radio broadcasts carried the believe-it-or-not account to audiences around the world. Hundreds of letters poured into the mother house, some in praise, many in protest. Though such an act of boldness was sure to happen somewhere at some time, given the pressures to update the habit, the traditional culture of the Roman Catholic Church, which included most nuns, wasn't prepared for it. Less conservative Catholics, on the other hand, were apt to find it more palatable if not immediately to their liking. The most scathing criticisms came from the portion of the laity most resistant to change. For many sisters who liked the revision, this rebuke was painful and surprising, a rebuff from the very Catholics they had taught and nursed back to health.

"When they saw the habit in the parish or school, in the hospital, or at the door of the convent when they rang the door bell, they felt secure," Mother McGrath wrote.

> Now this sudden threat to their security showed itself in angry denunci-ation of the whole thing. You can't do this to us. You can't take our nuns away from us. . . . The dress pictured was fixed as the adopted habit, not for Ursuline sisters alone, but for all sisters. They equated a new dress for re-ligious not only with the habit but with faith, decency, cessation of prayer and sacrifice, the devil and Communism, total lack of modesty, hence chastity. Length, style, high heels, nylons, and above all "a ribbon around the head of an old grey-haired nun" was the height of indecency.

The nuns who were part of the Paola Ursuline community at the time say that disapproval by laypeople toward this visual switch subsided rather quickly while among the nuns themselves the debate continued.

For a brief, momentous time, the debate placed Paola in the cross fire of Church politics. The bishop of the Diocese of Oklahoma, where the sisters taught, favored the change. Archbishop E. J. Hunkeler of Kansas City opposed it. A little more than a year later the Vatican Council would issue its statement on religious life that opened the door to experiments (Perfectae Caritatis). But before that came to pass, Rome ordered an end to Paola's trial run. The sisters ignored the order. Mother McGrath, the last superior elected before Vatican II, stuck by her convictions in the face of fierce antipathy, later viewing the in-cident as a turning point in the history of the Church. "Yes," she wrote, "it took a drastic step, the habit revolution, before the recognition of women re-ligious as having a place in the Church could even begin." All the while, Paola was acting virtually alone, as orders were wont to do, while other communi-ties were wrestling with similar habit questions in their own ways. Though others began to take tentative steps toward a modified habit, none served as a flash point as Paola had done.

After being rebuffed by Rome, the Ursuline sisters acted cautiously but never abandoned their plan to give the habit a more modern look. Among Mother McGrath's talents was political savvy. Even before taking a head count, she reckoned that support for the alterations was deep enough to permit her to go ahead. Despite trouble gaining Rome's required approval, the sisters designed an acceptable, streamlined model. Within a few years they had made the habit and veil totally optional partly because, as Mother McGrath wrote, "We were beginning to realize that, being women of various shapes and forms, we could never agree on one style." By 1966 most orders were going through the same process.

Rome had stepped in right away. Noting the press reports on the Ursulines in Oklahoma, the pope's representative to the United States, Egidio Cardinal Vagnozzi, in a letter dated February 4, 1966, ordered the community to stop the experiment. Effective appeal was out of the question. By this time, however, renewal of religious life had been sanctioned by Vatican II, so the Paola Ursulines began consultations about an acceptable new habit. Sisters were surveyed by their superior. Of the entire community of 110 who responded, 91 preferred a new habit or dress, and 100 wanted to remove all headwear except, in most cases, a shorter veil; only 10 wanted no change.

With their consensus established, the Ursuline sisters took steps to design a new habit. They created a number of choices. They had style shows. They disagreed. They took note of what other communities were trying. They went back again and again to the sewing machines and the seamstresses. Finally the sisters had something that won a solid consensus. It was, in Mother McGrath's words, a "black suit, mid-calf length, a white collar, a shoulder length black veil, beige hose, and black, medium heel shoes." Nice and conservative. The community sent a picture of a sister in this attire to Rome with a request for the approval of the Congregation of Religious. Soon came the answer from Cardinal Ildebrando Antoniutti of the Sacred Congregation of Religious. "The decision is," the cardinal wrote, "that the model presented, the 'tailleur' or tailored suit, with jacket and short skirt, is not distinctively religious enough to serve as a religious habit. . . . We know, dear Mother, that you and your sisters will accept this decision in the spirit of the decree 'Perfectae Caritatis.' "

The sisters did and they didn't. They did set aside that suit, but in a general chapter meeting in December 1966 they voted by a two-thirds majority after vigorous debate to adopt a new habit that turned out to be less conservative than the one that had been rejected by Rome. It consisted of a black or brown suit—skirt, jacket, blouse—with a short veil. Long hours of discussion and countless meetings went into selecting it. Whereas the old habit had obscured womanliness, the new clothes accented differences in the female form, so creating a single style that suited everyone was tricky. The final product was an agreeable compromise. But in less than ten years, the dress code would become more permissive still, and sisters would be allowed to choose a dress within a range of colors and styles with or without a simple veil—or a modified habit. Very few kept the habit. By that time the Ursulines had long since stopped asking Rome's opinion.

By the mid-1990s, the community was not always sure what to make of the flare-up over the habit. For Sister Grosdidier, the dramatic step now seemed "not that important," but she remembered with fondness the excitement of the community being thrust into the limelight. The title of Mother McGrath's book—*Yes Heard Round the World*—testifies to its place as a defining moment. Mother McGrath clearly likened the initial skirmish in the movement to free nuns from the cumbersome habit to the first shot fired in the Revolutionary War. But there remained some skittishness among the sisters about the notoriety and Mother McGrath's feisty metaphor, because they feared that their community would be branded rebellious or too strong willed. They preferred to see the crisis as a spontaneous reaction rather than as a calculated response to what the Oklahoma City nuns felt they were called to do; and Mother McGrath's response as one expressing faithfulness to her responsibility as superior to her sisters' needs rather than establishing herself as a firebrand taking aim at the surrogate redcoats.

In any event, normalcy returned to the Paola Ursulines soon after the newsmaking flare had been sent aloft, and nothing much extraordinary has happened since. Sister Grosdidier taught her children and raised her flowers through it all. The habit revolution was only the first salvo.

By the mid-1960s, convents all across the United States were edging toward something similar, in fits and starts, prodded by the convergence of forces culminating in the Second Vatican Council. By no coincidence, perhaps, styles were changing throughout U.S. society at the same time, trending toward informality and the shedding of the gray flannel suit in favor of expressing more personal flair.

But the habit, of course, *was* very special, a source of recognition, fright, adoration, mystery, and consolation. Because it loomed so large in Catholic eyes and evoked so many strong feelings in Catholic hearts, any effort to remake it would surely become the symbolic battleground in the struggle to recast religious life in the image of Vatican II. Some saw the change in habit as sacrilege; others, as liberation.

Only six months after the Vatican Council instructed nuns on renewal, Sister Mary Bonaventure, O.S.F., a professor at the University of Detroit, wrote in the periodical *Review for Religious:* "No phase of renewal has precipitated so much re-examination, appraisal, dialogue and even heated debate as the question of change or adaptation of the religious habit."

Every move was magnified by the fact that nuns stood out so starkly—they were the sole Church group explicitly instructed to revamp their ways and the only Catholic women cloaked so oddly in the fashion of a distant past. Priests and other laypeople were required to follow new forms of liturgy and daily practice, including the Mass in English, but otherwise their personal routines such as dress were left pretty much untouched. When it came to proper attire, priests had already simply adapted their everyday wear as they saw fit, most exchanging the traditional cassock for black business suits and clerical collar to blend more smoothly into the mainstream of American life.

Nuns were treated differently. They were set apart as "Brides of Christ," packaged as monastics; encased in yards of dark fabric so as to blot out their sexuality and erase most of their identity; heads wrapped so tightly in linen that they were known to develop ear infections; waists bound by a cincture from which hung an industrial-strength rosary that rustled as they walked. As a trademark symbol, the habit had become as recognizable to the public as, for instance, the standard uniform of the Salvation Army, registered nurses, letter carriers, and railroad conductors. Although the nun was synonymous with the habit, there were rare, notable exceptions to a rule that, in reality, was not ironclad law. A celebrated case was that of Mary Frances Clarke, the eighteenth-century founder of the Blessed Virgin Mary Sisters of Dubuque, Iowa. Mother Clarke never wore a habit during her lifetime, although her community later insisted on burying her in one and commissioned a fully habited portrait of her, to the consternation of many of her admirers. Mother Bruner of the Precious Blood Sisters of Dayton, Ohio, was another nonconformist. To her, a religious uniform was a hindrance to her ability to serve. Accordingly, she remained habit-free.

Though habits looked similar and served the same purpose, they were as different as the gowns at a policeman's ball. The instinct for creativity and distinctive markings had not stopped at the convent door. Each order had its own design and accessories that often stood out starkly in both large and small ways from others. The grandeur and astonishing variety were regularly on display to compare and contrast in a book called *Guide to the Catholic Sisterhoods in the United States,* compiled by the Reverend Thomas P. McCarthy. Each page of McCarthy's book contained facts about a particular order along with a picture of a nun in the habit and distinct, sometimes exotic, headgear of the order. Nuns referred to this gallery of headpieces as "the bird book." No women's collections at Saks Fifth Avenue or Bergdorf's ever had more range. Many habits were aesthetically pleasing, as the communities that wore them were not so shy about boasting, and flowed gracefully; others were homely, cluttered, ungainly, and ugly. The reviews from onlookers were predictably contrasting. "There was no sight to compare with a Holy Cross Sister standing in front of the classroom with the sun shining translucently through her headdress," one woman recalled of her student days in the 1950s. An anonymous sister registered a different impression from the same years: "Some of the garbs are outrageous. If I were not a religious, I might be tempted to run the other way." Colors ran from white (Dominicans) to blue (Religious of the Sacred Heart of Mary) to brown (Carmelites) to gray (Maryknoll Sisters) to purple (the Grey Nuns of the Cross) to pink (Adorers of the Holy Spirit). Some had ominous pointy widow's peak headpieces, others broad "Flying Nun" hats, still others enormous hoods that cut off most all peripheral vision. Some had capes, others did not. Scapulars differed in width and length. Veils might extend far down the back or to the neck. And so on. The sole standard, it seemed, was the general assumption that the body should be covered except for the hands and the face.

Veils predated the Church, of course. Women in Greek and Roman societies wore them in classical times. As some Christian women were consecrated for spiritual purposes, ideas about common, distinct forms of dress that went beyond the veil were floated about by male authorities. Such self-appointed arbiters of ecclesiastical design as Jerome, Clement of Alexandria, Cyprian of Carthage, and Tertullian all freely dispensed advice to the virgins and widows who clustered in the early women's communities. Although the suggestions never melded into an exact code, the patriarchs did prescribe a general pattern: that is, black dresses. When the first monastery for women was founded by

St. Syncletica in the fourth century, the practice of wearing common garb took solid root. By the middle of the following century, St. Augustine, bishop of Hippo, required that the monastery his sister had entered follow the same practice. Customs and styles changed greatly over time. Habits worn by most orders in the twentieth century had origins in the plain clothing of women who lived at the time the order was founded, most likely in the eighteenth or nineteenth century, many of them modeled on widows' dresses. St. Vincent de Paul garbed the first Daughters of Charity in the style of Paris peasant girls, for instance, and borrowed the winged headpiece, or cornette as it was called— worn by television's "Flying Nun"—from the French sunbonnet. Yet while the dress of common women moved on with the fashions of the culture, nuns' garb remained anchored in an earlier time, subject to the approval and adaptation by the Church hierarchy—Bishop James E. Walsh's design of the habit for the Maryknoll order he founded, for example, or Baltimore cardinal James Gibbons's creation of the headdress for the Missionary Helpers of the Sacred Heart.

Not surprisingly, the fashion of a distant age lent an increasingly costume-party mystique to the already otherworldly image of the nun. What had been very everyday clothing at the time of an order's founding, the daily apparel of ordinary women, had come to epitomize the otherworldly. For many both inside and outside religious communities, the garb marked nuns as both separate and special. It also acted as a barrier, placing sisters beyond ordinary life and making their life forbidding and unapproachable. It tended to identify the nun more with what she wore than who she was. By the middle of the twentieth century, the otherwordly baggage was weighing too heavily on the worldly mission of the nuns.

Pope Pius XII's 1950 appeal to nuns to update their customs and procedures was tacit recognition by the Church's supreme earthly ruler that the nun was indeed estranged from the modern world. Exhorting the orders to narrow the gap, Pius opened a door, although his directions lacked specifics. The process of acting on the pope's wishes in redesigning the habit therefore went nowhere in the decade after the pope's urging, as if everyone were waiting for someone else to make the first move, in the absence of a clear signal from Rome. In the United States, nuns had found their own voices, their own orientation to the world through Sister Formation. For many sisters, that bridge to modernity helped render certain aspects of their traditional life obsolete without ever focusing on the habit. Enrolled in colleges and universities as never before, exposed to a broader curriculum than ever permitted, they were moving closer to the contemporary world of the laity and further from the cloistered life that many orders had espoused since medieval times. To many nuns, the habit thus was becoming less important in defining their vocation.

Not everybody, of course, was led to that way of thinking. Sister Penet, the inspiration behind the Sister Formation Conference, for example, was among those who believed that any move to discard the habit in the effort to update religious life was misguided. Her painful break with her closest colleagues, Sisters Walters and Bradley, resulted primarily from differences over that issue and subsequently involved broader aspects of renewal.

But the momentum was clearly on the side of change.

Most significantly, Cardinal Suenens's salty warning against retaining the old habit had added force to revisionism just before Vatican II. Then the Council dispatched the sisters to the drawing boards. "The religious habit," said Perfectae Caritatis, "an outward mark of consecration to God, should be simple and modest, poor and at the same time becoming. In addition, it must meet the requirements of health and be suited to the circumstances of time and place and to the needs of ministry involved."

It could be argued that the Council fathers would never have placed the matter on the agenda without Pius's prompting more than a decade before. Perhaps they purposely left the directions vague in order to give the sisters maximum flexibility. Or maybe they treated the matter halfheartedly in expectation that the sisters would move cautiously, trimming around the edges while leaving the habit basically intact. It is safe to say that few if any bishops foresaw the eventual outcome; neither did the sisters. The fact was that the Council's call for renewal had granted the sisters what they believed to be, for good reason, great latitude. Though Sister Penet deeply regretted the lengths to which her movement went, Sister Formation had taught sisters to respect their ability to think and decide. Now they were ready to act.

The inseparable connection between habit and nun meant that the ensuing struggle over the fate of the habit would pose the first great test of how far renewal would go and how distressed Rome would become by this symbolic shake-up.

The debate that unfolded was principally about what the habit stood for and how important its meaning was to the sister's vocation. Nuns had always been placed in their own holy, otherworldly, perfectionist realm but without a distinguishing sacrament or a voice in the structure of the Church. Did habits provide, therefore, a necessary and irreplaceable symbol of their special status? The Second Vatican Council had robbed them of their special claim to the pursuit of holiness and placed them on an equal footing with the laity, the common herd of holiness pursuers. Had the habit, therefore, lost its purpose? What else did the members of a religious community have to establish their unique identity? By making the sister visible, didn't the habit enable her to carry out her ministry more effectively? What would it mean to be a sister if she looked just like non-vowed laywomen?

Nearly everyone had been ready for some degree of alteration in the traditional garb. The availability of new lighter-weight fabrics was a godsend. Mother McGrath, for example, recalled that she and her Paola Ursulines loved their habits although it took a good half a day's work to wash and iron them. They had rejoiced when cottons and synthetic materials became fashionable. On the first day of 1958, the community switched to a new headpiece that eliminated starch and stiffness, she writes, but retained the coif and complete head covering with no hair showing.

Likewise, the Sisters of Charity of Convent Station, New Jersey, had simplified their habit, adopting a softer version in 1960. Among other things, they discarded the headpiece that had framed their faces in fluted rectangles after a car accident killed a nun whose vision had been impaired while driving. (Connecticut, where the accident took place, soon outlawed anything that so impaired a driver's vision.)

After Vatican II, minor alteration became major tailoring, sometimes quickly, often gradually. The Sisters of Charity in New Jersey, for example, had agreed to permit both blue suits and full habits by the late 1960s, and by the early 1970s some sisters had dropped the veil. Mother Elizabeth Seton, the revered founder of the order, had not adopted the veil herself.

The next step involved to the growing number of sisters who practiced their professions outside Church institutions. They were allowed to wear clothing they judged appropriate. As result, a decade after the Council, a large table of nuns gathered for dinner would run the gamut from old garb to secular dress and gradations in between—a trim of the veil or a slight raise of the hem. Everyone, it seemed, had a habit tale or quip. One former nun fondly recalled visiting a convent filled with nuns on a hot summer day. The nuns were, as usual, dressed in their bulky wool habits and there was nothing to cool the air. "It was like walking into a room full of wet sheep," the ex-nun remembered.

A year before Vatican II fired up the debate, Sister M. Claudelle Miller, S.C.L., of St. Joseph's convent in Leavenworth, Kansas, sampled lay personnel, sisters, and students at Catholic institutions as part of the research on renewal for her community. She asked if laypersons liked or disliked traditional dress. Did sisters and laypeople think the sisters' clothing should be changed? How important was religious garb to the sisters' work? Two-thirds (65 percent) of sisters and laypeople favored at least some change. Better-educated Catholics were more likely to favor change. Older sisters, over age forty-five, were more in favor of change than were those who were younger; while younger laity, twenty-five to forty-four, wanted change more than older laity. Said one sister in the survey: "Religious habits that lack simplicity often repel rather than attract others to their ideals." The tension identified in the survey was between daily work, which habits could make more difficult, and the religious symbolism of community identity and otherworldliness, areas that seemed to benefit from the habit. The symbolism Sister Miller found was deeply ingrained. Her question, therefore, was how far alteration could go without ruining symbolism.

Perhaps sensing the storm that was about to break, Sister Mary Wilma, superior of the Sisters of Charity Community in Leavenworth, Kansas, approvingly emphasized that Pope Paul VI had reminded the superiors general of the world in Rome on May 23, 1964, that nuns "at all times and in all places" were "subject principally to the Roman Pontiff, as to their highest superior." Did the pope have a premonition that nuns would sorely test Roman authority? Was this, in other words, a preemptive strike? Sister Mary Bonaventure, a professor at the University of Detroit who early on marveled at the depth and breadth of the habit crisis, also counseled caution. The ills of religious life could not be blamed solely on the habit as some were wont to do, she asserted, and throwing it out would therefore be folly. "We only need apply the test of street logic to note the enormity of the fallacy," Sister Bonaventure said. "I have a severe headache which I wish to alleviate; I should cut off my head to effect a permanent cure."

Communities suffered a long night of tension and anguish in their efforts to strike that balance between change and tradition. The personal impact was often wrenching. "The first time sisters came to breakfast without a veil," said a sister of the Sacred Heart, "some of our older sisters got up and left. They just cried and cried and cried."

The process of setting standards was messier than it had been before the Council because the religious superior could no longer make unilateral declarations. Superiors were instructed to convoke a general chapter meeting to consider all aspects of renewal. To the superiors was entrusted much of the responsibility to move the community toward greater democracy as well as to an elected representative government that took on considerably greater authority. This was asking a lot of many superiors who were holdovers from the pre–Vatican II days. The transition often entailed giving up the title of mother superior or its equivalent in favor of a simpler designation, and facilitating decisions rather than issuing directives. Some welcomed the change; others did not; still others were replaced in the normal cycle of office by leaders who embraced the collaborative style. Out of sight but hardly out of mind was the power of Rome to disrupt the most carefully laid plans.

Mother McGrath, as superior of the Paola Ursulines, knew the perils full well. She had taken the lead with changing the habit before getting the hierarchy's go-ahead and paid a price. Her first shock was how vociferously laypeople had reacted against her granting permission to two of her Paola Ursulines to experiment with the habit in Oklahoma. "Their fixed image of a sister had been shattered," she wrote with a trace of bitterness.

> *Sisters were always there, in their own little quarters, to teach their children, to relieve them of responsibilities they just didn't think of assuming themselves because the sisters would do it; to nurse them when they got sick; to be a sign of prayer and goodness which somehow seemed necessary for everyone but, if the sisters were around, it would somehow rub off sufficiently to ensure their future glory too, and the sign of all this was the habit.*

Suddenly, a simple change in habit had caused them to be branded agents of "the devil and Communism," by angry Catholics, she lamented.

For the Ursulines and hundreds of communities, the changes in the habit became a litmus test that divided nuns who wanted to move faster from those who wanted to go slower or stay where they were. Many of those who felt their sisters balk at reform walked away from the convent (one sign of a sister's imminent departure: her hair under the veil began to grow out). On the other hand, some sisters who resisted the changes left for contemplative communities that were under no such mandate to reform. Those in the middle—the tens of thousands of sisters who felt both the excitement and anxiety of that open moment—felt the pressures from both sides, took part in the debate, made adjustments, and muddled on. For many nuns, memories of those years remain painful.

The group of Sisters of Charity in Convent Station, New Jersey, seated at a long table beside a large window on the second floor of their mother house, remembered the shocks of thirty years ago.

Sister A: "The sixties. I'd like to forget it."

Sister B: "It was a great controversy—the habit or not the habit. I remember a potluck supper one night. There was a full habited nun sitting next to a nun in shorts. It was a shock."

Sister C: "Yet for all the conflict none of it was personal."

Sister A: "The talk was over. We'd all received the same letter stating the new, freer rules."

Sister B: "I think of a remark one nun in a traditional habit made when she saw two other sisters in skirt suits. 'Well, you won't trip on that,' she said. I suppose it was a little sarcasm hiding her hurt, but, you know, nobody had ever made comments like that even in fun."

Sister E: "I never opposed the change in habit; I just never really chose it. I don't like change, but there we were. One day we were in our blue habits, the next day we could be in contemporary dress. I wore a habit until the Snow White Company stopped making them. Now I'm not against a uniform but I don't want anybody telling me what to do."

Sister C: "It was also an inspiring time, especially the great chapter of change guided by Mother Marie. She was amazing, inviting people to state their views on all this, listening carefully, saying, 'I hadn't thought of that.' To see her changing helped us move along."

And move along they did; like so many other orders, the Sisters of Charity switched to a new habit soon after the Second Vatican Council and to optional dress just a few years later. In the process, some answers began to emerge for American sisterhoods. Sisters became more convinced that they had been too identified by the habit. Said one Franciscan sister: "There was value to being identified and the simplicity of the lifestyle which the habit brought but I'm not hung up on the idea of the 'holy habit.' The clothes are not what make you." And a Dominican nun summed up what many nuns felt was the false symbolism of the habit: "I don't want to be a flawless figurine who looks as if she has it all together, which I don't. The habit also brings with it the temptation to look at oneself that way." Inevitably, perhaps, it was easier to shed the cause of the excess than to preserve a healthy sense of spirituality or otherworldliness. The outdated, even bizarre aspects of nuns' clothing were consigned to the used clothing bin but little had been found to replace the habit. For some, anonymity was in keeping with Vatican II's elimination of their special status and they were enthusiastic about it. But others missed the presence of a common symbol of commitment and community that went beyond the pins and other discreet emblems they now attached to their dresses, two-piece ensembles, and pantsuits. The symbolism dilemma remained unresolved.

Meanwhile, on the front lines, attention turned to practical decisions such as how much to spend on ordinary clothes. Some felt it important to dress with dignity in the likes of Hart Shaffner & Marx, a fashion industry leader. Others headed for bargain basements or sought the assistance of consultants provided by their orders. The superior of the Blessed Virgin Mary nuns of Dubuque, Iowa, for example, purchased clothing from jobbers and made it available to sisters at a boutique. Despite dropping the required habit, nuns did take on a distinct look distinguished by short, unstyled hair and modest skirts and blouses or conservative suits in subdued colors or polyester pantsuits. Identity as a nun in a particular community was commonly signified by a simple wedding band or a cross on the collar of the blouse. The discerning eye could pick a nun out of most groups of people.

Stories of how the wardrobe switch went over were legion. One sister

walked into her classroom for the first time in civilian clothes to the startled reaction of one boy. "You look twenty years younger, sister," gasped the boy. She
was then twenty-two years old. Another sister asked if anyone in her class no-
ticed anything new about her wholly revised appearance. After some moments
of silence, a girl ventured, "Your shoes?" And everywhere in the Catholic
world the discovery that nuns had arms and legs prompted curiosity and shock.
A dedicated minority held out for traditional garb. None was more articulate
than Mother Vincent Marie Finnegan, superior of the Carmelites of Alhambra, California, and head of a group of sisters opposed to mainstream developments in religious life. "It's more important to have the habit now than at any
other time in my lifetime," she said. "I don't have a problem with modified
habits; I just like to know you ARE religious. When people know, they have
reverence. If women are in a habit, don't you just assume they live together
and pray together? If they're wearing jeans or a skirt and a blouse, you probably think they live in an apartment and do their own thing. It's still true that if
you want to start a bonfire, start talking about the habit."

A steady diet of nostalgia, piety, and satire still fed the popular imagination
with images of nuns in habits. Movies, television, books, dolls, advertisements
held to the old, in part because it was the only image of nuns the media knew.
It was also the only one many Catholics remember; by the dawn of the twenty-
first century church people were much less likely to be able to spot nuns in a
crowd or on the street. Unfortunately, the old stereotypes prevailed. The old-
fashioned nun could be a ruler-wielding despot or a silly girl or a totally spiritual being without human traits. These have been for the most part benign
associations with imagined sisters who ranged from helpful to tough.

On another level, however, bitterness was still occasionally voiced by
Catholics who believed that a habit-less nun was an uppity woman. A scene
from *Dead Man Walking,* the moving account of the ministry of Sister Helen
Prejean to death-row inmates (the film version of which is probably the finest
portrayal of a modern nun on the screen), illustrated the pervasiveness of the
hard feelings. As Sister Prejean enters Angola penitentiary for the first time, the
Catholic prison chaplain advises her darkly to put on a habit when she visits.
She recalls him saying, "The inmates know that the pope has requested nuns to
wear habits, and for you to flout authority will only encourage them to do the

same." Indeed, John Paul II had long favored more traditional dress for nuns, but he never prescribed a certain style or tried to revoke the choices granted by Vatican II. In accord with her community, therefore, Sister Prejean adopted ordinary dress in 1968 and notes in her book that she hadn't had "one of these 'habit' conversations in a long while." At the time of the change, some Catholics who saw the habit as the dress of "angels" were upset, she remembered, but that had died down. Now she is confronted by the chaplain. His entreaty amazes her because she has "serious doubts that Angola inmates know—or care—what dress code the pope recommends for nuns." Besides, she adds, half whimsically, the habit had been life-threatening in her early days when she did wear one. Her veil had once caught on fire from a candle, and it had often yanked her to a halt after catching on doorknobs. In response to this chiding chaplain who refers to inmates as "the scum of the earth," she places her experience as a nun over papal admonitions.

Sister Prejean's encounter reflects the continuing contretemps between nuns and the hierarchy. During the flurry of the 1960s, as habits were simplified, cast aside, and generally demoted as a factor in religious life, officials in the Roman Curia grew increasingly outraged by these developments. To many of them, renewal had run amok. Early attempts to contain it had failed as the sisters acted on what they saw as a higher duty to run with the implications of Vatican II. Their resistance to Rome, based on this sense of transcendent purpose, was not unlike Vietnam War protesters invoking higher conscience in resisting the draft. But Rome continued to fume over what its officials saw as growing extremism, and matters finally came to a head when Cardinal Antoniutti wrote a letter to the Vatican's ambassadors throughout the world in January 1972, ordering nuns to return to a uniform habit and to wear it in public. John Cardinal Krol forwarded the letter to the Leadership Conference of Women Religious for distribution to major superiors. Sister Thomas Aquinas, who later took back her birth name, Elizabeth Carroll, was then president of the conference and one of the most widely respected Catholics in America. She distributed the letter to the superiors, as requested, but attached to it her response, which sharply disagreed with the cardinal. The intended effect of the Vatican's initiative was, therefore, effectively blunted. Strident attempts at arm-twisting ceased, although the grievance remained. Such demands, periodic and unrelenting, came too late to reverse the tide, but the need to fend off a steady stream of criticism cost many sisters deep anguish and undermined their morale.

Fifteen years after the Council, nuns in the United States had seized upon the freedom to choose their own style of dress. Changing the habit had become a statement of emancipation from male authority in the face of angry opposition from the highest reaches of the Church. By 1982, according to the second of three exhaustive Sister Surveys conducted by Harvard-educated sociologist Sister Marie Augusta Neal, three out of five orders (57 percent) had made major adaptations in the habit and another third (34 percent) had abandoned it altogether as a requirement, although some form of the habit often remained optional. Only about 10 percent of sisters wore anything like a pre–Vatican II habit.

The first Sister Survey (1966–68), which reached nearly all 180,000 nuns in the United States, found that two-thirds of the respondents (63 percent) were opposed to allowing sisters freedom to choose to wear secular clothes on some occasions and (64 percent) were opposed to sisters being allowed to wear contemporary dress at all times. In 1982, just fourteen years later, the ground had almost totally shifted. Thirty-nine percent believed in freedom to choose the style of dress, another 17 percent said it was sufficient to wear a symbol of the community, and another 7 percent thought no identity was necessary. The reversal boiled down to three basic reasons: (1) rejection of the habit as a symbol of elitism and privilege; (2) pragmatism; (3) refusal to accept the concept of a standard uniform.

But if the turnabout was a victory, it was largely pyrrhic. Sisters had left their communities in droves, not driven by changes in habit policies in themselves but by the broader changes in direction that were signaled by the change in habit. Decisions over habits set precedents that disposed communities to act with greater or lesser boldness on other issues. The period was a sort of "veil of tears" from which no order emerged unscathed. Meanwhile, priests and bishops in the parishes and dioceses where the nuns lived and worked often voiced intense disapproval of nuns' efforts to replace the habit. For the most part, the sisters went ahead anyway, but the climate between themselves and the male clerics grew increasingly negatively charged, with long-range implications.

Chapter Six

Breaking the Convent Mold

I n the wake of the Second Vatican Council, tension and strife over the
habit coincided with a powerful surge of optimism within American
communities of sisters. The old ways would not be surrendered without
a fight—and the fights were often bitter. But the larger force was a promise
of liberation. Creative energy burst through the communities like the brilliant glow of a supernova signaling the breakup of a distant star, and like that
celestial phenomenon, it was only partially visible to the outside observer.
Few nuns denied that religious life needed alteration. The dispute was over
how much renewal Vatican II had called for or really wanted.

Surface changes in dress and prayer were obvious. Far less so were the
dramatic shifts in how sisters viewed religious life. Also obscured from public
view were the wrenching debates that took place over the course of months
and years that left lasting impressions and scars on the minds and hearts of
thousands of sisters working to create something new. Not unlike the
founders of the nation, who faced the daunting task of conceiving and con-
structing a new form of government after the Revolutionary War, the sisters
prepared to rewrite their constitutions almost, as they understood it, from
scratch. The difference was that the nuns, unlike the founders of the nation,
were operating within only a semblance of freedom, ambiguous and conditional. It took their resolve to define what that freedom meant.

Communities had a long history of chapter meetings where important business was conducted. Most nuns, or their representatives, had traditionally elected their superiors but otherwise had a negligible influence over their community's affairs. The superior's authority over all matters great and small had been nearly absolute by virtue of the "grace of office" that was assumed to invest the mother superior's decisions with nothing less than the authority of the will of God. Chapter meetings, therefore, were usually exercises in rubber-stamping.

Vatican II thinking required different assumptions and procedures. Privilege, superior status, and strict top-down government would no longer suffice. Long hours were devoted to remaking the concept of chapters and representation and limitations on authority. Power would flow to the sisters and away from the community leaders. In a nutshell, sisters in general would have many more choices, and the control device known as "permissions," by which nuns had to ask for everything from a bar of soap to clearance to attend a family funeral, was abolished.

It should be no surprise, then, that an explosion followed the removal of such restraints. Although the existence of "permissions" within religious orders had been celebrated for encouraging conformity and facelessness, creating an environment in which sisters had nothing much to decide for themselves, the sisters were now living in a society that increasingly emphasized personal freedom and choice. That climate had become harder to escape when they entered the convent, although religious life, in general, still stoutly rejected the dominant culture's values of self-determination. Pent-up energy still built behind convent walls to the point that even Vatican II's amorphous instruction provided an outlet for release.

The quickening that enlivened those momentous post–Vatican II general chapter meetings was largely but not always positive. Enthusiasm mingled with anxiety and confusion and dismay. Forward motion caused reaction. Factions arose within most communities, pitting traditionalists against progressives and leaving a big group in the middle feeling torn. Although a majority of sisters appeared to seize the moment as liberating, a sizable minority saw alteration as misguided and destructive. The years of perceived repression made some nuns want to run faster than their communities were ready to— and many would leave unsatisfied. At the other extreme, all that conditioning, all that loyalty to the old rule, all that comfort with a role that had clear rewards, left other sisters with the conviction that wholesale reform would kill any true religious life. The opposing factions tended to exist in inchoate form before the proposals hit the floor of the special chapter meetings. Before and during those meetings, which could last several days, spirits and energies ran high as the opposing sides spelled out their claims. Despite considerable fear and foreboding, however, the atmosphere at those fateful meetings was suffused with excitement. At stake was revitalization. Every nun favored that, no matter what her definition of renewal. In the headiness of the post–Vatican II Catholic world, "hope" was the byword on all sides, however much the sisters differed on means and ends.

The tradition of cleansing and clarifying was as old as Christianity. Renewal, or quite literally "making new again," was linked to the dynamism of repentance, forgiveness, and the shedding of obstacles to reach a deeper and more authentic life of faith. It was the centuries-old yearning to return to basic purposes that had somewhere along the way become compromised or displaced. The Second Vatican Council and Pope Paul VI had given explicit instructions that nuns (and men's religious orders, though they were far less bound by rules) call the equivalent of "constitutional conventions" to renew themselves. "They shall accomplish this," wrote Pope Paul VI in setting the standards, "especially by means of general chapters."

But, of course, the process had already begun before Vatican II. Pius XII, as noted, had provided the first nudge; the Sister Formation movement had hastened it along by promoting education and ending isolation by bringing orders into contact with one another; and Cardinal Suenens's book *Nun in the World,* part of which had been published in the *Sister Formation Bulletin,* had acted as a major spur from a highly placed source. For each community, the pace and extent of renewal was different, of course, owing to its level of autonomy and its individual traditions. Some moved very quickly; others, often badly split, took a long time. The surprising thing was how much agreement did arise over such a short period of time.

The story of one group of Benedictines who generally belonged somewhere between the progressives and the conservatives reveals much about the spirited struggle undertaken by a wide range of orders. The Benedictine sisters are one of the oldest women's orders, rooted in Benedict of Nursia's monastic rule (its formal, historical name defining the character of the order) of the sixth century. Several Benedictine communities were planted by Germans in the United States in the nineteenth century. Many of these convents with a common heritage banded together. The Federation of St. Scholastica was one of the big ones. In the mid-1970s, the Federation had 2,200 sisters affiliated with twenty-three convents from Pennsylvania to Louisiana to California to Mexico City.

From 1966 to 1974, representatives of the Federation's member communities met five times as a decision-making chapter to confront the challenge of renewal. The first order of business in 1966 was to remove the obligation to say the prayers of Prime (in the order of the day, it was the second gathering for prayer) promptly at 6:10 a.m. The sisters had been previously expected to pray together six times a day for as many as five hours in addition to putting in a full workday, usually in the classroom, doing household duties, attending Mass, and taking meals in silence while fellow nuns read from spiritual classics. Eliminating Prime began the process of relaxing formal prayer and increasing private devotions. Other early decisions ended the choral office during which nuns had sung Gregorian chant at intervals during the day; discontinued the Wednesday fast; began the process of modifying the habit; and spaced chapter meetings every three years instead of six (to meet the particular needs of renewal, the next chapter actually convened in 1968, after only two years). Power was redistributed to encourage further participation—downward from superiors and outward toward members. At the Benedictine convents, the election of a prioress and community advisory council to fixed terms by all members became standard. In addition, the council was enlarged and its authority increased. Meanwhile, the number of delegates elected to the chapter on the Federation level nearly doubled between 1966 and 1968. Self-study, an instrument of critical analysis that had been foreign to convents of the past, became a key ingredient in the renewal chapters. At the close of the renewal phase in 1974, the Benedictines had rearranged most of the furniture of their religious household, symbolic and otherwise. Sisters had the option of wearing the habit but could choose not to; they were freer to pray on their own; and they had much more control over where they lived and what kind of work they did. All of this was achieved through strong consensus, but the results were not an unqualified triumph. Sister Stephanie Campbell, O.S.B., a contributor to the book *Climb Along the Cutting Edge,* which analyzes the renewal in the Federation, writes: "Some communities experienced polarization over change; friends with differing views found themselves at odds with one another; 'liberal' sisters were considered suspect by the more 'conservative.' . . . There were wounded sisters in every community; the price of renewal was not cheap." Two Federation communities split in half and went their separate ways. In the seven years ending in 1969, nearly a fifth, or four hundred, of the Benedictine sisters left Federation convents for reasons that, in one way or another, stemmed from the upheavals that sprang up around renewal.

Researchers in the order sought to know more about the 80 percent who stayed. One measure was a survey of the delegates to the chapter meetings on renewal from 1966 to 1974, the results of which were reported in *Climb Along the Cutting Edge.* Of the 158 sisters picked to represent the convents, 142 responded. Nearly 70 percent of them held a master's degree and another 16 percent had a B.A. or B.S. Nearly half (47 percent) said they had been much or somewhat happier during the renewal process than they had expected to be. An overwhelming 95 percent were optimistic about the future of their community.

Asked to describe religious life before Vatican II by choosing from a list of adjectives, the respondents praised the old convent for offering stability (96 percent), security (94 percent), and a sense of reverence (89 percent). They also remembered the old convent as being both a respectful (81 percent) and a happy (80 percent) place. Among the negative qualities of the old convent that stood out for them: restricted (90 percent), frugal (85 percent), impersonal (66 percent), elitist (60 percent), and adolescent (56 percent). What did they like about life during renewal? Among the traits they most often selected were positive (97 percent), hopeful (96 percent), open (95 percent), liberating (94 percent), meaningful (92 percent), enthusiastic (88 percent), and happy (88 percent). The chief drawbacks they saw were that renewal had brought both a state of confusion (56 percent) and a fragmentation in the community (47 percent). Most delegates said that documents of Vatican II had propelled change but that the Church at the diocesan and parish levels often had not encouraged it. A third said that in their experience clergy had actually tried to hamper change.

The Benedictine survey of the 80 percent who had stayed through the shake-up shows unflagging support for the post–Vatican II reforms despite the pain; those who left were divided about the changes—some rejected them but most were generally believed to favor them or want even greater alterations. Although still enamored of much that the convent of the past had to offer—and without scoffing at it—the sisters who stayed were embracing the new forms and uncertainties with greater fervor. The greatest threat the survey detected was their own fear of the unknown.

This remarkable transition from one set of values to another would have proved impossible without a tidal shift in thinking. What the Benedictines found in their surveys mirrored the pattern in other communities: that nuns had done their homework by studying their order's history and tradition along with Vatican II's statements on the nature of the Church, Catholicism's relationship to the world, and, of course, Perfectae Caritatis, which was addressed to them.

Among the questions that emerged from their study were how to define what it meant to be a nun, how she should live, and what work she should do, all within an atmosphere of freedom that nuns had never before known. The search, in their terms, was for a community that had a human face, that paid more attention to the needs of the person.

Many of these questions were deeply theological—and as such, nuns were generally poorly educated to handle them. Among the oldest traditions in Catholicism was the judgment that women were emotional creatures incapable of the rational inquiry needed to examine theology. Using that rationale, the hierarchy had forbidden women from studying theology. Access to theological knowledge was quite clearly linked to positions of power; ergo, the women were excluded from positions of power. A decade before Vatican II, the only place women could study theology was at St. Mary's College in South Bend, Indiana, where the enterprising Sister Madeleva Wolff had begun granting doctorates in sacred studies to women in the 1940s.

For hundreds of sisters, the scarcity of opportunities for theological study was not the only obstacle; they were also deterred by an embedded self-image that steered them away from such a traditionally masculine pursuit. In order to move ahead, nuns had to overcome a deeply ingrained bias that told them they were incapable of meeting the challenge, a variation on the "feminine mystique" that Betty Friedan had recently introduced to the wider American population. In the sisterhood, the Sister Formation Conference had helped derail this myth by instilling a greater sense of personal competence and intellectuality. It had also weakened the strains of dependency and deference. To prime the pump, the *Sister Formation Bulletin* included pieces by well-known contemporary theologians in the 1950s—a bold decision at the time. But Vatican II had provided no further theology for building on this foundation. It had provided the thinking behind a new vision in many key areas of doctrine regarding the nature and purpose of the Church and the new relationship of Catholicism to justice in the world. In an effort to respond to the pleas for greater relevancy from Pope Pius XII and others, the nuns were given general guidelines intended to better adapt them to the modern world. But the Second Vatican Council failed to offer those in religious life a grounding in theology that provided a rationale for the direction they were supposed to take. Instead, it resorted to old concepts that had elevated the sisterhood to a perfect, privileged status, a concept that had been discredited earlier in the Council's most weighty document, the Dogmatic Constitution on the Church. It was like providing nuns with a new ship with outmoded navigation tools.

The major work was done after the Council as women religious grappled with their identities. Nothing in the history of the post-Council renewal of religious life can perhaps compare to the turnabout in the lives of so many sisters as they toppled the stereotypes of themselves as inferior versions of men. It was an astonishing revision of identity without which the rest of the reforms would have been impossible.

By 1967, as the first massive Sister Survey of 139,000 U.S. nuns (all sisters were invited to reply) reveals, sisters were reading the leading theologians of the time, many of whom were architects of Vatican II. Heading the list of luminaries, many of whom had been silenced by Rome before Vatican II on grounds of violating orthodox thinking, were Pierre Teilhard de Chardin, the futuristic paleontologist and theologian; Henri de Lubac, the French Jesuit who emphasized the sacramental nature of the Church; Karl Rahner, the German theologian who contributed to a new understanding of the Church's relationship to the world; Bernard Haering, the German ethics professor who helped redefine morality more in terms of personal relations and less by inflexible rules; Edward Schillebeeckx, the Dutch theologian whose massive texts on the nature of the Church and Christ had a profound Vatican II flavor; Bernard Cooke, the American Jesuit who emphasized the sacramental implications of the Council; Charles Curran, the American moral theologian who rethought the Church's teachings on sexuality from a Vatican II perspective; Hans Küng, the modernist Swiss theologian and Vatican II architect whose views on the papacy would later result in his censure by the Vatican; Gerard Sloyan, the American champion of the Council; Gregory Baum, the Canadian Jesuit who championed dialogue between the Church and the world; and Hans Urs von Balthasar, the Swiss-born theologian with the most majestic name in the group whose theology was imbued with a supernatural, mystical flavor. That a woman could be included in that select circle was still, of course, a far-fetched notion. Having dipped into these deep waters, however, sisters were better prepared to grasp the thinking behind the Council's documents. To say that they took these documents quite seriously, no longer being willing to allow male clergy to do their theology for them, is an understatement. The greater sense of autonomy and intellectual freedom generated considerable exhilaration. For the first time, nuns saw the possibility of arriving at their own vision of the religious vocation. The awareness buoyed them, as a 1967 Benedictine questionnaire revealed. Eighteen of twenty communities in the Federation of St. Scholastica took part; 1,539 of the total membership of nearly 2,200 sisters responded. As this survey of a rather conventional order shows, firm theological convictions were taking shape, some touching the foundations of religious life. Outward behavior, from the freedom to choose with whom to sit at meals to leaving the convent for a drive by oneself, was normally undergirded by theological principle. The surveyed sisters reflected a much bigger reality. Two-thirds (66 percent) now disagreed with the concept that taking vows gives the nun "special holiness." More generally, they spurned the "state of perfection" image that had set nuns apart before Vatican II, embracing instead the Council's "universal call to holiness." To many nuns, the demands of living apart in a superior state, even with its privileges, were a burden, and the removal of this special status brought comfort. They thought about authority in a new way. Previously, power flowed vertically from Rome through the local superior. The emerging perspective, by contrast, saw the source of authority as the Holy Spirit who speaks within the whole body of the Church, empowering those who are presumed to be left out. In the old system, nuns were warned against "particular friendships" and against anything that would detract from self-sacrifice (essentially the "model wife" concept including the "Bride of Christ" imagery). Suddenly friendship was blessed as a cornerstone of community life, and the development and nurturing of the self were considered essential.

Regarding the purpose of religious life, the Benedictine survey respondents were more unsettled. The most favored definitions on the list were "gospel life, no more, no less" (21 percent) or "to witness to the existence of another world than this one" (19 percent); another 40 percent preferred both, apparently reflecting the effort to merge worldly and otherworldly purposes. The lack of clarity is understandable, given the disruption inherent in the collapse of an old, entrenched system. Still, a solid majority (59 percent) said post–Vatican II life was confusing. Enthusiasm had sustained many nuns in a journey of great uncertainty.

But the path ahead was rocky, strewn with ambiguities. "It was one thing to lighten the prayer load, another to share faith," wrote Benedictine Sister Joan Chittister. "It was one thing to be a work force, another to be prophetic. It was one thing to train women to conform, another to call forth personal and communal commitment. It was one thing to build the institutions, another to rebuild or raze them."

In the initial spectacle of renewal's supernova, however, the evidence signaled strong approval but with significant dissent. Two years after the Second Vatican Council ended, with renewal in its very first stages, the Sister Survey found that 55 percent of the nuns believed that the process was moving at a good pace, though another 23 percent saw it moving too slowly. Further, they saw its impact on communities as marginally positive. A third (32 percent) believed community morale had risen during the past five years while a quarter (25 percent) thought it had sunk; two out of five (39 percent) saw no basic change.

While the single impetus of reform had stirred an invigorating breeze through all the communities, no two responded alike. In later years, each group had a story to tell about those sometimes wild and woolly frontier days when everything broke loose and rising forces needed to be tamed. Most of that history exists as fragments of memory and anecdote. What a sister remembers depends largely on her age and circumstances at the time.

The paradox of the supernova implied an immense explosion of energy and light that was, in actuality, an implosion, a collapse of the mass into a denser unit.

Sisters of St. Joseph of Springfield, Massachusetts, Maxyne Schneider and Mary Hennon, from their home in Gardner, Massachusetts, in 1995, for example, look back at those topsy-turvy years as many nuns do, as a sort of a second formation process that oriented them to a new way of life. Sister Schneider had entered the St. Joseph community in 1960 and was not quite finished with her initial formation in the old ways before renewal came along. She would go on to earn a Ph.D. in chemistry and to teach in the community's Elms College. More recently she joined Sister Hennon and three other of her sisters in establishing a center for helping abused women cope with problems such as violence, poverty, and childrearing. It was a form of innovative religious ministry Sister Schneider says she couldn't have imagined when she first entered religious life. By comparison, Sister Hennon, now in her seventies, had become a postulant in 1939, the year Eugenio Pacelli became Pope Pius XII. Her superiors had steered her away from her first choice, teaching English, in favor of their desire that she obtain a doctorate in science education. She had been a professor, dean of Elms College, administrator of the order, and leader of an antipoverty project in Kentucky before beginning her new venture with Sister Schneider.

Sister Schneider reflected on the years of change with humor and dispassion. She recalled the buildup to the first foray into renewal, a chapter meeting scheduled in 1965. At the time, she had finished her novitiate but was still studying and had not yet taken final vows. She remembers the excitement on the eve of the meeting. Sisters were asked to submit the topics they wished to discuss. The suggestions flowed. Never having observed a chapter, Sister Schneider asked a superior how long it would likely take. "A day," she was told. That seemed an awfully short amount of time to her, but there was still the topic list with its meaty subjects. "I was anticipating major issues," said the upbeat dark-haired, brown-eyed nun, "then it was all over and all those important things didn't show up." As had been the custom, the bishop ran the meeting with dispatch—it was the last time a bishop would preside—and the session remains memorable to Sister Schneider for its two major resolutions that allowed the sisters to wear pajamas and wristwatches, replacing crinkley nightgowns and pocket watches on a string. The outcome had been a letdown, a trivialized chapter meeting, although later the changes that were allowed did seem to hold some meaning. "After all, those things were tokens of the world," she said of the newly approved items, "and they replaced the leftover trappings of an old-fashioned time. What the chapter did was a little leading edge as to what was to come."

Sister Hennon's recollections were more painful, in part because she had served as a Sister of St. Joseph in the old ways for a quarter century before renewal came about. As she explained it, the strain arose mainly from the loss of friends who took their leave in subsequent years and from the sudden need to confront issues of authority and the treatment of women that had either lain dormant or had never been addressed, creating a reservoir of discontent ready to burst. Sister Hennon, like many older nuns, welcomed the revolution, regarding it as a kind of liberation, but dreaded the ordeal.

What stood out for her was the obstructionism of the old system. The diocesan bishop, Christopher J. Weldon, intruded into the renewal chapters in two blatant ways. In an effort to gain another six-year term for the convent's current superior (he had single-handedly appointed her to two previous six-year terms), he tried to block a move by the community to open up the election process, allowing more time for sisters to consider candidates. He had also attempted to seat two delegates of his own among the elected representatives to the chapter meeting. Stalemated, the sisters refused to leave the mother house in Holyoke until he came to speak with them about resolving the issues. The reverend mother lost an open election, thereby becoming the last mother superior. From then on, the head of the community would dress in civilian clothes and be called president.

"Those were very painful chapter sessions," said Sister Hennon with a tinge of resonant emotion.

> *There were tensions over small group living, which the bishop opposed, and over changing the habit and the prayer schedule. Some people wanted to move ahead; some people didn't. We had very big losses. From 1965 to 1975 we went from eight hundred sisters to six hundred. But it was our willingness to talk through these issues that gave us a sense of what the community was all about. We came to know where we were going together. Where were we going? Wherever we felt the freedom of the Spirit of God.*

We looked for the signs of the times. In the Gospel that meant going among the poor.

The two nuns were living at the time they were interviewed in a poor area serving poor women. They themselves were scraping by with help from SHARE, a self-help food coop that allowed them to purchase $35 worth of groceries for $14 and two hours of volunteer work a month.

Without that bonding time of renewal between 1965 and 1975, neither sister believed the mission would have continued as strongly as it has. "Mary was in her mid-forties during the special chapters of the late 1960s," said Sister Schneider. "She found it very painful. I was too young and naive to be sensitized to pain. But one thing stands out. When we were preparing for special chapters for two summers, we went away to a Maine inn. We stayed together, prayed together, sang together. If you're praying, playing, and laughing together it's hard to have strong divisions."

Internal forces caused splits in most communities struggling to direct new energies toward consensus. But for some orders, like the Sisters of St. Joseph, there was also an outside force: intervention from bishops and priests. Some of this intrusion had little effect on strategy but cost communities time and energy that might have been more profitably spent. Some of it provoked conflict.

Of the battles, none proved so costly or significant as the standoff between James Cardinal McIntyre of Los Angeles and one of the best-known orders in his archdiocese, the Immaculate Heart of Mary (IHM) sisters. The outcome of that battle would send a chilling wind over the renewal efforts in every part of the country. At the same time, it would galvanize sisters who were least inclined to allow institutional Church authorities to define their religious lives.

The IHMs of L.A. were a strong community of more than six hundred sisters who were known for their teaching skills in the archdiocesan schools, their innovations in ministries to the poor, their stands against racial injustice and war, and their general progressive stance toward the sisterhood. They ran a college. One of their sisters, an artist named Corita Kent, became nationally known for her fanciful designs, including the immensely popular red "LOVE" heart that was used on a U.S. Postal Service stamp. The IHMs were the first sisters in the United States permitted by Rome to drive cars and to go out alone.

In 1963, the IHMs were ahead of the curve: they had approved several adjustments to their community life. Among the more whimsical actions of that year's general chapter meeting was to approve the use of Dr. Scholl's sandals as official garb. Four years later, the community met again and went much further, eliminating all mandatory standards with regard to dress, prayer schedule, and the kind of work a sister did. Sisters claimed the right to choose their own professions, with or without the approval of the archdiocese.

Cardinal McIntyre was known to be unsympathetic to the Second Vatican Council. He had stayed home for most of it, citing poor health. He had also complained repeatedly that the IHM college was too liberal. Faculty and administration efforts to integrate the city's housing, for example, had drawn his legendary ire. Like most prelates of the largest dioceses of his time, he held fast to the prerogatives of authority that had rarely been challenged for nearly a century in this country. He was a "prince of the church" in a Catholic culture that still accepted the exercise of vast power. It was not unusual that when confronted by, of all things, nuns who usually had been the first to obey, he would reflexively respond with an assertion of that vested authority.

When the IHMs brought the cardinal the results of their 1967 general chapter, therefore, its declaration of independence from most areas of hierarchical power met with his scorn. There began a protracted struggle between the cardinal, the great majority of sisters who sided with their superior, Sister Anita Caspary, and defended the charges, and a minority of sisters who rejected the main outlines of renewal. The cardinal insisted that the community submit to regulation of dress (adoption of some kind of common habit), hold specified times of community prayer rather than leaving prayer up to the individual, allow the archdiocese to approve the professional work assignments of sisters, and pledge obedience to the cardinal of Los Angeles. He demanded, in other words, the old monastic disciplines, Vatican II or no Vatican II. Most in the IHM community rejected these conditions. The pope's ambassador to the United States sent a delegate to try to work out the conflict. The national conference of bishops appointed a committee to look into the matter.

A quarter century later Anita Caspary remembered her charged sessions with the cardinal. "It was like going into a great palace, feeling like a little kid," she said. "We were scared by the power. It was a threat to our institutions. The greatest fear is that we would lose everything. Usually we were kept waiting and that only increased the fear of what would happen.

"The cardinal was always very critical of us for not dressing properly, [for] wearing conservative black suits instead of habits. In most cases, when there was an arguable point, I'd put forth what I wanted, and he'd simply say, 'You're wrong.' He said our decrees, which were beautifully written, were just not correct. He'd get red in the face, stand up, make angry gestures. 'Why aren't you being obedient?' he'd say. 'Why don't you understand?' "

Neither could speak to the other over a yawning cultural divide that had validity on both sides. The cardinal could probably not have done other than he did, given his inheritance. Neither could the nuns, in their reborn posture.

The joust began soon after the national committee of bishops, acting on Rome's behalf, forced the question of whether the IHMs intended to abide by the tenets of religious life prescribed by the hierarchy. The nuns refused. More than 90 percent of those who balked were dismissed from the archdiocesan schools (bishops in other dioceses where IHMs taught did not require them to leave) and given dispensations from religious life. Most of the nuns took the dispensations, then marched straight to the community chapel to retake their vows in silence. From this demolition sprouted a new Immaculate Heart Community with no formal ties to the institutional church. It was not what most sisters wanted because to be outside the official fold, to be what is called a noncanonical community, is to cease having influence within that very institution to which sisters had vowed fealty. It is to be an outsider, however freeing the new setting may prove to be. The IHMs had already felt the sting of rejection and ostracism. In 1968, the Conference of Major Superiors of Women, the most powerful voice of nuns, had failed by a single vote to back the IHMs in their stand against the cardinal. It was a crushing defeat, an extraordinary moment. Only a clash of this magnitude—an order that had attained such renown and influence pitted against a cardinal of such strength and ability—would have made it to the floor of the CMSW meeting. The stakes were believed to be high for all sisters.

The sisters retained the support of many CMSW leaders, and accounts of this test of wills were printed and broadcast nationwide. Twenty-five thousand laypeople signed a petition backing the sisters' cause. *Pageant* and other magazines documented the drama, as did many other mass circulation newspapers, including the *L.A. Times*. The battle was perhaps inevitably pitched as the combat of virtuous, disarming nuns against the bully cardinal, a band of Davids versus Goliath. While there was a measure of truth to this characterization, it does inadequate justice to the reality that both the cardinal and the sisters were operating on a sincere, passionate set of convictions about the Church. Cardinal McIntyre held fast to the version that predated Vatican II; his defenders said he was being vilified for simply doing the job the Church installed him to do. The sisters, meanwhile, were burning with the fires of renewal.

The outcome fractured the IHMs into two parts, a small remnant of forty or so loyalists and the remainder, who were stripped of their identity as official sisters and continued as an experiment in noncanonical viability. Survive they did. In 1995 the Immaculate Heart Community returned to its original home by a decision of the bishops' committee and celebrated its twenty-fifth anniversary. The same year, the Leadership Conference of Women Religious belatedly apologized for refusing to side with the community during the fracas. Surviving members of the IHM were honored at a party thrown by the conference in Anaheim, California. A tearful guest declared it a "glorious day," a moment of vindication.

But the encounter and the smashing setback at the hands of the L.A. archdiocese sent a cautionary message throughout the American sisterhood. Sisters across the spectrum of orders registered shock. There was little doubt that, as sisters sought a voice for their reforms, they would be looking over their shoulders.

Chapter Seven

Storming the Exits

The chilling expulsion of the Los Angeles Immaculate Heart of Mary sisters from the ranks of the Church's approved sisterhoods both exposed the growing restlessness in religious orders and anticipated a mightier explosion. Three dozen IHM sisters—about one-tenth of the total—obeyed the cardinal and formed their own IHM loyalist convent. The rest, the decertified ones, had hastened back to their community chapel to retake the same vows, this time to a new, noncanonical—unapproved—entity called the Immaculate Heart Community. Everything remained essentially intact except that the cardinal now forbade them from teaching in the archdiocesan schools and they now existed outside the Church system. They still practiced the customs of the old order, but they no longer answered to Rome. Theirs was an improvised middle way, born of strife, grit, and ingenuity.

Although the IHM model of establishing an alternative community was rarely copied, the revolt of such a prominent and influential community helped convince nuns across the country that severing their formal ties to religious life was possible. The rush of sisters out the doors of the convent during the late 1960s was the most spectacular in the history of the United States. Thousands of nuns simply exited with or without Rome's permission (a letter of dispensation), leaving hundreds of communities weakened and emotionally wrecked. The defectors were driven by a cluster of causes: among them, tensions over whether renewal was going too fast or too slowly; a loss of special status that had conferred on religious life a higher calling than that given to marriage; and conflicts arising from tactics by Church authorities to restrain the sisters' emerging independence. There is no sure way of knowing to what degree the bishops' countermeasures caused the flight, but their reactions most certainly helped worsen frictions within the convents, dampening the hopes of many sisters that renewal would continue. Did the hierarchy purposely try to goad liberal nuns to leave by blunting progress? No such common effort seems to have existed, but such bishops as McIntyre saw "troublemakers" in their way and were glad to see them leave. In the great exodus, progressive nuns were the most likely to go; perhaps they would have departed under any conditions, but the opposition of male authorities certainly didn't help. In any event, the rush to the door cost religious communities some of their most talented and capable sisters, the very sisters who might have provided leadership for a brighter future.

In the decade ending in the nation's Bicentennial year, U.S. orders lost more than 50,000 sisters. By then, when the worst of the hemorrhaging slowed, from a quarter to a third of American nuns had quit. In 1966, according to *The National Catholic Directory,* there were 181,421 nuns across the country; ten years later that total had dropped to 130,995. Death accounted for some of that loss, but many of the sisters who left were relatively young and healthy. The vast majority of the losses were due to sisters who simply walked away because religious life no longer made any sense to them.

Sisters can usually give you hard numbers that add poignancy to the decline. They recall exactly how many women had entered with them and how many, usually a handful, if even that, have stayed. Sister Patricia Wittberg, a widely respected Indiana University sociologist, was one of fifty-nine postulants in her Sisters of Charity community of Cincinnati. Six remain. Sister Catherine Gardner of the Sisters of St. Joseph of Springfield, Massachusetts, recalls with a palpable immediacy the "painful" decade starting in 1965 when the order's rolls dropped from eight hundred to six hundred. Sister Anna Marie Megeo entered the Beech Grove, Indiana, Benedictines in 1965, just as the storm was breaking, with five other women. She alone has stayed.

The effect on communities was catastrophic. It was as if a city roughly the present size of Orlando, Florida, or Fort Wayne, Indiana, had lost nearly three out of every ten of its citizens. Numbers told only part of the story, of course.

In the folklore of sisterhoods, the departures swept away much of the leadership corps of early- to late-middle-aged women who served as models and guides to young sisters.

The loss of skilled professional teachers, nurses, doctors, and administrators dealt a severe blow to many schools, hospitals, and service agencies run by the sisters. The trend toward allowing sisters to choose their own work rather than being assigned to their orders' institutions had begun to weaken a closed system, so the exodus of worker-nuns only hastened the process of shutting the institutions down.

To women bound together in a complex web of vows, duties, mission, worship, and the warp and woof of daily life, the scope of abandonment—empty places at the table where their closest friends had sat—was nothing short of traumatic. Some nuns had always left, of course, for a variety of personal reasons, but before the renewal began those who left were very few in number. Moreover, departure had always been viewed with embarrassment bordering on fright, as if the news of a departure might spread a contagion and thus needed to be kept a secret from those who remained. Sisters just disappeared. As change came, the process broke into the open.

Scarcely any sister who witnessed the change of those ten years can forget it. The exodus looms in the memory of sisters and ex-sisters with the vividness and punch of an earthquake. "Everyone seemed to be going out the door when I was coming in," said one Franciscan nun who was a postulant in 1968. "It was traumatic." What had been a bedrock of stable routine and a cluster of constant companions became, instead, a vista of shifting sands and vanishing soul mates. A sister eating lunch at a long community table could vanish by dinner. Superiors were beset with feelings of failure and grief when they couldn't talk sisters out of leaving. Many of the sisters who stayed behind were badly shaken by this assault on their assumptions about stability that had become part of their mind-set when they took their vows. They lost dearest friends, models of leadership, and delightful housemates. Rightly or wrongly, a largely unspoken assumption was that the best and brightest were the ones who were exiting, leaving behind the dregs and causing widespread demoralization. For some of those who left, the moment was a means of breaking away from a life they had come to see as a mistaken calling. Others were impatient for greater freedoms than renewal appeared to be offering. Many conservatives, by contrast, were stunned by how far the revisions had gone and felt estranged from the religious life they had loved: standard habits, prayer schedules, work assignments, and coexistence under the same roof. Some switched to more traditional orders.

Sister Mary Jeremy Daigler, a Mercy Sister in Maryland who has served as a campus minister and top college administrator since her first years in the convent in the 1960s, recalled the shift: "Before Vatican II, a sister simply wouldn't be in choir or in the refectory. You'd hear crying in the dormitory the night before and she wouldn't be in class the next day. Somebody probably said something like, 'Sister has returned to Savannah.' After the Vatican Council it felt like people were leaving all the time; it seemed like a tidal wave. The people who were leaving came to tell us a couple months ahead of time. It was healthier. We'd have a farewell party for her; we'd help her get a wardrobe together. But when she left we didn't know if we'd have any contact with her, so when she did leave, it felt like death.

"So many types were leaving. The older sisters had a difficult time, fearing for and worrying about how our ministries could hold up with so many deserting them and wondering if there would be a community for them much longer.

"Middle-aged sisters were filled with anger about the leaving because, I guess, they were going through their own midlife transition. Where the older ones felt saddened, the middle-aged ones felt betrayed."

Although "particular friendships" had been outlawed under the old regimen, the law was, of course, unenforceable on its face. Sisters had friends, good friends, and many of them bolted, leaving sorrow and emptiness behind. Some actual biological sisters separated, one staying, the other going, causing agony that did not easily subside. Nuns who had never thought about the stability of their community became anxious and vigilant. "When you saw a sister letting her hair grow," mused one sister, "you knew she'd soon be gone."

Sister Mary Margaret Funk, a vibrant Benedictine with a strong philosophical bent from the Beech Grove community in Indianapolis, remembered as if it had just happened the day in 1978 when her sister left the order. Through all her work for the community in subsequent years, including a term as prioress, she has missed her sister. "Her reasons for leaving were mine for staying," she said. "I knew God was here and that this kind of life could be done. She didn't. We represented two paths of the heart. She's married to a Jewish man and says the sign of the cross is cruel. I see the total value in that but I'm not going to argue. But her leaving had to hurt. She left fourteen years ago. It's the worst separation I've ever had."

For Sister Patricia Lynch, the circumspect leader of the Paola Ursulines, the anguish lingers thirty years after her sister vacated the convent in 1968. Her best friend walked out the same year. "I was devastated and saddened," she says, her voice trailing off. "My sister, Peggy, wanted to be a nurse. She told me that her experience in the novitiate hindered her."

Some who walked away, then, did so with the blessings of their community; some went quietly with scant comment; some took their leave in a maelstrom of anger and hurt. Why did they go? A popular assumption is that they quit to get married. Many did, but marriage was one factor among many, and only sometimes was it decisive. Opportunity certainly knocked. Vatican II had opened the convent to the world, affording contact with a wider assortment of eligible men. Many sisters had known priests as distant collaborators in parish ministry, but after Vatican II socializing between them became possible. Attractions were the natural outcome of the range of encounters in the climate of social and organizational experimentation that marked the post-Council Church. Sister Lynch's sister, for example, had begun a relationship with her future husband before she left the order. Pastors and nuns went off into the sunset together and a romantic colorful tradition was born. Among the stories fitting that tradition was that of the Sister of Providence who taught and lived at a high school that was broken into one night. When the police arrived, one of the officers took a shine to her, and she to him. They married a year later. Or the Sister of Charity who, still dressed in her habit, introduced her future husband at a social gathering at the convent.

Sisters were enrolling in graduate studies as never before. In doing so, they were exposed to the love-in climate that pervaded the youth culture of the universities during the 1960s and 1970s. All of this commingling was conducive to matchmaking and an exchange of wedding rings, but the high visibility of that choice tended to exaggerate its prevalence. When religious superiors were asked in 1966 to choose from a list of reasons they believed sisters were leaving, "prefers marriage" was given as a reason for only a third (33 percent) of the defections by those who had not yet taken final vows and just

20 percent of those who had. In the same survey of 423 leaders, unhappiness with community life ranked much higher than marriage as a cause attributed to the defection of both those who hadn't taken their final vows and those who had. By 1982, after the great winnowing had eliminated many whose departures were related to issues centered on renewal, leaders responding to a similar survey estimated that roughly half of the dropouts had chosen to marry.

Vatican II had even flattened the playing field regarding vocations, lowering the status of a nun or upgrading the vocation of marriage, depending on one's perspective. Whatever the interpretation, it was certain that the pedestal the nun had stood on, above and holier than her non–nun sisters, had been removed, putting sisters and wives on the same plane, vocationally speaking. Why remain a nun when it was possible to accomplish comparable goals in service and holiness as a woman outside religious life, married or single? What was the advantage if sisters were supposed to seek the same kind of spirituality as other women?

Marriage was the option that, for women, still promised the greatest idealism and social approval, but the desire to wed appears only weakly related to unhappiness with the vow of celibacy. Abundant anecdotal material strongly indicates that sisters objected much more to the exercise of power in their communities (emanating from the male hierarchy) than to prohibitions on sexual behavior. Marriage was important, but apparently not dominant for the nuns. An Ursuline sample may be illustrative. Seven young women entered in 1967. All left the convent. Three subsequently married, four didn't. While priests reported chafing under the vow of celibacy, nuns complained most about the vow of obedience. For all the usual association of the sister exodus with marriage, then, a broad consensus shows that what affected sisters much more than the appeals of marriage, family, and sex was the perception that Church authority was too heavy-handed, oppressive, and inhibiting.

The resistance to renewal by James Cardinal McIntyre and other hierarchical heavyweights lent credence to sisters' conviction that the Church's ruling authority was determined to contain the process and perhaps roll it back. Before the Council had even issued its constitution on religious life, Perfectae Caritatis, Pope Paul VI sounded a cautionary note to a gathering of superiors general on May 23, 1964. "For the members of these religious institutes," the pope said, "are *at all times and in all places subject principally to the Roman Pontiff,* as to their highest superior" (italics mine). The Vatican's guidelines by which sister communities were to conduct their renewal were contained in an Apostolic Letter called Ecclesiae Sanctae, which was issued after the Council had spoken. No other group in Catholicism had received such far-ranging directions for redesigning their basic structures and routines. The nature and scope of this directive had unintended consequences, of course, but many Church leaders didn't see the document's implicit potential for wholesale revision. On the other hand, perhaps the pope's reminder to the superiors signaled Vatican fears that things could quickly race beyond the hierarchy's control.

Such premonitions were justified. It soon became clear that the Second Vatican Council's instructions set in motion a process of revamping communities in a democratic direction that would lead many nuns to explicitly challenge the pope's claim that the vow of obedience necessarily meant heeding the pope. It was one sign of the vast storehouse of pent-up frustration at overly regulated convents. A growing number of nuns came to believe that they owed primary allegiance to God rather than to any human superior who claimed to speak God's will. But in the atmosphere of frayed nerves and heated conflicts between traditionalists and progressives within religious communities, the pressures against reform exerted by conservative bishops and priests became another serious source of discouragement and conflict for nuns who had been thinking of leaving. As alluded to earlier, hierarchical reaction was perhaps rarely the sole reason for nuns to walk away, but it sometimes contributed to a mood of frustration and defeat, leaving sisters feeling unable to work out their own community destiny without the meddling clergy fighting change every step of the way. For sisters who longed for a faster pace of renewal, the interference was an especially big factor in their decision to leave.

By the early 1970s, nerves were on edge and tempers were rising. In an attempt to stave off major collisions, the U.S. bishops formed a liaison committee to negotiate with representatives of the Conference of Major Superiors of Women. The committee asked all bishops what troubled them most about how the nuns were changing. Their report went to the 1971 meeting of the CMSW. Among the complaints: a "negative" attitude toward the Vatican and "inordinate criticism" of the Church hierarchy by some sisters; irritation with the increase in the number of sisters living away from the convent; "heartache and worry" over sisters walking away from teaching in Catholic schools after more than a century of serving as teaching staff at bargain-basement salaries. Despite these and other gripes, the bishops extended their "prayerful gratitude and affectionate esteem" through clenched teeth.

The bishops' critique threw hefty political support behind those sisters who were resisting changes. Pressure from the highest authorities was being brought to bear to sway the debate and coerce a reversal of renewal, but it was all done in the spirit of paternalistic concern that the sisters were "misinterpreting" Vatican II.

Sister Jeanne Knoerle, a Sister of Providence of the Mary-of-the-Woods convent in Indiana and former program officer for the Lilly Endowment, watched the lid come off her community when renewal hit. "Everything came unglued," she said. "I think there were people who left my community because they thought change wouldn't happen soon enough. They felt unhappy and stuck and left to find new horizons. Some of those stayed but left later on. Some just stayed out of inertia."

But countless others felt displaced by the overturning of tradition and suffered the fate of the spiritually homeless. One former nun who found herself in this exile described the sentiments of those like herself at the time as being "like children whose parents have died," lost and in exile. Yet in their grieving they knew that it was impossible to go back to the way things had been.

The strains that accompanied the tumult tested a sister's commitment to stay the course, and some found their resolve sorely wanting. In contrast to sisters who felt their calling so strongly that they could make concessions, the ambivalent ones found little reason to compromise. Many had come to religious orders during the flood of candidates during the 1950s and 1960s when momentum in American Catholicism made joining a popular thing to do. Until the post-Council crunch, it had been relatively easy for these sisters to blend in. Now, in renewal, the comfort zone had largely disappeared. Everything was new, sorely testing a sister's dedication and resolve. Though some of the most resourceful sisters decided to go, others who were ill suited to religious life in the first place hung on. Superiors knew them well: nuns impaired by emotional deficiencies that had rendered them dependent personalities who, for one reason or another, sought the apparent security and surrogate family represented by the convent. They had entered for the wrong reasons, unable to make a mature choice, and relied with quiet desperation on the goodness of the convent. Some of these sisters were pushed out by the insecurity of renewal, but those who stayed, never embracing or even comprehending the shifts, often retarded progress through passive resistance, all while requiring a great deal of care. One superior had a rule of thumb: "We can only really protect, care for, and love ten sisters who are chronic emotional problems," she said. "They are like the weak people in a family." Although nuns don't normally use such language, these hangers-on were deadwood.

Sudden strikes from Rome could plunge a community into a downward spiral. Such was the case at the Mt. St. Angel Benedictine monastery in the rich farmland of Oregon's Willamette Valley, whose cerebral prioress, Mother Gemma Piennett, had run afoul of Church bigwigs by protesting the Vatican's attempt to cripple the Sister Formation movement. Mother Piennett, who held a doctorate and two master's degrees, had first been elected prioress in 1955. She presided forcefully over a domain that included a four-year college, a nursing home, and a center for migrant workers. Some sisters believed that her passion for education and special projects caused her to neglect some other aspects of community life, but she was reelected and widely admired. Then in 1966, barely three years after her sole defense of Sister Formation at the National Catholic Educational Association meeting in Cincinnati, she received notice that Rome was deputizing a Benedictine priest to investigate the monastery. After a perfunctory examination, he bluntly deposed Mother Piennett and her leadership council. They asked why. The priest said no reason would be given. "Not even criminals are treated this way," responded a sister who had served as president of the college. "This," the priest replied curtly, "was not a court proceeding." Archbishop Edward D. Howard descended from Portland to announce the coup to the assembled Benedictine sisters.

Shock, anger, disillusionment followed. Some sisters left the community; others were troubled but remained Benedictines and distanced themselves from the monastery by taking jobs elsewhere. One sister, for example, vacated her post as a history professor at the community's college and joined the faculty of a state university. There was no act of protest against Church authorities, however, no movement to rebuff Rome's intrusion. The assumption was that Rome's Sacred Congregation of Religious had exercised its rightful function. Without interference, the sisters might have voted Mother Piennett out at the congregation's next election, but that election had been denied them, and they accepted the ruling without complaint. The anger was internalized. Dismayed sisters chose to bolt the hall in silent protest rather than stand with Mother Piennett in her last-ditch support for Sister Formation. Psychologically, the passivity represented a turning inward, sapping the energies and strength of the community.

From the conservative side, nuns who believed that renewal had raced out of control—going way beyond acceptable limits—blamed the blockbuster 1967 Sister Survey for spurring the exodus. Nothing like it had ever been attempted. Its aim was nothing less than enlisting every sister in the nation to fill out a marathon questionnaire containing a whopping 645 items (at a steady, quick rate of ten per minute, it was more than an hour's work). Surveyors wanted to know what sisters believed, how they felt about renewal, what they read, their views on race and non-Catholics, living arrangements, the vows, their leaders, practically everything except what they ate for breakfast. Heading the project was a brilliant Sister of Notre Dame de Namur, Sister Marie Augusta Neal, one of the first women to earn a Ph.D. from Harvard University and a professor of sociology at her order's college, Emmanuel, in Boston. Sister Neal's doctoral dissertation had examined how well Boston's priests were prepared for the Catholic Church envisioned by Vatican II. Her goal in the Sister Survey was a variation on that theme, but with two critical differences. First, renewal had advanced much further by the time the Sister Survey was under way. She sought to know how sisters were responding to where Vatican II had already taken them. Second, the Vatican Council had posed general directives for nuns (Perfectae Caritatis); no such direction for updating had been handed to priests. Much more was expected of the sisters, and the Sister Survey set out to read their reactions in the early stages of implementation. Only someone with Sister Neal's outstanding reputation as a scholar could have created and implemented a project of the size and scope of the Sister Survey. Financing would be based on a charge of $1 for every sister taking the survey.

In this case, the nun's training in compliance worked in favor of the survey takers. The results were astonishing then and remain so. Every sister was sent a thick questionnaire: 139,691 were returned, an astounding 88 percent rate of participation. Looking back to that labor-intensive task more than thirty years later (every form required key-punch recording on a new IBM processing device), Sister Neal said the survey provided sisters with an invaluable resource for shaping renewal. As she spoke, she sat in a robin's egg blue rocking chair, wearing a flower print dress and occasionally gazing out the window of her home, a second-story apartment of a wood-frame building typical of the working-class neighborhood of Boston where she had grown up.

The hardest lesson for Rome to learn back then, she said, was that sisters finally needed to hear the authority of their own voices, singly and collectively, as part of heeding the Holy Spirit's counsel in directing them in renewal. The survey allowed sisters to hear one another and to pay attention to how the Holy Spirit might be speaking through that means. "Surveys were a new way of doing obedience," she said. "It is part of a new exchange. Carrying out this mandate requires a different understanding from the one you've had. By carrying out this mandate, you change the whole structure of the [hierarchical] Church."

The Sister Survey projected a striking message on a broad, public canvas, becoming the kind of billboard from sisters that Sister Neal had hoped for. Its findings contributed to virtually every major discussion of how sisterhoods should chart their course, including most of the pivotal chapter sessions on renewal that rewrote the book on community life. A large majority of sisters, according to the survey, favored the collaborative process by which their communities were being transformed and enthusiastically embraced their community's goals. Basic concepts concerning how they lived, what kind of work they did, the circumstances in which they prayed, even the meaning of the vows, had already undergone widespread redefinitions. Large numbers of sisters had already absorbed—perhaps even anticipated—the salient tenets of Vatican II, including the universal call to holiness that essentially did away with the differences in status (especially the appeals to sisterly perfection) between themselves and other Catholics. From the survey, it is clear that two-thirds of the sisters believed that their communities should be governed much more democratically. Automatic deference to the chain of command was a thing of the past. In particular, the luster of the superior's alleged special authority—to dispense God's will to the sisters by her "grace of office"—had largely vanished. The very term "superior" had already been dropped in many orders and others would follow suit. The most ardent advocates of change were community leaders, sisters in charge of training younger members.

Questions about the vows also revealed evolving views about poverty, chastity, and obedience—rules *against* certain behaviors were being replaced by actions in support of positive goals. Poverty had meant not spending a penny without permission from the superior; increasingly, sisters interpreted it as choosing for themselves a manner of simple living. Nearly three out of five agreed that the vow of poverty meant daring "to live precariously, setting out like Abraham who did not know where he was going." Chastity had meant simply *no sex;* the trend was to view that vow as seeking loving, caring, and nonexploitative relationships (without sex). Asked whether the "traditional way of presenting chastity allowed the development of isolation and false mysticism," two-thirds (63 percent) agreed. Obedience had formerly meant doing what one was told, whereas in the renewal climate it meant finding the will of the collective spirit. Barely 10 percent of respondents believed they owed their superior absolute obedience. More than three-quarters (78 percent) agreed that the traditional teaching on obedience stifled a sister's personal responsibility, and two-thirds (64 percent) called for a drastic overhaul of the community's decision-making processes. Seven out of ten sisters said that their habits were being modified or made optional. Barely one in ten wanted to retain the traditional habit. Despite the upheaval in the convent, 75 percent said they hadn't considered leaving during the previous two years.

All in all, the survey was a consciousness raiser, signaling that renewal was operating under a full head of steam. The results sketched a profile of a largely progressive network of U.S. sisters that had transcended the old barriers among orders. From this benchmark research tool, the evidence seemed indisputable: nuns in this country not only had accepted the mandate of Vatican II but had grabbed hold of it and run with it. Energies for reform that had been gathering since the pioneering Sister Formation Conference in the 1950s had clearly found a creative outlet, primed by a document prepared by, of all people, a world assembly of bishops, few of whom had any such eventuality in mind.

But the rejoicing over the survey's results was limited mostly to progressives, who numbered perhaps from a third to half of nuns. Many conservatives had a different slant on what the Sister Survey had done. A few had totally refused to cooperate with it on grounds that sisters' attitudes and opinions should have no bearing on policies shaping religious life. Truth was truth, they argued, regardless of how sisters might or might not feel about it. The broader version of that argument was promulgated by some bishops who insisted that the Church was decidedly not a democracy but a hierarchical conduit for living the truth as revealed by the Holy Spirit. Surveys were ground-level, egalitarian constructs that had a vaguely Protestant character whereby the Holy Spirit was believed to emerge from the pew. Although the guiding metaphor of Vatican II—the Church as the people of God—carried a similar connotation, it was still, in fact, outweighed by dogma that placed the "sacred deposit of faith" in the hands of the pope. Traditionalists, then, were wont to regard surveys as a ploy to substitute a sound scientific lesser authority for a far greater one. So they would have no part in it.

A far more trenchant objection from the conservative side was that the survey instrument itself had been used as a means of dividing sisters and pressuring them to accept a more progressive stance than they had held before completing it. By asking nuns how they viewed each significant aspect of their lives, the critics said, the survey exposed nuns to new ways of thinking that almost invariably seemed more "acceptable" than the traditional views that had surrounded them. According to this analysis, the survey swayed sisters to oppose their own time-tested traditions. Some contended, for example, that the many survey questions that asked sisters to choose between teachings before and after Vatican II were, by definition, biased against the "old" in favor of the "new." In any event, the results showed widespread rejection of the old. Given the growing trend toward ending daily prayer schedules for the entire community, for example, conservatives argued that the survey's underlying support for this change increased the sisters' willingness to go along with the change. The same applied to such issues as whether sisters should be required to live together (the trend was away from it) and the trend toward permitting sisters to choose the kind of work they did. Subliminally, the critics argued, sisters knew that the survey was steering them toward the "good" side—the progressive, aggressive renewal side. Many conservatives became convinced, therefore, that the Sister Survey went beyond merely tracking the course of religious renewal and became, instead, a factor in its direction and pace. That influence, in the critics' view, in turn hastened the departure of disillusioned members. Moreover, they contended that the survey process deepened the divisions over renewal in many communities by harshly exposing sisters to a picture of conflict in clear percentages, something they could read in black and white, thereby heightening dissatisfaction. Some sisters wavering on the threshold of the convent saw themselves on the "losing" side and left. Certain others, disappointed by what they considered to be too much opposition to renewal, left.

The resistance to change by convent conservatives reflected—and often voiced—the defiance of priests and bishops, perhaps a solid majority of them. Fear, even panic, had gripped the clergy at the prospect of creating a more fluid model of the religious community that would result in sisters' making choices that would destabilize convent routines and weaken Church institutions by reducing the numbers of members who elected to work in them. Lillanna Kopp, an accomplished sociologist, saw dire effects from what she considered the clergy's anti-renewal bullying. Kopp had entered the Sisters of the Holy Name of Jesus and Mary in 1940; thirty years later she left to form the independent sisterhood, Sisters for a Christian Community. "The story of the travail of the renewal of religious life would be an inauthentic, whitewashed account," she wrote in *Midwives of the Future,* "were it not recorded for historical purposes that much renewal enthusiasm and expertise was silenced and censored. Hundreds of sisters threatening to the status quo were invited to 'put up, shut up, or get out.' "

Criticisms notwithstanding, the Sister Survey itself became a factor in the larger debate over renewal. Some critics continued to brand the survey as a biased tool designed to advance progressivism. Others maintained the suspicion that the results were aimed at exploiting the liberal-conservative rift. "When people said that the survey had caused this or that to happen," Sister Kopp recalled that "it prevented them off from doing anything about it. They would simply withdraw. Many congregations split. Some asked me to come and talk. Those who resisted the survey also resisted the Vatican Council's document on renewal."

But the sharp complaints about the survey were far outnumbered by praise for its method and results. Nuns had never held this kind of a mirror up to themselves. Following the dictates of Vatican II, they were supposed to review their mission both in terms of the intentions of their founders and in light of the Gospels. The survey was one measure—a dramatic one—of how they understood the underpinnings of the life they had committed themselves to. From that point forward, they would possess a yardstick by which to assess how they felt communally about the most significant aspect of their vocations. They would have the data to blunt attacks from those who made purely personal or self-interested claims about religious life without facts to back up their opinions. Inevitably, in helping find solutions to the inner conflicts that had beset religious life, the survey would also become part of the problem, making the quarrels among the sisters stand out starkly and vividly. Those at both extremes of the pro- and anti-renewal groups walked away.

The departure of beloved sisters—fellow workers, fellow sufferers, fellow worshipers, housemates—was often shattering to the stability of those still holding the fort. Self-doubt seized many sisters who had been supremely secure about their vocations. Anger flooded those who had lost good friends and had little hope of ever seeing them again. The soul-searching that resulted was the most wrenching and decisive that many nuns had ever undergone. Often the question boiled down to finding a reason to stay when an admired friend had just left. To some it seemed that the brightest and most mature members were more likely to go. Was there something wrong with being among those who stayed? But many sisters found reassuring answers. A Daughter of Charity recalled her moment of truth. "I was soaking in the tub one day," she said. "I thought, 'Everyone is leaving; why am I staying?' It's then I realized that I know I have a vocation and can't pretend I don't."

Sister Margaret Brennan, a leading intellectual and personal influence on her community, the Immaculate Heart of Mary of Monroe, Michigan, and on the national and international spheres of religious life, personally interviewed two hundred women who were exiting from Monroe during her tenure as superior. "Listening to them challenged me personally," she said. "What was the meaning of God's will for *my* life? I received grace to be faithful to that. It was my biggest challenge. Leaving, as it turned out, had not been an option, but you could lose your vocation by not being faithful. Of those leaving, however, I wouldn't say they were unfaithful or didn't have a vocation in the first place. They were struggling. Many wanted to leave; others simply came to it, wanted to do good for others and began to see the Church as the people of God, another way of serving God." On the other hand, a Sister of St. Joseph saw many nuns in her community panicking as the trumpets sounded the prospect of changes at the close of Vatican II. "They thought that religious life would never last," she said quietly, "and they wanted to get out before it collapsed." Another sister, a Benedictine, said succinctly, "When someone left I'd say, 'Why am I here?' It was appropriate to reevaluate. Everyone went through that because it seemed that everyone was leaving."

Sisters across a broad spectrum of orders now faced a bald choice. The unthinkable had become the thinkable. What had been a remote option became a real possibility, as sanctions against leaving weakened and the sheer volume of defectors created momentum. Many, like Sister Brennan, found their personal commitment to the vows sorely tested by the rapid exodus and emerged from the trial with new certainty, clarity, and resolve. They were also exposed to their feelings and attitudes toward those who left. The ability to act with charity toward those who had decided to leave was often a function of grasping the meaning of the Vatican Council's declaration that all Catholics were equally called to holiness. The struggle was to shift one's perspective from judging those who had abandoned the "higher" calling to accepting those who chose to follow a vocation of equal value in other parts of the lay world. It was an adjustment that sometimes took years, even decades, to resolve. A sister of St. Francis reminisced one day in the spring of 1997 in an old stone convent in the Midwest about the fact that "it was sometimes still painful to me. I'm not sure some should have left. Some never married. They taught. They say some prayers. But now they're elderly and they're alone." She paused. "I may disagree with every sister around my table at dinner," she said, "but I'd trust my life to anyone at that table."

A joke that made the rounds of the convents at the time points up the pervasive streak of ambivalence. On the campus of a Catholic women's college, a nun meets a Jesuit. She complains that the Vatican II changes bother

her. "Too many, too fast," she says. "That's okay," he says. "It shows you had deep training in the traditions." He then sees her a few days later and asks how she's doing with her problem. "Not well," she answers. "I find that I'm judging those who are leaving and that shows my training isn't very deep."

Sometimes the mending took a long time. Sister Carita Prendagast was ninety-five years old at the time she was interviewed in 1999 at the Sisters of Charity center in Convent Station, New Jersey. She was an elegant, prim, white-haired portrait of enduring vitality, the kind that the religious life can afford, adorned in a trim blue suit, white blouse, and a silk scarf of white, orange, and green. She peered out from behind silver-rimmed glasses with an alert, curious look tinged with sadness. Soon after entering religious life in 1933, she became one of the first sisters to serve in China, learning Chinese from Protestant missionaries whom she still referred to as "the Prots." During the invasion of Japan, she had run an orphanage. She still bore the painful memory of the day she turned a baby away because the home was already filled beyond capacity and food was scarce. The next day, the baby was found dead in the stream across from the orphanage, apparently drowned by the desperate mother. Awash in her own tears, she vowed never to let that happen again. After returning to the United States, she took various leadership positions, serving as an effective and much beloved superior during the topsy-turvy 1960s. Of the exodus, she said she now believes "it was the work of the Holy Spirit." But when the sisters started leaving she said she had felt "it was my fault—perhaps I had stressed education above piety. I felt that I had failed."

The guilt lingered for many years. The turning point was the Sisters of Charity's reunion twenty years after the Council, when former sisters returned to Convent Station for festivities on the spread of lawn behind the juniorate. It was a grand time, nuns mingling with former nuns who brought their husbands and children. "I saw these beautiful children of former priests and nuns who had been called 'spoiled' by those who criticized them for leaving," said Sister Prendagast deliberately. "I suddenly realized that those beautiful boys and girls wouldn't have had a life if their parents had stayed. I realized that their leaving hadn't hurt the Holy Roman Catholic Church in any way."

Chapter Eight

Seeking Justice

Never was the play of forces between religion and society more dramatic than during the frenzied decades of the 1960s and 1970s. Call it convergence or the ripening of historical consciousness or simply a series of moments whose time had come; the revolts in cultural values and behavior reshaped both society and religion, at the same time increasing the interaction between the two spheres. This seismic stirring helped propel onto the world stage two dazzling figures, President John F. Kennedy and Pope John XXIII, both progressives in the popular mind. Different circumstances had driven them, of course. A changing post–World War II political climate helped JFK gain the White House, whereas the reluctance of the College of Cardinals to push ahead with modernization led them, mistakenly it turned out, to elect Pope John XXIII, an old man who was widely assumed to have no ideas but who would competently mind the store as an interim pope. By 1960, the two leaders stood side by side as symbols of a hope that embraced both. They were outsized figures who reached toward the future without being lashed to the past. Within those separate domains of church and state arose calls for justice that differed somewhat in focus and emphasis but were, in the end, mutually reinforcing.

For the Roman Catholic Church, the fathers of the Second Vatican Council had made justice a central theme of the Pastoral Constitution on the

Church in the Modern World as part of opening the old medieval institution to the modern world. Since nuns had always been among the most responsive to initiatives at the highest levels of Church governance, many of them were among the first to respond to the Council's appeal to serve the poor and the oppressed.

Until Vatican II, sisters had followed the long tradition of keeping largely to themselves, maintaining an insular way of life minutely regulated by rules. It was a world deliberately withdrawn from the flow of society, circumscribed by convent routines, demanding duties in Catholic schools or hospitals, and daily routines of communal prayer. The outside world was discouraged from impinging on this self-contained structure. The first significant crack in the wall opened when the Sister Formation movement, as a consequence of its campaign to provide sisters with higher education, inevitably exposed them in limited fashion to the wider society. That crack had contributed to minor changes in clothing and routines. The Council constitution directing the sister communities to renew themselves (Perfectae Caritatis) gave them a mandate to begin a wholesale review of their communities that triggered an instability that led to thousands of defections.

Together with those internal strains came the mandate that called upon sisters—indeed all Catholics—to take up the cause of justice and human need. The Council document the Pastoral Constitution of the Church in the Modern World (Gaudium et Spes) proclaimed that the Church must get its collective hands dirty by fighting against anything that abuses or devalues human beings. This turn outward toward the cause of human dignity was defined as essential work of preaching the Gospel. To an institution that had been closed in on itself for the previous hundred years, this call, contained in the longest document issued by the Council, gave the Church institutions spectacular new marching orders.

Sisters, of course, were paying close attention. Justice was now on the official agenda. The Council document echoed papal letters by Pope John XXIII, most notably Pacem in Terris (Peace in the World, 1963) and Mater et Magistra (Christianity and Social Progress, 1961), and preceded Pope Paul VI's encyclical Populorum Progressio (On the Development of Peoples) that built on those themes. By 1971, the world Synod of Bishops had put the matter at the top of its concerns, releasing a major appeal, "Justice in the

World," and Paul VI reinforced that stance in Octagesima Adveniens ("The Eightieth Year," marking the anniversary of the first papal letter on social issues, Rerum Novarum, by Pope Leo XIII in 1891) in which he referred to the "new social questions" of justice to which the Church must address itself, such as mass poverty and nuclear war. In addition to underscoring this theme, the Synod of Bishops inserted a key phrase in its document that was to become the I-beam of the social justice cause. Taking up the banner of justice was not just an optional, extracurricular activity for Catholics, the bishops said, but a "constitutive element of the Gospel," at the very heart of it. Promoting justice was what it meant "carry out" the Gospel and couldn't be left out or skipped over. Pope Paul VI reinforced his earlier pastoral letter with a special exhortation to nuns in 1971. "How then," asked the pope, "will the cry of the poor find an echo in your lives?"

One other signal that caught the attention of many sisters was the appeal from a 1968 meeting of Latin American bishops in Medellín, Colombia. In a region of the world where Church hierarchy so often sided with the rich and the powerful, the leadership of the bishops did a striking about-face, boldly calling on Catholics to join them in making cause with the suffering masses. The phrase that stuck was the bishops' plea to the Church to show "a preferential option for the poor." The formal, legalistic-sounding phrase signified the bishops' simpler conviction that Jesus favored ministering to the poor and found God's presence among them in a special way. To those sisters who had worked in Latin America—or would do so shortly—the phrase was a dramatic rallying cry. To many others it defined a standard by which to measure their work as individuals and as communities of sisters. Once the curtain on injustice had risen, sisters increasingly saw themselves as part of the problem, not just as ministers to the inequalities "out there."

Not surprisingly, perhaps, the universal Church's plea to work for human rights coincided with the drive to free the convent from piles of legal strictures. Layers of rules and regulations were being discarded in the name of Vatican II, allowing sisters choices they scarcely could have imagined a decade before. Renewal was synonymous with greater democracy in deciding purpose and policy. Increasingly, the selection of professional identity, manner of dress, and living arrangements, even apart from the convent, were matters left to the individual nun. Though this spectacle of breaking out of a tightly controlled existence caused acute anxiety and fear among many nuns, others reacted with relief, even exuberance. Those who felt liberated from a procrustean bed of sorts often saw the urgings by the Council, popes, and bishops to seek justice and freedom as a natural extension of what they had learned from their own experience. A distinct psychology of liberation, that is, was found to apply to conditions both inside the convent and beyond. The correlation was a natural one, although it was not always subjected to conceptual analysis. The affinities were expressed more in action than in words. Where sisters embraced freedom inside their communities, they were likely to bring that fervor to the downtrodden. The ground might not have been familiar as they went forth; the underlying theme was.

While communities were turning their attention to how to do social justice ministry in addition to all the other demands being made of them in this period of flux (the Sister Survey of 1980 found that 49 percent of the communities had made social justice the chief item of a general chapter meeting), American society was convulsed by efforts to end racial segregation and the Vietnam War. For a growing number of sisters, both causes became arenas for pursuing social justice. This rush to activism demonstrated how much the ground had shifted in terms of what it meant to seek justice. In the nineteenth-century Church, the leadership had finally supported the right of workers to form unions for the benefit of millions of Catholic laborers—but only after many years of heated debate among the bishops. Along the way, the American Catholic Church had likewise defended Catholic immigrants against discrimination. But the poor and nonwhite elements of society at large had never come under such broad consideration and protection, especially if supporting their cause involved fighting the established order. That is, serving the poor rarely became a fight for their rights. By the 1950s, for example, Mother Katherine Drexel, the Philadelphia aristocrat-turned-nun who was declared a saint by Pope John Paul II, had distinguished herself by building schools for African-Americans and Native Americans across the country. Her benevolence and spirituality became legendary. At the same time, however, she refrained from protesting the systematic segregation and coercive bias that touched the people whose children attended her schools, crippling the lives of the minority groups she served so lovingly. African-American women who sought admission to Mother Drexel's own community before World War II were referred to an all-black order in Baltimore. At the dawn of the civil rights movement in America, black women did become welcome and have exercised key leadership in the community. Whether Mother Drexel is seen simply as a product of those segregationist times who tried her best to challenge those strictures or as someone who failed to grasp an element of Gospel justice, the fact is that she was viewed as a pioneer in her own time.

By the late 1960s, the definition of what it meant to do justice in scores of communities involved challenging the status quo and risking confrontation with the authorities. A few sisters had plunged into action earlier in the decade. In 1963 scores marched at Selma, Alabama, with Martin Luther King Jr. and in the huge civil rights march on the Washington Mall. Certain communities such as the Lorettos were far ahead of the religious pack in latching on to these causes. Sister Mary Luke Tobin, the esteemed head of the Sisters of Lorettos and one of the few nuns to attend Vatican II, had been drawn to social justice by a document written in the late 1890s by Pope Leo XIII. Called Rerum Novarum (Rights and Duties of Capital and Labor), it was the first encyclical in Church history devoted largely to human rights. Sister Tobin found it compelling. When a sister called Sister Tobin in 1968 to ask if she should go to Selma to march with Dr. King, Sister Tobin's calm answer was "Of course." Others likewise hardly needed to ask permission of their superiors. On the other front, a smattering of nuns also appeared at early anti–Vietnam War rallies.

The social justice theme wove its way into the process of freeing up life within the community. The normal setting for this drama was the momentous chapter meetings on renewal. By late 1967–68, these sessions, sometimes long and acrimonious, were fully under way. The chapter became the setting where change became written down in constitutions, where each community had to define the renewal in the most concrete terms, such as how meals were to be conducted and vacations awarded in a climate freed from endless "permissions." At the same time, many communities such as the Lorettos and the Dominicans seized the moment to dedicate themselves boldly to wiping out poverty and discrimination of all kinds.

Such pledges, drawing heavily on the relevant Vatican and papal documents, were embedded in the community's constitution. The passion and energy for this social justice initiative most notably flowed from sisters who had tasted their own kind of freedom sweetly and wished, implicitly at least, and under circumstances of a very different kind in the world, to pass it on. Some sisters also saw a different kind of incentive at work. Their concern for promoting human dignity, they noted, came at a time when some sisters felt uneasiness as a result of losing the privileges and special status they had held before Vatican II and feeling uncertain about how they would be treated during the transition to something new. Status seemed suddenly a good deal more fragile and maintaining one's dignity amid such uncertainties made the concept of human dignity very real. Accordingly, renewal had left them vulnerable, hence more sensitive to the plight of others.

The Council had, with a certain naivete perhaps, told sisters to rummage through their past to rediscover the who and why of their founding. That meant, in some cases surprisingly enough, rediscovering the true identity of the founder. To the shock of some, certain founders had, in effect, been deleted from Church records. In such cases, the community's history had been falsified to show that a priest or bishop had started the community instead of listing the woman who actually deserved the credit. This was done because of the genuine founder's unwillingness to obey Church authority without question. Because of this balking, she had been deemed an unworthy example for the community by her clerical superiors. Such were the circumstances, for example, surrounding Theresa Maxis, who started an Immaculate Heart of Mary convent in Monroe, Michigan. Her heritage was largely African-American. After surviving the natural rigors of the early days, she ran into friction with authorities over the future of the community and was driven from her post. She lived in exile from her community thereafter. She was no longer acknowledged as the community's founder and was effectively banished from memory until a post–Vatican II review revived her. The innocent-sounding request to explore the original intentions of the founder could produce startling results.

That was shockingly true for the Sisters of St. Joseph of Peace, which expanded from its original base in Jersey City, New Jersey. Before Vatican II, the name of Margaret Anna Cusack was virtually unknown among the sisters at St. Joseph. Since her founding of the community in the late nineteenth century, her name and the character her prodigious works had lent to the order had been lost. Following the Vatican II mandate, one of the sisters, Dorothy Vidulich, an accomplished writer and social activist, brought Mother Cusack to light again by digging through layers of official Church forgetfulness. Mother Cusack, it turned out, had been a brilliant author and a thorn in the side of certain bishops and clerics. Most significantly, when the truth came out she became a model of unjust treatment by male clerics. Born in Ireland, the daughter of a doctor, she had joined the Poor Clares before getting the call to begin her own community based in social justice. She eventually moved to Jersey City, where she lived with her community and tried unsuccessfully to gain a foothold in New York City. The archbishop of New York, Michael Corrigan, rebuffed her efforts to minister in the city.

A prolific author, an advocate of women's rights, and an ardent foe of the forces that maintain poverty, she deeply impressed a wide variety of Catholics. In her 1874 book, *Women's Work,* she had written: "Give women their rights, then, for those rights are justice—just to men as well as women, for the interests of men and women cannot be separated. Let women have the possession, and the control, of their own property; it is a necessary right for the rich as well as the poor."

Regarding the desperate plight of the poor in Ireland, she wrote, in a passage that has a contemporary application: "It has always been to me perfectly incomprehensible why Irish landlords, whether Roman Catholic or Protestant, and the English government, whether liberal or conservative, could not see that if one-half of the money spent on coercion, special commissions, and famine funds, were expended in opening up industrial resources for the people, which would enable them to earn the money to pay their rents, there would be some ground to hope for the peaceful conclusion of the Irish question."

Her boldness, intelligence, and independence as a woman placed her at odds with the autocratic Archbishop Corrigan and other hierarchs. The bishops saw her outspoken advocacy of rights for women and the poor as proof that she was a dangerous reformer and a socialist. As a result, she was banished to the fringes of Catholicism. She eventually left the Catholic Church to become an Anglican, the religious tradition in which she had been raised. During her exile as a virtual nonperson in Catholic history, such was the antipathy toward her that the Sisters of St. Joseph of Peace were forbidden to assign the name "Clare" to any of their sisters. "She was indeed the skeleton in our congregational closet," Sister Vidulich has written, "and the church of Rome had succeeded by a direct command to have both her name and her memory effaced from our history." Mother Cusack remained out of mind until Sister Vidulich found her. Once restored, Mother Cusack became not only the subject of her community's respect but a source of inspiration and conviction for many others.

Mother Cusack's restoration to her proper place in her community's history should be accompanied by a note of caution: while Church authorities may applaud good works done in the name of the Church to benefit society's unfortunates, they would likely fight feminist measures aimed at raising women's status *within* the Church. Mother Cusack pleased her superiors only so long as she stayed within the strictures defined by the hierarchy. When she went beyond those boundaries, she became uppity. She exposed a deep-seated split that would reemerge painfully a century later among sisters all over the United States.

With her resuscitated model before them once again, the Sisters of St. Joseph embarked on a thorough reshaping of their ministry that was quite simply centered on social justice. At their meetings devoted to putting Vatican II into effect, they quickly tackled the problem of racism and how to address it. By 1974, they had made peace a special priority. "It was overwhelming," Sister Vidulich recalled, "considering that we'd never done anything like that before." Sisters marched for racial justice and civil rights in Selma and Washington, D.C.; they marched for peace, demonstrating against the Vietnam War (Sister Vidulich remembers holding a placard that read HONK IF YOU WANT JUSTICE during a demonstration on the George Washington Bridge); they established peace and justice centers. Following Mother Cusack's legacy, they also, more quietly, nurtured feminism. One young woman had deliberately taken her vows without a Mass in protest against the exclusion of women from the priesthood. Another said she organized small group prayer services to avoid ever taking part in a liturgy in which only males can preside. But these moves have been made rather covertly, without fanfare, in an effort to sustain feminism while steering clear of confrontation with Church authorities.

The pattern at St. Joseph was repeated in many of the most vigorous communities. Sometimes the disconnect between the community and the founder's legacy seemed clearly a deliberate attempt to hide truths that embarrassed or offended Church authorities. In other instances, it seemed to be more a matter of carelessness or benign neglect. In the case of the Sisters of St. Joseph, as the real story was unearthed, some sisters felt shocked and angry at being robbed of their own heritage. As such stories circulated, distrust between nuns and Church leaders intensified. Social justice was officially considered an acceptable goal outside the Church but it was seen as one that was generally unacceptable inside the Church. Key bishops and theologians argued that God had created the Church as a hierarchy of authority, whereas the world was run by political arrangements on a human level. According to this thinking, the Church worked in a top-down fashion, God revealing sacred truths through the pope and the "teaching authority" of the bishops downward to the people. It wasn't for ordinary Catholics to bring their own standards of social justice to these truths, which included a ban on women priests and rejection of artificial birth control. Those things, the Church authorities had decided, were beyond categories of social justice; they were what they were because God said so.

By the early 1970s the most powerful Catholic voices—popes, Synods of Bishops, the Latin American hierarchy—had called for Catholics to make social justice in the *world* a mission priority. For many sisters, that emphasis had already been built into the recasting of their community constitutions. The enthusiastic support for this ministry from the top leaders of the Church was widely welcomed: it added both support and legitimacy to those working on the front lines of struggle. Knowing that Pope Paul VI was in the trenches with the activists, theologically at least, provided spiritual uplift and a needed morale boost. A few high-profile members of the hierarchy took on the social justice cause in the very thick of the strife, as in the case of Dom Helder Camara, bishop of Recife, Brazil.

The voices of the sympathizers and the rationale of the Vatican II documents, important as they were, could never substitute, of course, for the dedication and grit of nuns themselves. Opposition to racism, war, economic exploitation, poverty, and related issues grew among sisters across communities. In an age of coalitions by Americans fighting a variety of causes, nuns organized their own.

The year 1971 was pivotal, due in large part to the loud calls for action by Paul VI and the Synod of Bishops in Rome.

The Leadership Conference of Women Religious (LCWR), the broad umbrella group representing about 90 percent of American sisters, revised its bylaws that year to reflect social justice as a priority. The action came during its annual assembly, whose theme was, significantly, "The Church Is for the World." The commitment was echoed in a wide variety of conference programs, workshops, seminars, and leadership initiatives. The annual assembly was the takeoff point for a bold, accelerated effort that altered the character of the LCWR. Many conservative orders bolted, forming their own, competing association called, after the Vatican II document for religious, Consortium Perfectae Caritatis. Among the new group's chief criticisms of the larger conference was that spiritual concerns were being sacrificed for political goals.

Late that year, a group of forty-seven nuns met in Washington to launch an activist center eventually named NETWORK. Its purpose would be to press the U.S. Congress on behalf of sisters' concerns for social justice. Under the guidance of Sister Carol Coston, a bright, resourceful Adrian Dominican, the project quickly planted roots in the Washington scene and, as the first licensed Catholic lobbying agency in the United States, established a reputation for commitment and integrity.

Ten years after its founding, NETWORK was confident in its direction. Sister Nancy Sylvester, the Immaculate Heart of Mary sister who succeeded Sister Coston as director in 1982, looked back at that first decade in an article celebrating the agency on its tenth anniversary. NETWORK, Sister Sylvester wrote, had in its first decade "named its value criteria as seeking justice, peace, empowerment of the poor, systematic change, participation in the decisions that affect one's life, mutuality in relationships (i.e., nonhierarchical forms of relating), stewardship of global resources and the environment, integration of human needs and human rights (i.e., a holistic view), interdependence of people and a preferred social vision (i.e., seeking creative alternatives)."

LCWR and NETWORK were largely free to set their own courses, but they were officially linked to the Church, which meant that, in a broader sense, they were structurally accountable to the hierarchy, ultimately Rome.

They both passed a vital litmus test by being listed in the annual Kenedy Directory (aka *The Official Catholic Directory*) of the U.S. Church. Bearing this seal of approval was obviously both an advantage and a burden.

Dozens of other social justice efforts, however, took place out of the national spotlight, beyond the scrutiny of Church authorities. This lack of sanction didn't make them illicit or unworthy of approval, only less visible. Sisters marched for housing, sat on antipoverty boards, tutored children, sheltered battered women, petitioned governors, protested job discrimination, decried the criminal justice system, became thorns in the sides of people in power and friends to the powerless. Many communities either sponsored such efforts or supported sisters who did. Some chose single issues; others pursued many. Some of their activities lasted years; others a much shorter time.

The two official organizations—NETWORK and LCWR—and most of the smaller ones stuck closely to an agenda that sought social justice in the world. That was the most pragmatic course. Raising social justice questions about the Church itself could risk the enterprise. NETWORK, most notably, steered its mission self-consciously away from Church issues as a means of safeguarding its work, according to Sister Sylvester.

Another highly motivated group, however, broke the mold. The National Association of Women Religious (NAWR), a bolder, on-the-fringe alternative, got off and running on the social justice front even before the LCWR or NETWORK did. The sister most responsible was Marjorie Tuitte, a daunting Dominican nun who crusaded for social justice both inside and outside of the Church. Among her admirers, she ranks at the top of American Catholic exemplars of social justice. Her detractors saw her as blunt, even shocking, in the tactics she chose to win attention for her causes. She was formidable (larger than life in the experience of many of those who say their lives were turned around by her), smart and effective, a tireless firebrand and a superb indoctrinator. Trained in the methods of Saul Alinsky, the controversial strategist of social change through confrontation, she imparted often sharp-tongued lessons to sisters across the country, urging upon them the distinction between working for charity, which essentially kept the system in place, and working for justice, which meant changing the status quo. Her basic point was Alinsky's conclusion that crises usually boil down to the way in which power is exercised. Traditionally, power has flowed from top to bottom—from king to vassals, emperor to serfs, bishops to flock—in hierarchical, pyramidal fashion. The goal was to transform this top-down domination, substituting a circle of collaboration by equals. Sister Tuitte imparted these principles in withering fashion, a style that made her both irresistible and intimidating. She was instrumental in the founding of NETWORK, but NAWR gave her the freedom to employ her prodigious talents outside the confines, strictly speaking, of Church approval. Whereas LCWR and NETWORK were linked to the Church hierarchy by virtue of their inclusion in *The Official Catholic Directory,* NAWR was subject to no formal pressures or sanctions, nor was it, of course, in any way protected or privileged. It set its own course and defined its own character to avoid being coopted by the bishops. Individual nuns who belonged to the group might be subject to Church authority but NAWR itself was not, much like the small number of communities that were established, such as the Los Angeles IHMs, without official or "canonical" status. The same was true for two other like-minded groups, the National Coalition of American Nuns and the National Black Sisters Conference, which spoke out and took action largely as they saw fit.

This outburst of activism was inextricably bound to shifting views of the vows of poverty, chastity, and obedience. More broadly, the search for what the vows meant in a contemporary setting had become a central focus of renewal itself. The vows had so often in the past seemed straightforward, yet with promptings of Vatican II they were now far from self-evident to many sisters. They had been packaged largely in the logic of classical philosophy, abstract and world rejecting, static and self-denying, sealing a commitment that made the nun's vocation heroic in the eyes of many Catholics. Sister Patricia Wittberg, S.C., a sociologist at the Indiana University at Indianapolis, has noted that the vows had survived virtually unchallenged by major developments in Western thinking until the second half of the twentieth century. For example, she said, the concept of chastity had bypassed Freud; an understanding of obedience hadn't taken the revolution of liberal democracy into account; and the pledge of poverty had neglected Marx's analysis of the root causes of poverty. Impelled by Vatican II, sisters' conceptions of their vows tangled with these and other streams of modern thought. Sisters within and among communities came to different conclusions about what these promises meant in the contemporary world. Traditionalists such as Carmelites

tended to hold fast to past concepts. Among the revisionists, while no interpretation was universal, the trend was clear. The vows had implied a rejection of one's instincts—self-determination, sex, and material comfort—for
the sake of seeking perfection in a life *inside,* closed off from the world. For a
growing number of liberal-minded sisters, the vows now took on a positive
cast: they became a way to enhance, rather than diminish, the self, directing
sisters to be open toward the world and to nurture a loving dedication to it.
The first huge Sister Survey in 1967 (nearly 140,000 respondents) bears this
out. Barely 10 percent of the sisters still believed that they owed absolute
obedience to their superiors; 46 percent rejected the idea that seeking perfect
love with Christ ruled out "all partial loves" (32 percent said chastity did
mean that); 55 percent refused to accept the concept that religious life meant
continually resisting one's own wants and desires (34 percent disagreed); half
(49 percent) were unwilling to rank seeking personal holiness above doing
the ministry of the community.

The translation of vows into action altered the work sisters did—often
drawing them from classrooms to antipoverty programs and peace centers—
and the purposes of their ministries, from seeking holiness to pursuing social
justice. Countless discussions and debates accompanied the transition. In
1974, for example, a major part of the LCWR's annual convention was devoted to exploring the growing ferment over how the old vow of poverty fit
the new circumstances.

No two communities responded to this revisionism in exactly the same
way, and many showed no desire at all to to make social justice work their
mission. Although the array of orders shared a core heritage, they had ac-
quired distinct instincts, routines, styles, and focus by dint of the circumstances that had brought them into existence and the influences that had
nurtured them. Accordingly, they approached the enormous challenge of renewal with varying amounts of enthusiasm and receptivity. The appeal to do
social justice work exposed these differences among the orders and also divided sisters within the same order. Many of those who opposed this initiative claimed that it would replace a traditionally spiritual vocation with one
aimed at political and moral causes for which nuns had not been consecrated.
In the decade following Vatican II, commitment to social justice couldn't
simply be presumed to exist in most religious communities; it often came

slowly and partially, engendering great controversy and being tagged by some as the *radical* alternative to the conventional mission. In the wrangling over the proper place of this issue within the mission of convents, many conservative sisters decided they could no longer remain in a climate that was so vastly remaking the life they had entered.

Evidence from the Sister Survey suggests that activism for social justice had gained widespread approval among sisters. A solid 44 percent agreed that sisters should be "witnessing to Christ on the picket line and speaking out on controversial issues," compared to 32 percent who did not believe so. Even in a cultural climate in which masses of Americans had embraced the cause of racial justice and Lyndon Baines Johnson was rallying the U.S. Congress behind a bold anti-poverty program—in other words, in a country significantly pervaded by a reform spirit—the fact that nearly half of all nuns, who had been shielded from the world just a few years before, now believed that engaging in social activism was vital to their vocation represented an astonishing shift in fundamental beliefs.

Rhetoric begat deeds. As a social justice imperative found its way into the constitutions and chapter meetings, a concrete agenda took shape. Sisters across a broad spectrum of communities unfurled antiwar placards, demanded an end to racial bigotry, provided soup and tutoring for the poor, registered voters, mobilized neighborhoods against police brutality and for improvement of city services, and found many other expressions of advocacy. A second Sister Survey in 1982 found that 55 percent of the sisters said that their communities had created new social justice programs since 1965, and 30 percent said theirs had not. Among the specific areas mentioned most were work with the poor, efforts to improve health, and direct action on behalf of social justice.

Although sisters reported widespread action, the survey also showed that only a relatively small minority were actually involved in these ministries. Administrators in the communities responded that just 8 percent of their members worked on such projects. In her book based on the second survey, *Catholic Sisters in Transition,* Sister Neal concludes that "although there has been much discussion of new works and much action toward choice of ministry, discussion and action are not moving large numbers of sisters into ministries more consonant with their new mission statements." The fact that "some clergy and religious adopted the social gospel and others did not," Sister Neal added, was a problem that the Church needed to address. Although the percentage was small compared to the large number of sympathizers, it was probably fairly typical of the portion of any group—church, senior citizens club, parent-teacher association—that actually does the work.

The disparity reflected two critical factors. One was that many social justice–oriented sisters quit religious life because they found it too confining and lacking in devotion to that ministry. Another is that, by the mid-1970s, many American sisters felt that the Church had subjected them to forms of injustice that they couldn't ignore. There was a growing awareness that they, too, had suffered at the hands of a male hierarchical system that was robbing them of a measure of their humanity. Meanwhile, Rome had clearly signaled its unhappiness, even scorn, at the direction that sister communities had taken in the United States, toward greater autonomy and independence of mind. A seemingly trivial matter signaled that displeasure: Rome's attempt to stop the national association of sisters from changing its name. It was an important fight over symbolism. Originally organized in 1956 as the Conference of Major Superiors of Women (CMSW), the organization proposed renaming itself the Leadership Conference of Women Religious in 1971. The flash point was the word "leadership," which implied that the group was taking matters into its own hands, deferring less to the male authorities. To the defenders of tradition, this proposal signified renewal gone wrong. Although Vatican II's call for activism on behalf of social justice presumably applied to nuns no less than to the rest of the Church, the assertiveness signaled by the name change could make it more difficult to limit sisters to issues *outside* the Church. The superiors at the annual meeting rebuffed Rome, voting 356–39 to adopt new bylaws that approved the new name. But by that time those who rejected the conference's break with tradition, about 10 percent of the membership, had formed a competing group, Consortium Perfectae Caritatis, that sought to keep Vatican II renewal within much stricter limits.

Friction over giving the upstart CMSW a more commanding title was never resolved by discussion between conference officials and Rome because Vatican officials refused to agree to talks. After the conference went ahead with the name change in 1971, its leaders regularly trekked to Rome and asked to meet with the pope and other authorities. The requests were repeatedly denied.

Sister Margaret Brennan, an Immaculate Heart of Mary sister and one of the conference's leading intellectual lights, was president during 1972–73. She recalled the experience two decades later.

"What we found was shocking," Sister Brennan said. "The Church had called us to renewal, and we took it seriously. When we began to live it out, however, we became a threat to the centrist church. In dealing with Rome, their insistence was that we weren't obeying. I can't count the times we met in Rome and tried to speak our voice to the Holy Father—not to complain, just to explain who we are and why we're doing what we're doing—but our requests were never granted."

In an effort to ease the mounting tensions, Sister Brennan wrote to the Vatican secretary of state to ask for an audience with Pope Paul VI. The reply was sent to the head of the U.S. Conference of Catholic Bishops rather than to her, a move widely interpreted as a deliberate insult. The president of the bishops' conference, the redoubtable John Cardinal Krol of Philadelphia, passed along to her the message that her request had been refused. "I called the cardinal to ask why the letter from Rome hadn't been sent to us and that being denied was stressful to us," Sister Brennan said. "He said, 'Maybe if you were more obedient you'd get in.' It was very shattering for me. After years of studying in Europe, my own theology was very deeply rooted in the Church as the Body of Christ. I hadn't had a problem with that. Then this hit. Our experience had not been reverenced; there wasn't even any real discussion. I kept wanting to say that the Church shouldn't be this narrow. Those were traumatic years."

The surge of social activism among sisters did not by itself, of course, account for the resistance from Rome. The sisters' activism was a component, another indication to keepers of a pre–Vatican II mentality at the Church's highest levels, that renewal had let the proverbial cat out of the bag and now there was no going back. Social justice ministry invited the kind of independent thought and self-determined action that paid less heed to formal ecclesiastical authority. But much of the objection from Church officials was ambiguous. Sister Brennan and other leaders rarely received a clear indica-

tion of what specifically disturbed the hierarchy. The atmosphere was permeated by anxiety and suppressed anger on both sides, apart from occasional instances of rebellion when sisters lashed out against the system. The mixture
of confusion and subliminal disapproval undoubtedly had a chilling effect on
sisters' willingness to go further. The pressure would grow more intense as
Church officials worried that the cause of seeking justice was being extended
into the Church itself. The founding of the independent Women's Ordination in 1975 became a major force in fanning those fears.

The call to justice touched off personal soul-searching and endless discussion and debate within sister communities over how to formulate that
mission into their constitutions and make it work. For a relatively small number of sisters, the challenge was life changing, providing them an outlet they
had lacked for exercising their energies and ideals.

Sister Jeanne Knoerle illustrates the dynamism and continual evaluation
that this new priority could stimulate over time. A Sister of Providence, former president of Saint Mary-of-the-Woods College, and program officer for
the Lilly Endowment, Sister Knoerle looked back in 1984 at how her mind
had changed. A decade before, she had helped write a community statement
that urged the sisters "to raise our awareness of the causes of poverty and
powerlessness so that, as a result of reflection and inner conviction, our lives
and ministries may assist in the elimination of those causes and their effects."
In an unpublished paper for her community called "Ministry: Focus and Direction," she said that in retrospect "we erred" in fixing on that goal, not because it wasn't important, but because it was too narrow. Just as crucial but
neglected, she added, was "our traditional role as religious to assist others
with compassion and love to cope with the painful realities of their lives."

"I felt then, as I do now, that besides working to create a more just and
humane world, we need to recognize the continuing, inescapable human reality of sin and injustice and pain and recognize that we have an important
role to play in helping people deal with the effects of those evils," she wrote.

She could coexist with those who fought for social change, she said,
"But if 'bonding together to empower the poor' has come to mean 'destroy-
ing the system' and if as a Sister of Providence I am publicly committed to
doing that, I cannot, in conscience, do it. I have chosen to believe I do not
need to."

Continuing, she wrote, "Attempting to create a more just world—assisting persons to live in an unjust world—these are simply different ways of focusing our activities. Life does not preclude doing both, but time and energy generally does. Some want to change the world by changing our economic and political and social systems. Some, including myself, want to improve the world where they can, but more importantly want to help people cope with what they feel will be the injustices that will exist, no matter what system prevails."

The sisters' commitment to social activism was seldom en masse or unequivocal, but rather scattered and fitful. Some sisters and whole congregations got caught up in it, while others refrained from any significant involvement. Nuns, then, were probably more likely to find their way toward activism on their own, or in the company of a small number of others.

Sister Florence Deacon, now a history professor at Cardinal Stritch University, was a young teacher in a Milwaukee parish school in the mid-1960s when her own evolution began. The previously all-white school was rapidly becoming black. Sensitized by the Church's justice appeals, she identified with the plight of her black students by joining the intensifying civil rights movement in the city, among whose leaders was the high-profile priest the Reverend James Groppi. She soon joined the Archdiocesan Sisters' Council, made up of members of the many orders in the area, and by 1970 she was head of its social responsibility committee.

At about the same time, some of the leaders of her congregation, the School Sisters of St. Francis, began pushing for social justice education. The result was the formation of a "ministry for justice" program for Sister Deacon and more than a dozen other members of the community. For the entire summer of 1973, the sisters were tutored in the rough-and-tumble of real-world power by the redoubtable Sister Marjorie Tuitte from Chicago, who had been brought in to conduct the mixture of instruction and indoctrination. It was a moment of transformation for Sister Deacon. "We learned social analysis and organizing, liberation theology [the Latin American grassroots ministry focused on providing poor people the spiritual and political resources to take greater charge of their lives], the political system, etc.," she recalled. "We continued to meet for several years after and later expanded to the Peace and Justice Committee for the congregation."

Trouble began when this group of sisters attempted to extend social justice themes to life within their own congregation. Congregational authorities had by then heard warnings from inside and outside that too much revision of Church structures could threaten the community and the Church. Sister Deacon's superior refused her request to hold a series of informal meetings to discuss such matters. "This was in the midst of the post-Vatican renewal in religious life," she remembered, "and there was a lot of distrust and formation of factions in many congregations. The possibility of a split was in people's minds, since this was happening in several communities.

"When I was 'commanded under holy obedience' not to hold the coffee hour meetings, I had a moral dilemma, which I finally resolved in favor of congregational unity."

She and others were considered radical for their social activism, she said, although ideas that were "radical became accepted and actually became directives for the entire congregation. In my mind there is about an eight-year lag between when a new idea is first suggested and when it becomes commonly accepted."

For every action, there was a reaction, although not exactly proportional as Newton saw it in the physical world. Sisters Quinonez and Turner in their book, *The Transformation of American Sisters,* determined that by the early 1970s "enlarged participation in civil spheres, the exercise of power to secure one's purposes, the right of self-determination, and the worth of each individual's contribution were finding their way into the ethos of religious communities." But a backlash had set in. "The opposition of Vatican and American authorities to these developments hastened the awakening of the women leaders to the fact of their institutional exclusion from and their impotence in the polity of the church."

Chapter Nine

Sister Sisterhood

O f all the justice issues burning in the 1960s, none seemed more relevant to religious sisters than the rights of women. Nuns had been pioneers, after a fashion, running schools, colleges, social agencies, and hospitals before most other American women had even dreamed of taking such responsibilities. To be sure, their roles had been circumscribed within the broader boundaries of Church authority, and their power didn't extend to the councils of hierarchical authority, but they were distinguished leaders in charge of big, complex structures. They were, in short, the CEOs of institutions before women were CEOs of institutions.

Practicing professions hitherto reserved for men, a goal embraced by the women's movement in the 1960s and 1970s, nuns had therefore prefigured the cause of women's rights and become at the very least implicit feminists. Abetting this process, starting in the mid-1950s, had been the Sister Formation movement's success in enabling thousands of young sisters to earn college degrees and, more important, respect for their intellectual talents. This large cadre of educated Catholic women took their knowledge and skills into a growing variety of professions. A rising number of sisters began enrolling in graduate school, particularly in the humanities and sciences, in order to become college professors and administrators or to offer other specialized services. The total of doctorates awarded to sisters more than doubled in twenty years, from 302 in the 1950s to 632 in the 1970s.

Being pioneers didn't necessarily mean sisters were feminists. Looking back, most sisters say their goal in gaining professional competence was to serve people entrusted to their care rather than to promote women in career fields. For the most part, then, they say they weren't seeking to become heads of anthropology departments and psychiatric units for the sake of exercising personal authority or to gain professional prestige. Most of them ardently embraced the religious mission of their communities as it applied to the institutions they served.

Coincidentally, however, sisters were pursuing degrees and taking leadership positions in professional fields (or in some cases fulfilling roles that sisters had long occupied) at the same time that many American women were stirring to the cause of ending sex bias and stereotyping. Women's rights emerged on a national scale alongside racial equality and opposition to the war in Vietnam as a cluster of issues that many social activists increasingly identified as rooted in similar sources of injustice. On those other fronts, sisters had long since entered the fray.

On women's issues, sisters had more direct experience of the problem. Though they were outside the cultural mainstream of marriage, family, and breadwinner, their vantage points as intimate observers of Catholic family life gave them a special angle of vision on the tensions women faced. They also knew firsthand the consequences of living within a religious version of the feminine mystique. They had, for example, known the female "pedestal" within the Church structure—with its special privileges and regulated autonomy—while being aware that their existence was tightly restricted within a ghetto defined ultimately by male clerics. Until the Second Vatican Council knocked the props out from under their elevated status, they had been considered superior in a pure "perfect" society, not unlike the idealization that some of their sisters and mothers had been accorded by the patriarchal order. At the same time, they had felt the sting of condescension and subordination from superiors, both male and female, that often undercut their self-worth. By comparison, then, while civil rights and peace marches involved causes beyond the direct experience of most nuns, feminism at least theoretically touched issues closer to home, that is, the treatment of women. Their own life experience, and the growing restiveness among American women, appeared to provide fertile ground for a surge of feminism among sisters.

It did and it didn't.

By the late 1960s, the broader women's movement had begun to seep into religious communities, indirectly as if through osmosis. Nuns were, of course, susceptible to this wider cultural current just as they had absorbed other influences such as the cause for racial justice. But internal factors also began to stoke these embers. As they struggled to renew their communities according to Vatican II's guidelines, friction arose between their desire to do the job as they saw fit and the reluctance of some priests and bishops to let them. The greatest cataclysm of those early years was the assault by James Cardinal McIntyre of Los Angeles on the progressive policies of one of the nation's best educated and most vibrant communities, the Immaculate Heart of Mary sisters. The dramatic, highly publicized showdown, which resulted in the dissolution of the IHM's formal ties to the Church, jolted many sisters across the land. Lillanna Kopp, a sociologist and former Holy Name sister who founded the independent Sisters for a Christian Community, painted the aftermath in stark, progressive terms. "Thanks to a reactionary and authoritarian bishop," she said in a 1998 interview, "one congregation was destroyed, while thousands of sisters were radicalized, and mobilized, by what they saw." Not everyone agreed with that assessment. Some saw the IHM's behavior as shocking and scandalous. But sympathy for feminist arguments churned among nuns who had previously ignored the cause. They now saw the cardinal's crackdown as a dramatic example of male oppression. One of those for whom this was a turning point was Sister Elizabeth Carroll, a Mercy sister who was one of the most respected nuns in the country. Aghast at the cardinal's treatment of the sisters in L.A., Sister Carroll found herself more committed than ever to feminist principles. At the annual meeting of the Conference of Major Superiors of Women, it was Sister Carroll who submitted the proposal to support the IHM cause against the cardinal, an initiative that fell short of passing by a single vote.

But from these early stages, a fault line was forming between two spheres. One concerned the pursuit of women's rights and dignity within secular society. On this front, there appeared to be considerable support by nuns for such things as equal pay for equal work for their sisters and mothers outside their communities. The other sphere focused on the Church and was more controversial. How should women religious think about their treatment within the Church? Was it a God-given set of beliefs and policies that kept women from presiding at the Eucharist or taking part in decisions that affected the whole church? Or were these "laws," as it were, man-made?

Though important, such questions were marginal. By the end of the 1960s, no significant women's movement had emerged among the sisters. One reason, explained Sister Miriam Ukeritis, a psychology professor and co-conductor of the landmark 1992 study of religious orders, was that the defection of nuns to opportunities opening for women in secular employment had drained religious communities of feminist strength. Some nuns recoiled from the sharp feminist critique on grounds that it impugned them as victims of oppression or was basically unchristian. "The rise of the women's movement was accompanied by resistance to looking at women religious," said Sister Ukeritis, a St. Joseph of Carondelet sister and faculty member at DePaul University in Chicago. "There was reluctance to look at questions like how you deal with oppression in the Church and how can you belong to a group suffering oppression."

Nothing in nuns' other social justice activism should have implied that they would naturally gravitate to women's liberation. While social justice was a common thread, each cause had its own constituency. Many civil rights crusaders never ventured into the peace movement, and, while substantial overlaps certainly existed, the women's movement attracted those who had been involved in neither of the other two causes. Nuns who saw such connections often balked at plunging into feminism because of the many possible repercussions it might trigger. The Second Vatican Council had provided them justification for antiracism and antipoverty efforts—especially in the Pastoral Constitution on the Church in the Modern World (Gaudium et Spes)—but the hierarchy in Rome still held a decidedly traditional view of woman as wife and mother that did not admit of the term "liberation." The drive for women's equality took root outside the Catholic Church; the same had been true of the appeal for racial equality. The first internal support for attending to the women's cause came from that legendary mold-breaker Pope John XXIII. In his 1963 encyclical Pacem in Terris (On Establishing Universal Peace in Truth, Justice, Charity, and Liberty) the pope declared that justice for women was one of the paramount "signs of the times." "Women are becoming ever more conscious of their human dignity," he said, and the rights they fought for were "befitting a human person both in domestic and public life." That surprising opening to the feminist movement abruptly closed, however. When his successors did discuss the subject of women, the rhetoric rarely sounded hospitable to women's liberation as it had become known in the wider culture.

In practical terms, any bold advocacy of "the advancement of women" within the Church threatened the absolute rule of men. Nuns under vows of obedience who espoused such views were, therefore, taking a perilous step, especially at a time when conflicts were erupting between nuns and prelates over the direction of religious communities. Those who unfurled that revolutionary banner sometimes arrived at the troubling question of whether they or other sisters could, in good conscience, embody feminism while living within the conventional rules of the Church. Many others felt the weight of Catholic tradition shoving such matters aside.

For a few sisters, the women's movement embraced women both inside and outside the convent. But not many saw it that way. Most advocated women's equality in society with regard to areas such education and employment (the areas at the heart of the Equal Rights Amendment), but their initiatives generally stopped at the motherhouse door. One exception was the rash of disputes over nuns' pay in schools and hospitals—salaries had been scandalously low. But even in these struggles the association with the wider women's movement was mostly tenuous and indirect rather than overt.

Sister Theresa Kane, the Sister of Mercy who became indelibly linked with women's rights in the Church by appealing directly to Pope John Paul II in 1979 for full equality in all ordained ministries, believes most nuns were conditioned to think feminism was inimical to their lives as consecrated women. It was foreign, a fly in the soup; nonsensical, lacking context. "Instinctively," she explained, "feminism didn't seem religious to them. It seemed more like a secular movement. At its root, feminism is really spiritual, though I've seen it worked out mostly economically and politically. But theology began to struggle with the question of God, to develop a feminist spirituality and a spiritual feminism." In the minds of some Catholic feminists, feminism within the Holy Roman Catholic Church was quite distinct from the question of ordination. To some, feminism meant solidarity with all Catholic women to combat a heritage of patriarchy. Apart from achieving that goal, they said, ordination of women, though theoretically a good idea, was totally beside the point. Others preferred ordination into the male-dominated church sooner rather than later.

The other obstacle, Sister Kane said, was that "women in general have been so conditioned to be servants, to be volunteers, to always be giving, that the feminist idea of promoting oneself sounded too selfish to them. We'd never think of doing that to a man." Many nuns could not embrace feminism because of their suspicion that it involved man-hating, and this reluctance has persisted for a quarter century. Sister Ellen Joyce, a historian at St. Elizabeth's College in Convent Station, New Jersey, occupied every top office in her Sisters of Charity community during the years of renewal turmoil. While she asserts that feminism instilled a valuable sense of pride in women and ended some unfair treatment of sisters, she claims it often went too far by "branding" the Church the "chief oppressor." While most middle-of-the-road nuns wanted to accomplish basic justice, she says, they balked at endorsing a line of thought that sounded politically or ideologically motivated toward overthrowing male authority. "I'm not sure you can be a Christian and an ideologue," she said. "I'm influenced by [the late German theologian] Karl Rahner, S.J., that when you turn Christianity into ideology, it's no longer Christianity.

"I do think women are treated unjustly. I've seen it. I've heard of it. I'm just inclined to think of feminism as flawed theory, the assertion that women are compassionate and men are not. The answer is justice, not feminism. I'm for women but I don't consider myself a feminist."

Over time, then, many sisters worked out their own accommodation with feminist principles even if they refused to identify with the movement. That included some of the most notable conservatives, such as Mother Vincent Marie Finnegan, a Carmelite sister who led the Consortium Perfectae Caritatis, the group that split off from the more liberal Leadership Conference of Women Religious, partly over feminist issues, in 1970–71. Mother Finnegan was a spirited, cheerful, voluble woman in full habit who espoused a variety of feminism she attributed to Pope John Paul II. "There is a positive feminist movement from the Holy Father," she said. "He needs to be heard. We're beyond a far-out feminism. There have been gains for women in the workplace and in society and the Church needs to be addressed and has been addressed. There's been a lot of dialogue and improvements in the relation of women in general and in the Church. There *is* a proper feminism." In the view the pope espoused, women have a place that deserves respect and dignity, and sexual oppression needs to stop. Accordingly, this platform called for justice for women in the workplace and other areas of public and private life. On the other hand, it rejected what it scorned as a "unisex" concept of gender equality and stood by the Church's tradition of reserving ecclesiastical authority to men. Women and men were "complementary," the pope contended, rather than equal. Each had a place and a role; a common humanity, but different natures. It was a separate-but-equal, takes-both-to-complete-each-other policy. Women were still seen principally as wives and mothers; fathers as household leaders and breadwinners. The priesthood and principal decision-making must remain in the hands of men, the argument went, because God said so. Papal pronouncements and Vatican statements attempted to close the discussion by declaring that the Church fathers were simply "unable" to change these rules, no matter, they implied, how much they might want to, because the rules were revealed truths.

Mother Vincent's highly qualified brand of feminism represented perhaps the most prevalent strain among women religious in the 1970s. It was a divided view; it contained a large measure of support for women's efforts to gain equality in the secular world, but reluctance to challenge the status quo in the Church, at least openly, apart from modest adjustments. That mind-set has held in the intervening decades. The women's movement simply had difficulty reaching into internal matters of the Church.

At the same time, sympathy for feminism differed in intensity and scope from place to place among American nuns, from tepid support for some basic economic and legal rights in society, to commitment to wholesale reform of both secular and Church institutions. But the movement was making some inroads, starting in the 1970s, and that small beginning eventually gained some momentum.

At a critical level, a significant crossover was taking place that would stretch over many years, thanks to a dedicated group of feminist scholars and activists. They supplied research and ideas that eventually made intellectual and practical headway in building a consensus that embraced both Church and society. They were the loyal opposition insofar as while they called themselves Catholics they also followed out the implications of a more militant feminism than most nuns were ready to endorse. They were, like all revolutionary groups, a small minority with large minds and steadfast courage. Collectively, they built models and rationale for a kind of feminism that reached the interiors of Christian existence.

Mary Daly provided the first crash course. A theologian at Boston College, Professor Daly launched a scathing attack on Catholicism's treatment of women in her 1968 book, *The Church and the Second Sex.* It was, at base, a rigorous assault on patriarchy; Daly felt so strongly about the issue that she renounced Catholicism altogether. Nevertheless, she inspired a generation of Catholic feminist scholars who came to prominence during the next twenty years. Among them were Elisabeth Scheussler Fiorenza, a New Testament professor at Harvard Divinity School; Rosemary Radford Reuther, a theologian at Northwestern; Elizabeth A. Johnson, a Sister of Joseph and theology professor at Fordham; and Sandra M. Schneiders, an Immaculate Heart of Mary (Monroe, Michigan) sister and professor of New Testament and Christian spirituality at the Jesuit School of Theology at Berkeley.

The combined influence of these and other noted thinkers and activists had, by the mid-1980s, triggered alarms in Rome. Suddenly Vatican officials were branding U.S. sisters "radical feminists," although the huge majority of sisters weren't any such thing. Noting the irony, feminists were inclined to believe that the Vatican's stereotyping revealed a hysterical overreaction and a heavy-handedness that could help prove the feminist case. Many other sisters across the country were appalled. To their dismay, the Vatican had apparently lumped them in with the fringe extremists who pressed women's rights way too far. To cite Cardinal Josef Ratzinger of the Congregation for the Doctrine of the Faith (now Pope Benedict XVI), "a feminist mentality" had invaded women's orders. It was "particularly evident, even in its extreme forms, on the North American continent," he said. Among the signs of this degeneracy were creeping "professionalism," the absorption of secular values to replace religious ones, and the use of psychotherapy in the convent. Such trends, according to the cardinal, were the main reasons for the orders' troubles.

In her landmark 1991 book, *Beyond Patching,* Sister Schneiders took stock of the types of feminism that had taken root in the United States and the degree to which they were having an effect in the Catholic Church since Professor Daly's 1968 salvo. Her analysis was a collection of dazzling lectures accomplished succinctly in 112 pages, including a section in which she brilliantly considers how male dominance in the Bible represents a triumph of patriarchy.

Sister Schneiders reviewed the terminology most often associated with the cause. The "women's movement," the most broad-based term, implied the overall improvement of the status of women. "Women's emancipation" referred to efforts to free women from particular legal or political restrictions that kept them from being equal, goals associated largely with the proposed Equal Rights Amendment (although, as she pointed out, some women believe women should have such rights but not claim "equality" with men). Finally, "women's liberation" meant to Sister Schneiders the "liberation of women (and men) into the fullness of human personhood and the freedom to exercise that personhood." This last concept was clearly the closest to her position. So long as maleness defined the nature of what it meant to be a person, she explained, women's rights meant little more than the ability of women to be like men, or, in her words, that "the best way to be a woman is to be like a man." She went further, in a comment on Pope John Paul II's pastoral letter Mulieres Dignitatem (on the Dignity of Women) that had extolled women as mothers and refrained from mentioning women's roles in the Church. "Women have been seen to complete men the way a second coat of paint completes a house," she wrote, "whereas men have been seen to complete women the way a motor completes a car."

Sister Schneiders thought that the most recent upsurge of feminism could be divided into distinct, though overlapping, camps: liberal, cultural, socialist, and radical. The liberals stuck with the basic agenda of removing legal and political barriers in order to give women equal opportunity. The cultural types sought to promote those "special contributions of women to the construction of a better world," supplementing the hitherto dominant male traits such as aggression with female virtues such as cooperativeness. The goal of this effort was to displace some of those male qualities or to balance them with "superior" female characteristics. Socialist feminists saw economic and class injustice as the root of sexual oppression, and were convinced that the ending of capitalistic structures would eradicate male domination.

Radical feminism, the alternative most favored by Sister Schneiders, rejected both the assurance of the liberal and cultural wings that adjusting the system would suffice and the class-based explanation of the socialists. This radical stance demanded, instead, recognition that the pattern of male supremacy permeated all aspects of society, based on sex rather than simply cultural or legal inequalities. The systematic, patriarchal subjugation of women, therefore, had to be dismantled and replaced by a belief in the dignity of each person without assumptions of superiority or inferiority. Patriarchy, said the radicals, could not be remedied by resorting only to formal remedies. As a faith that accounted for the distribution of power, status, and function, patriarchy could successfully be displaced only by another faith.

By the criteria of radical feminism, Sister Schneiders asserted, the Roman Catholic Church was "perhaps the most patriarchal structure in the Western world" and therefore had good reason to be nervous that some nuns and other Catholic women were taking this highly critical approach. The Church justified its all-male hierarchy as rooted in God's plan, and that stance had in the eyes of radical feminists become the source of *all* oppression, not just oppression in the Church, Sister Schneiders wrote. Their solution, she continued, lay in "resolute anti-hierarchicalism, or, to phrase it positively, in fundamental egalitarianism."

The radical feminists' indictment of the Church was far-reaching. Church officials had excluded women from authority—from administering the sacraments and making decisions about Church policy—and had placed them at the periphery of Church life, performing vital and difficult functions without corresponding respect and leadership roles. But Catholic influence had also pushed women into secondary roles in the home by making obligatory the roles of wife and mother under the domination of husbands and fathers, an arrangement legitimized by the Church. Simply put, men ruled with the blessing and rationale of Roman Catholicism.

All these complaints would be moot to devout Catholics if, as the Church had taught, God intended that men be in charge and had, in effect, ordained a patriarchal system. The basic question, Sister Schneiders said, was, "Is the church patriarchal by merely human or by divine authority? In other words, did God in Christ ordain women's secondary and subordinate position in Christianity, or have male hierarchs distorted the Christian message in their own patriarchal image?" If God did it, then "women can only remain Catholics at the price of their self-respect as humans and believers." But if humans had twisted the Gospel's message to build an all-male system, she added, "then Catholic feminists have an enormous and exhausting task on their hands, viz. the radical transformation of the church, but it makes sense for those who can endure the pain to remain and to struggle until the church becomes the 'discipleship of equals' which Jesus initiated." Sister Schneiders and many other nuns were inclined to believe that historical and biblical research would finally prove that the Gospels' message had been distorted at the expense of women. But for the moment, anyway, they were staying in the Church.

A flare-up in 1984 fanned debate over whether nuns could honestly promote total revision of the hierarchical church and remain, at the same time, members of communities under Rome's jurisdiction. The spark that ignited the fire sprang from a full-page ad in the October 7, 1984, edition of the *New York Times* in which twenty-four nuns, two priests, two religious brothers, and sixty-seven lay Catholics challenged the Vatican's claim that the Church's teaching on abortion—total condemnation—was unassailable. In the ad, the signers acknowledged that Rome indeed had a fixed teaching on abortion, reinforced by popes, but the signatories insisted that other legitimate views could arise from the experience of other Catholics. There were *many* valid views on the subject, not just one. Moreover, they said, abortion could be, under certain circumstances, "a moral choice." They therefore called for a "respectful discussion" over what they saw as a legitimate "diversity of opinion." This public bombshell would produce years of anguish for signatories and Church officials, particularly because the Vatican took action to punish the so-called canonical nuns who had in their judgment signed a statement of unacceptable dissent. As the result of these sometimes bitter clashes, more nuns began to question whether they should stay in communities that were so vulnerable to hierarchical attack.

In the spring issue of the *Journal of Feminist Studies in Religion*, in an article titled "The *New York Times* Ad," two key promoters of the ad, Mary Hunt, a feminist activist, and Frances Kissling, head of Catholics for a Free Choice, the group that sponsored the initiative, proclaimed that it was time for religious communities to declare their independence from Rome. "It seems clear to us," said the two women, neither of them nuns, "that the days of canonical religious communities . . . bound to patriarchal organizations on these organizations' terms, is over."

If sisters were to devote themselves to creating a church in which pyramids of authority would be replaced by a "discipleship of equals," the authors said, then religious communities "cannot be part of a patriarchal structure." To Hunt and Kissling, the same stumbling block interfered with the campaign for women's ordination. Ordaining women would give "some women a kind of position that is contingent on patriarchal approval," they wrote. Feminists elsewhere amplified and expanded this theme, opposing the ordination of women on grounds that it would simply make women part of the oppressive hierarchical structure. Advocates of women's ordination contended that allowing women clergy would help transform the structures in feminist directions.

As an unexpected consequence of the divisive *New York Times* ad, therefore, the fault line between the separationists and the integrationists widened and deepened dramatically. A relatively small number of radicals urged sisters to disconnect from the male authority; a larger number, the gradualists, wanted to work for change by remaining inside the system and pressing for women priests. By the late 1980s, the debates emanating from the ad and other conflicts had at the very least inserted feminism into the forums in which most nuns took part. Promoting the expansion of women's roles in the Church was now part of the conversation in most communities. The two very distinct approaches—one a radical restructuring of the entire Church order into a community of equals and another the fight to gain admission to all the ordained ministries of the system as it basically existed—have stood in tension with each other in the ensuing years. There is overlap between these groups, of course, as well as a middle ground that rejects women's ordination unless the priesthood and hierarchy are totally overhauled to rid them of "clericalism," the exercise of special powers and privileges that have accrued to that special status. Critics have demanded an end to what they saw as elitist practices that hindered Christian ministry and insisted that these and other symbols of domination be shorn from the priesthood before women even considered ordination. Most advocates of ordination opposed "merely the right for women to obtain access to the sacrament of Holy Orders [ordination] as it exists today," wrote Dr. Margaret Susan Thompson, professor of history at Syracuse University and an authority on religious communities. "The ultimate objective is not to substitute patriarchy with matriarchy but to do away with clerical elitism and classism entirely. They would replace it with a model of priesthood that stresses its 'servant' dimension."

A decade before the *Times* ad appeared, the focus was almost entirely on the question of ending the male monopoly on ordination. In 1975 an alliance of 1,200 supporters of women in the priesthood—a large percentage of them nuns—rallied for their cause in Detroit. Hundreds more were turned away. The specter of such a resolute and enthusiastic group publicly calling for an end to an all-male priesthood—a subject that was unthinkable, even taboo to many Catholics—created an enormous stir within the Church and drew extensive media attention. If anyone thought that the participants would retreat from a hard-line position on the issue, the eminent theologian Rosemary Radford Reuther dispelled doubts in her keynote speech. She denounced the "present clerical and institutional structure" as "demonic and so opposed to the Gospel that to try to join it is contrary to our very commitments." She blasted clericalism as "deeply rooted in sexist symbols of domination and passivity." Those practices had to go, she declared, before women could be ordained. Some nuns passionately applauded; others rejected the premise that ordaining women was part of God's plan. The hierarchy was nervous. Archbishop Joseph Bernardin of Cincinnati signaled that alarm as president of the U.S. Conference of Catholic Bishops by pointing out to the meeting's organizers on the eve of the gathering that the Church barred the ordination of women, in case anyone needed reminding.

From the Detroit assembly sprang the Women's Ordination Conference. Though ordination was its ostensible aim, the movement encompassed a wide variety of nuns, most all of them feminists to one degree or another, from those who sought to open greater opportunities to women under existing conditions to those who urged total renovation of the hierarchy. The conference became the common ground on which those who disagreed on some issues could thrash out differences while finding much to celebrate together in the interests of opening the Church to women. As time went on, serious splits developed over whether ordination was compatible at all with a church envisioned by some, such as the highly regarded scholar Dr. Elisabeth Schussler Fiorenza, as a "discipleship of equals."

Rome was still fretting. First, in the late 1960s nuns had pushed the boundaries of community renewal beyond what the Vatican had in mind as a minimalist touch-up on the old ways. Then in 1969 the Immaculate Heart of Mary sisters had faced a publicly embarrassing showdown with James Cardinal

McIntyre in an effort to institute extensive changes. Then the Conference of Major Superiors of Women had rankled the Vatican's Sacred Congregation of Religious in 1971 by renaming itself the Leadership Conference of Women Religious, a title that implied that the women would steer their own ship rather than take directions from Rome. The Sacred Congregation of Religious refused to recognize the new title for five years, begrudgingly doing so in 1975. Pushy women, it seemed to the distant cardinals in charge, were popping up everywhere. The Detroit Women's Ordination Conference was, therefore, seen by officialdom as a finger in the eye, a hugely public challenge to its authority.

The air of rebelliousness was thickening. Sister Marie Augusta Neal, whose pioneering sociological research had documented feminist sentiments and sexist attitudes, wrote in the prestigious theological journal *Concilium* in 1980 that the primary sexual problem in the Church was "men who manage the affairs of the church without recognition of their sisters whom they need if ministry, theology and clerical research are to be done adequately." On a wider scale, she wrote, echoing the earlier sentiments of Pope John XXIII that women's rights were a sign of the times: "Willingness of women to live in a male-dominated society will decrease rapidly as the rights of *paterfamilias* decline and the implications of full human rights develop."

Rome reacted to this defiance. To a growing number of Catholics, sexism in the Church went directly to the question of ordination. Nothing so raised the hierarchy's hackles or threatened clergy. If the proposal to ordain women were given too much legitimacy, the reasoning went, then the matter could get further out of hand. Ordination was the thread in the garment that, if pulled, could unravel it completely. Therefore, a year after the Detroit uprising, the Vatican issued a document stating flatly and unequivocally that priests must match the sexual identity of Jesus, anatomically speaking, and therefore must be men. On theological and Scriptural grounds, the argument was a tough sell and few bought it. The Pontifical Biblical Commission had already concluded that the New Testament contained no clear verdict for or against. Most theologians also lacked proof. But Rome had spoken and, for the time being at least, that was what mattered. The coterie of the highest Church leaders recognized a revolutionary idea when they saw one, although, of course, the formal effort to stamp out debate only inflamed it and drew more nuns to the cause.

At the crux of the ordination issue is the meaning and practice of the Eucharist. It is the Catholic Church's central sacrament, a meal in which, according to Church doctrine, the elements of bread and wine are transformed by the priest into the actual Body and Blood of Christ for the sake of incorporating believers into His Kingdom and imparting them grace. The Mass reenacts an age-old ritual of sacrifice and culminates in the reception of Communion by the people. The celebration of the Eucharist embodies the priest's symbolic and sacred roles in the Church. Catholics are taught that only priests can perform this and other sacramental functions because priests are empowered to do so supernaturally.

For those reasons, some nuns and other Catholic women questioned whether they should shun Eucharistic celebrations that, by definition, were presided over by men. It became an issue that divided nun from nun and solidified separate camps. A majority of sisters rejected such a boycott on grounds that the Mass belongs to the people and therefore holds significance for the faithful despite the obstacle of all-male monopoly. Many also saw absenting themselves as a form of "man-hating." Still others, taking a page from the reformist "underground" churches in the 1960s and 1970s, began creating Eucharistic celebrations for women by women outside the official church. Groups such as the National Association of Women Religious and the National Coalition of American Nuns encouraged this practice, as did many of the participants of the Women's Ordination Conference. From these and other quasi-revolutionary roots grew alternatives to the conventional Mass that were celebrated, in most cases, far from public view.

Nourishing this process was the ripening of feminist theology by a cluster of leading scholars, among them, Professors Mary Daly, Elizabeth A. Johnson, Elisabeth Schussler Fiorenza, Sandra M. Schneiders, and Rosemary Radford Reuther. Their collective works supplied both crucial intellectual analysis and an approach to worship as women that stood at odds with conventional Church teaching. With this formidable group arrayed against it, Rome had reason to worry. "Feminism had great impact," said Sister Johnson in her Fordham University office in the fall of 1995. "You don't mandate conformity to women who have had their selves denied them."

None of these scholars was more influential in both theory and practice than Professor Rosemary Radford Reuther. She was a respected and courageous thinker with a impressive record of scholarship. She was a top pick to become dean of Harvard Divinity School; the school stepped back from breaking its all-male tradition in the deanship by choosing instead George Rupp, who went on to become president of Rice, then Columbia. Professor Reuther went on teaching and producing a stack of books that spelled out in greater and greater depth and detail key aspects of the relation of feminism to Catholicism.

Professor Reuther's 1985 book, *Women-Church,* summed up the twin elements in this movement; it is both a briefing in Catholic feminism and a practical guide to creating and conducting feminist spirituality and worship. For scores of nuns scattered among communities across the nation, it became a handbook. In the analysis section, Professor Reuther drew a fundamental distinction between two ways of conceiving the Church that have competed with each other from the earliest centuries of Christianity. One was the "spirit-filled" view whereby the Church was called by the Holy Spirit to never-ending growth and renewal in a climate of freedom. The other was the "institutional" perspective that emphasized stability, vertical authority, and supernaturally fixed truths. The "institutional" approach fostered the kind of clericalism—the accumulation and holding of special power—that feminists blamed for most of the Church's ills. Clericalism became most visible, therefore most painful, during the celebration of the Church's most sacred sacrament, the Mass. Women sensitized to this tension thus faced a choice whether to stay or to leave.

Professor Reuther was a realist. Her book was aimed at a much broader audience than those who were prepared to quit going to the parish or community Mass. Some would take that route, she noted, but many others would choose against making a clean break. The latter were largely persuaded by feminist ideas but also retained loyalty to the institution. They kept one foot in the women-church movement, the other in the Church of their upbringing.

As sisters grappled with the conflict there was great anguish and heartbreak, with sisters moving in opposing directions, wrestling with their inner instincts and the catechisms they had unquestioningly accepted, to reach accommodation with the new feminist challenge. Some were frozen in a wilderness of confusion and contrasting feelings. A few had epiphanies.

Sister Elizabeth Johnson was one who had such an awakening. A Sister of St. Joseph of Brentwood, Long Island, she had followed a conventional path of service as a science and math teacher in Catholic middle and high schools. She said she had been aware of the women's movement largely because of the examples of Congresswoman Shirley Chisholm from Brooklyn and Gloria Steinem, the founder of *Ms.* magazine, but she hadn't considered how theology fit into this analysis until she went on a pilgrimage to Rome in 1972. On Palm Sunday, she was inside St. Peter's Basilica watching the entrance procession. "I never really knew it was all boys," she recalled in a hushed voice. "Priests, bishops, the pope and all the others. It took ten minutes to get down. I had an enormous sense of exclusion, the feeling that 'there is no room for me.' "

Her focus would never be the same. When her congregation decided to expand St. Joseph College, she was asked to prepare to join its faculty by earning a Ph.D. in theology. Delighted with the opportunity, she was accepted as the first woman in a theological doctoral program (the faculty at St. Joseph's remained solidly behind her). With her doctorate—awarded only after a harassing probe of her dissertation—she went on to become an eminent theologian whose book, *She Who Is,* is a staple of theology in general and feminist theology in particular.

One act of conscience cost her dearly, however. While waiting for Catholic University to decide on her strong bid for tenure, she signed a statement in support of the dissident theologian Reverend Charles Curran, who was under fire for certain theological views. She was subsequently turned down for tenure; Fordham thereafter welcomed her.

Another sister-scholar, Sister Margaret Brennan, told of a member of her community and a colleague at the Toronto School of Theology, Mary Malone, who was similarly jolted during her sabbatical in Ireland. One Sunday at Mass, as she heard the words of the Nicene Creed, "I believe in God the Father Almighty . . ." she recoiled as if hit by an electric charge. She sat down and left church exclaiming that she could no longer pray or worship in the Church. She made her views known in a public statement and soon lost her faculty job.

Devotional practice, with all its symbolism and central importance, often became the occasion for such turning points. As the drama has usually played out, a crisis of faith in the traditional ways of praying and worshiping precedes a break from the old and openness to emerging "forbidden" practices. Sister Mary Luke Tobin, the Sister of Loretto who alone among American nuns witnessed Vatican II and became an influential national leader, has noted the strong tie between "feminist solidarity and spirituality." A sister who remained in her congregation but quit going to Mass described the crossover. "You can experience trauma at first," she said of entering the realm of women's worship. "Then you break a taboo like celebrating the Eucharist as a woman. Once you do it, you're not afraid anymore."

Reuther's *Women-Church* was one of several books that gave voice to a rethinking of theology and spurred an explosion of liturgical experimentation that had been growing for more than a decade under the guidance, for the most part, of sisters. It was a process of discovering forms of worship that practiced equality and shared leadership while avoiding the habits of clericalism. Some concepts were tried and discarded; more often, groups entered into a continuing exercise in revision and reshaping. Most important, the custom of women gathering by themselves to pray and celebrate was taking root. By 1983 the momentum was sufficient to bring 1,200 feminists to Chicago for the first national "Womanchurch" assembly. The awkwardness of the separatist impulse was summed up in the title. Dr. Mary Jo Weaver, a noted feminist scholar from Indiana University, argued in her book, *New Catholic Women,* that the explanation was subtle but sure. "The key to understanding Womanchurch is its claim to be the church," Dr. Weaver wrote. "The participants in Chicago did not see themselves as exiles from the church but in exodus from patriarchy."

Not coincidentally, as Professor Margaret Susan Thompson of Syracuse points out, scores of Catholic bishops were simultaneously attending a "workshop on women." The themes of women's liberation were kicking up dust within the Church and the putative bearers of patriarchy had decided they needed to do something about it.

Meanwhile, the minority of radicals from the Chicago crowd and elsewhere was losing patience with what they regarded as the wishy-washy behavior of those in the middle. To the militant, nothing could justify ambivalence and compromise in the face of the crushing burden of patriarchy. Their appeal resonated with the civil rights movement's insistence on unqualified liberation. It was all or nothing, an ultimatum that demanded either a total overhaul of the Church's structures of ordained ministry and authority or withdrawal from its institutions. Some sisters were persuaded; most weren't, at least not entirely. Perhaps the solid majority held back for the reason that Sister Kane had described: feminism just wasn't considered religious. Whereas nuns increasingly acted in accord with objectives of women's liberation, they seldom did so on the grounds of feminism.

Attitudes toward male authorities varied greatly, of course, according to circumstance and personality. Most nuns had become accustomed to some kind of supervisory oversight by priests and/or bishops, providing a measure of security that even passionate feminists couldn't knock. One example was Sister Joyce Weller, the exuberant president of the Daughters of Charity of Los Altos, California. The Daughters of Charity order had stemmed from the movement founded in France by Vincent de Paul and had a strong heritage of working with the poor. The Los Altos community, with its mother house in the Bay Area hills, pursued that mission with vigor. Feminism had made a moderate impact, Sister Weller said. On that issue, she described the community as middle-of-the-road. One bone of contention among the sisters was the tradition of requiring a Vincentian priest as chaplain with responsibilities over certain key personnel and financial matters.

"When feminism first came along, some asked, why do we have these men?" Sister Weller said. The response from superiors was that the interaction between the Daughters of Charity and the priests was mutually supportive rather than top-down. "It was not a relationship to a hierarchy but to a brother on a horizontal plane. From the outside it might seem patriarchal, but it isn't patriarchal." The tension "lessened dramatically," she said, "because priests told us how much we mean to them."

The discomfort worked both ways, however. Perhaps for every sister who dismissed feminism as alien to the nature of her vocation, another felt that the need for feminist progress was shoving her in the direction of leaving her community. The dropouts agreed that the feminist mind-set clashed with the conventional meaning of religious vocation and justified abandoning the convent and, in many cases, the practice of Catholicism. "It's hard for me to speak of the Church as an organization," one ex-sister said mournfully. "I gave up church-going. It's just too painful." Nobody can tell for sure how many of the thousands of sisters who departed during the great exodus were motivated explicitly by feminist logic and perceptions of hierarchical counterattack, but many sisters believe a significant minority fit that description. Through feminist theology and worship many had become convinced that feminism *was* implicitly religious; what made them uneasy was that a valid feminist Christianity was incompatible with institutional Catholicism. That discomfort helped push them out of the institution.

As the influence of feminism spread, the lines separating radical reformers from moderate women's rights advocates and reactionaries became both clearer as polarities deepened and became more visible, and yet more blurry as sisters and ex-sisters often found themselves in states of uncertainty and ambiguity over which aspects of feminism to accept and which to reject. Were they called to remain inside religious communities? Did feminism demand leaving communities that were canonical, under Rome? What was acceptable worship? Had nuns' traditional roles as teachers and nurses exploited them? In these traditional settings were they being treated in keeping with their choice to sacrifice gladly and willingly to God—or were they victims of a sexist system that played upon their sense of guilt and institutional inferiority to keep the system humming? What could or couldn't be tolerated any longer in terms of working conditions and compensation? What about the male monopoly of the clergy? And so on. Whatever their feminist convictions—or lack thereof—feminist theology had turned over the earth under their feet like a plow digging a field.

The climate for change ushered in by the new scholarship and activism had significant, if modest impact, but one climactic event catapulted feminist concerns into the mainstream media. That was the salvo delivered by Sister Kane to Pope John Paul II before a national television audience in 1979. What was intended as a brief, routine greeting from the president of the Leadership Conference of Women Religious became an explosive moment that placed feminist concerns squarely, and literally, at the feet of the Church's highest authority.

The story begins when Sister Kane received a call in the fall of 1979 from an official of the National Shrine of the Immaculate Conception in Washington, D.C. John Paul would soon be visiting the shrine during his first papal trip to the United States. Could she welcome him on behalf of the Leadership Conference? Sister Kane agreed. "Nuns were so inconsequential [in these arrangements]," she recalled, "that the guy from the Shrine asked me what my title was, and then just said I was being put on the program. I asked how long?

'Very short,' he said. 'People are coming to hear the pope, not you.' " She agreed. "I felt sisters didn't get recognition," she said, "and they've done a tremendous amount for the Church."

This Mercy sister was the avatar of the unexpected. For years she had been a chosen leader of her congregation as well as national organizations of sisters, yet she projected no hint of ambition for such responsibilities. She was good-natured, good-humored, unassuming, bright, gracious, and accepting—and dedicated to toppling patriarchy. As she considered how to use her three-minute spot with the pope, she quickly discarded the usual stockpile of clichés and the niceties, deciding instead "to say something for women in the Church." She talked to Sister Elizabeth Carroll, the well-versed Mercy leader from Pittsburgh, and others. What began to emerge was a challenge to ideas the pope held sacred, though she anticipated that hierarchical censors would erase criticism of Church policy from the text she was required to submit in advance.

To her amazement, nobody asked to review her copy.

Then came the day. She processed up the aisle with the entourage and took her seat. Hers was the third welcome; a priest and a cardinal went before. As she waited, she wondered whether she could go through with it. "I thought if I got too nervous, I could leave it out," she said. "But that passed. It would be too cowardly."

On cue, she arose and began to speak. Her voice was steady and sure:

> As I share this privileged moment with you, Your Holiness, I urge you to be mindful of the intense suffering and pain which is part of the life of many women in the United States. I call upon you to listen with compassion and to hear the call of women who comprise half of humankind. As women, we have heard the powerful messages of our church addressing the dignity and reverence for all persons. As women, we have pondered these words. **Our contemplation leads us to state that the Church in its struggle to be faithful to its call for reverence and dignity for all persons must respond by providing the possibility of women as persons being included in all ministries of our church. I urge you, Your Holiness, to be open and respond to the voices coming from the women of this coun-**

*try who are desirous of serving in and through the Church as fully
participating members.*

Loud applause burst through the cathedral. It lasted nearly four minutes.
Fifty nuns rose to their feet to salute Sister Kane. All over the country, in convents and apartments, city town houses and suburban developments, Catholic
feminists cheered, staring at Sister Kane's sturdy countenance in disbelief. The
doughty sister from New York had unleashed a geyser of pent-up frustration
and grievance from those who longed for change and others who hadn't
known until that moment that they longed for change. In less time than it takes
to hard-boil an egg, Sister Kane had brought attention to the plight of Catholic
women as no other effort had ever done. The elation of her supporters was
matched by the scorn of her detractors, who called her actions wrongheaded
and insulting to the guest of honor. Not only had she spoken out of turn, her
critics said, but she had then defied protocol by boldly walking over to John
Paul after her oration to give him a personal greeting. The rules forbade such
gestures unless a person was summoned by the pope.

In the days following her short speech she was deluged by five thousand
letters and telegrams and four hundred phone calls. Soon the *Washington Post*
ran an entire section of letters, all against Sister Kane's appeal. She was pressed
to visit every cardinal in the country to explain herself.

The Catholic world was sharply divided over Sister Kane's outspoken advocacy. At the very least, it had been a breakthrough. From that point, the debate over women's role in the Church was public and highly visible. Her bold
statement also connected nuns and other Catholic feminists as they had never
been before. "Theresa Kane was the high point," Professor Margaret Susan
Thompson said. "She demonstrated that women can be strong. She helped
build bridges between those in religious life and those who were not. Those
who were not said, 'Wow, there's a sister doing this. We have much more that
joins us than separates us.' "

Chapter Ten

Backlash

I n 1995 John Cardinal O'Connor had a thing or two to say about nuns. The commanding archbishop of New York had recently returned from a high-profile trip to Rome. Pope John Paul II had picked him to be one of three prelates to preside over a thirty-day world Synod of Bishops on the topic of religious life. As he told his listeners, he had been seated right next to John Paul and escorted him to and from his vehicle, and he had had the opportunity to "chit-chat" with the pontiff. At the end, after making three hundred set speeches to the Synod, the cardinal said he had gathered his thoughts in an unpublished paper that he had chosen to disclose to this group in Chicago.

The cardinal's spirited defense of tradition, titled "The Significance of Bishops for the Rebirth of Religious Life," argued that too many nuns were trying to refashion religious life to their own liking in defiance of Church teaching and in an effort to steal power from priests and bishops. He alluded to a "relentless pursuit of power, power sought at the expense of faith, exclusive power to determine for ourselves" as the scourge of the allegedly rebellious nuns. The authority structure as it existed was divinely ordered, he said, and to threaten it was a sin. "Power is sought at the expense of faith," proclaimed the prelate, who had walked the corridors of Church power for most of his adult life. "Too often it is sought by those whose faith in God and in the Church has been seriously weakened." (Regardless of whether the nuns he was indicting lacked faith, they certainly couldn't claim to have grabbed much power over the centuries.)

If Cardinal O'Connor was the preacher, the audience was the choir at the 1995 national meeting of the Institute on Religious Life, an organization formed by traditionalists in 1974 to combat the liberalizing trends in religious life and to find ways to increase recruits. It was a movement close to the cardinal's heart. In 1991, he had founded his own religious order, the Sisters of Life, to show how a community could be run by strict adherence to the Vatican's stringent view of renewal, with emphasis on obedience to religious superiors and pre–Vatican II understanding of the vows. The Sisters of Life cared for AIDS patients and engaged in other charitable activities at the cardinal's behest. They wore habits. They assented to decisions made in their interest by those above them. They lived together in a community, not in twos or threes in apartments of their own choosing. They were like the nuns whom Catholics tended to remember, and they exhibited what Cardinal O'Connor, a conservative in all things theological, sometimes a contentious one, promoted in religious life.

Ever the superb orator and crowd charmer, the cardinal assumed the posture of a kindly judge who professed humility and sorrow before pronouncing life sentences on the guilty parties. Burdensome as his task might be, the judge would explain that he was compelled to do his distasteful duty. He took direct aim at all those sisters who ignored or disdained what the Institute on Religious Life stood for. He wanted *them* to get the message.

"The Church's 'nature,' " according to the cardinal, derived from a constitution that Christ had set down to guide the Church. "Of course, this is acceptable only to those who truly believe that the Church—One Holy Roman Catholic and Apostolic Church is in fact Christ's Church—the Church constituted by Christ, the Church illuminated by Christ and the Holy Spirit and that the Pope is the Vicar of Christ on earth." This set of instructions permits no amendments or changes. It is fixed and to be obeyed without question. By going off on their own misguided tangents, the cardinal was saying, nuns had strayed from the true path. Sisters were taking decisions away from bishops. They determined their own ministries rather than awaiting assignments from bishops. They shunned traditional authority and wandered off in "unconstitutional" directions, for example, instituting democratic forms of community government. They rejected the priest-centered Eucharist in favor of half-baked worship.

The premise behind the drive to push back the advances was that the Church's operating plans had been fixed from on high and couldn't be amended. As Cardinal O'Connor said that day in Chicago, Roman Catholicism was bound by a set of regulations set forth by Jesus.

Worse than the misled sisters, he added, were those who used "the occasion for true reform and renewal in order to accomplish their own objectives quite different from the objectives of Vatican II." The wayward had rebelled, in O'Connor's analysis, in part because the social revolution of the late 1960s and 1970s had produced, among other things, the ancient regime's greatest nemesis, feminism. "Radical feminism," the cardinal said, "emerged along with radical skepticism." True faith, embraced by true nuns, couldn't coincide with skepticism.

Some bishops also deserved a slap on the wrist for failing to make clear that Rome's presumed dictates on renewal were nonnegotiable. This was a variation on the great "confusion" theme, whereby foes of liberalism in the Church blame bad education instead of acknowledging that those with whom they disagree might choose to reject portions of what they had been taught. But perhaps they hadn't been taught well enough about the Church's prohibition against birth control; perhaps they had been taught well and found the teachings deficient. In any event, Cardinal O'Connor said, some nuns had been led to unrealistic expectations. "Many changes they introduced, sincerely believing them to be faithful to Vatican II," he said, "were ultimately rejected and indeed sincere religious themselves were even criticized for introducing such changes."

The former navy admiral told the adoring crowd that his words to them were his private thoughts, but anyone who had been as close as he had to the pope's ear for a month could reasonably be expected to be echoing the papal view as much as any bishop in the nation could. What he had to say reflected years of struggle by the Institute's constituency—representing between 10 and 20 percent of all priests, monks, and nuns—to overturn the changes brought on by the most ardent advocates of renewal. O'Connor appeared to be the Vatican's newest point man in this effort to roll back what many nuns called progress. The assaults from Rome on the course of that renewal in the United States ranged from muted to mailed fist. Renewal had been, to say the least, immeasurably damaged by the skirmishing.

Though trenchant, his argument was based on claims that were far from established facts. The "nature" of male and female, for example, was still a hotly debated topic. Opposing camps looked to the Bible or science, or both, for proof. Whole communities of sisters were seriously questioning the long-held conviction that sharply different sex roles were assigned by God. Further, Vatican II itself had discarded the cardinal's premise that "perfection" was still the standard for religious life.

Traditionalists argued that feminism undermined Church authority by distorting the self-image of women. As keepers of the old way, the traditionalists were dedicated to correcting what they saw as these grave errors. "In my judgment," O'Connor said, "so-called radical feminism is in reality a denial of the true nature of womanhood, in accordance with which one is constituted into Christ's body. Some are constituted as men; some constituted as women." Refusal to accept these distinct roles "leads to an unholy anger that we are not what 'we' want to be rather than what God has created us to be—again the sin of Adam and Eve."

But Cardinal O'Connor was declaring that the protracted war against the more open-ended interpretation of Vatican II renewal was still being waged after three decades. His rhetorical assertions held fast to pre-Council absolutes such as the superiority of religious life over the life of the rest of the laity ("[nuns] set aside as sacred for the exclusive service of the Church as distinct from even the holiest of lay persons") and abject subservience ("Those who are vowed to empty themselves as Christ emptied Himself, taking upon themselves the form of *slaves* [italics mine]"). Faith meant surrendering to the judgments of superiors ("even terminological changes can be significant, such as the exchange of the term 'superior' for 'president' [which many communities had done]"). The so-called democratic implications of such change undercut the structure of religious life ("In some cases the 'individual discernment' of the religious is considered sufficient for the superior to abandon a work deemed important by the bishop."). And, of course, they undercut the insistence that nuns must live together, wear the habit, and work where the bishop asks them to instead of figuring out a career for themselves.

In this view, truth entered the Church from the top and trickled down. It did not bubble up from the bottom, no matter what certain theologians of Vatican II might insist.

As O'Connor stated the case for those on the reactionary front—from the pope to prominent U.S. bishops—a case against what they saw as the wanton excesses of renewal threatening the Church—individualism, power seeking, and faithlessness were believed to be at the core of the rot. Their opponents weren't just contending over various possible interpretations of Vatican II's instructions to the nuns; they were the Church's mortal enemies, well-meaning, perhaps, but dim-witted and duped, having fallen prey to the most corrupt secular forces, not just wrongheaded dissidents against the official line but ultimately enemies of *God*. Confronting the central authority of the Church was tantamount to apostasy. Apparently nuns alone suffered from such temptations and had to be put back in their place. To O'Connor, this was just another skirmish in a long campaign to put the genie back in the bottle, but given his stature and his private access to the pope, his was more than just another salvo. It signaled the Vatican's univocal demands in the wake of the Synod on religious life, a bureaucratic exercise from which nothing was expected.

The central message: bishops must rule from the knowledge of truth that was conferred upon them alone by virtue of their office. Christ had given them supreme responsibility for keeping Catholics on course. If the Vatican Council's words were twisted or misread, bishops alone, in their capacity as final arbiters of the Church's truth—as the "Magisterium" invested by Christ—must root out the errors. Setting the Church straight was a tough job, Cardinal O'Connor told the audience, but, in effect, he and other bishops had to do it. "To fail to correct when correction is necessary," he said, ". . . is to fail God."

The campaign against this alleged "radical feminist anti-Church renewal" enlisted a formidable minority of bishops, priests, and nuns. Practically every progressive congregation, beginning in the 1960s, had run into resistance. Thirty years later, the strains of renewal had taken an incalculable toll on communities of nuns that were struggling for mere survival. The huge drop in numbers was, in part, a reflection of low morale from years of infighting between conservatives and liberals. The social turmoil of the times had also led to questioning and defection, with more young women turning to expanding career opportunities outside the Church. This attrition, of course, often crippled morale. But in the long run, Rome's continued opposition proved to be the most costly deterrent in the effort by congregations to complete renewal and restore vitality. In other circumstances the Vatican might have provided encouragement and assistance to speed the process. Some American bishops were sympathetic. But key members of the hierarchy from the pope down felt, conscientiously, that something was astir among U.S. sisters that threatened the very integrity of Roman Catholicism.

Without the need to fend off a stream of both blunt and excruciatingly polite assaults, the advocates of a more progressive renewal might have been able to move ahead with much greater vitality. Internal tensions would have remained, but the dynamic might have placed the Church's highest authority on the side of the majority rather than boosting the cause of reaction. As it was, valuable energies were spent keeping the opposition to renewal at bay. Renewal lacked the freedom from harassment to pursue its purposes. The haggling had retarded its growth.

The stark reality of that fight—and the key—was that Rome pumped moral, political, and perhaps financial support behind the campaign to roll back many of the vast changes in nuns' work, dress, living arrangements, and prayer practices. It was Rome's backing of the 10 to 20 percent traditionalist minority that kept reaction perking. In geopolitical terms, it was as if conservative U.S. nuns were Rome's client state contending with the more indigenous American drive to fulfill what it saw as the true promise of the Vatican Council's call for reform.

It was fundamentally a clash of cultures: hierarchical and traditional versus American and self-determined. Given what the Second Vatican Council Perfectae Caritatis said and left unsaid, it was a clash waiting to happen. What was said, albeit in terms often vague and incomplete, was that nuns were ordered to sweep the cobwebs from their communities and rediscover their purposes to suit their place in the modern world. They were told explicitly to refresh their understanding of the Gospels, to ascertain what their founder had intended them to do, and to experiment with means to achieve their ends. It was a big, open-ended assignment.

Priests and bishops received no such instructions, although the Council had dramatically revised the basic definition of the Church. Before the Council, Catholicism was essentially defined as the hierarchy, whence all truth and authority were believed to flow. It was the "perfect society" ruled over by those whose vocation was perfection (the image John Paul II invoked at the start of the Synod of Bishops on religious life, some would say anachronistically). Vatican II replaced the image of the upward triangle with the metaphor of the "people of God," a much more egalitarian concept buttressed by the belief that *everyone,* not just bishops, priests, and nuns, was engaged in the search for "holiness." Theoretically, there was no room for an elite or superiority based on rank.

But despite a dramatic shift in the basic metaphor, from monarchical and authoritarian to democratic and humble, the Council left untouched the ways in which the Church was actually governed. Even though Joe Catholic and John Paul II were equals in God's eyes, Joe Catholic still had nothing to say about what the Church taught and how it was taught. Bishops were exhorted to practice "shared authority" by which underlings were given a voice, but doing so was optional, and there were no guidelines on how it was to be done. In the end, decisions were the bishops' alone, save for their obligation to follow the dictates of their ecclesiastical superiors. At best, the consultative process could deliver advice that the bishop or the pope was free to accept or reject. The pope, for example, began consulting with Synods of Bishops soon after Vatican II. These sessions had produced reams of testimony and thousands of pleas and suggestions. But the pope, in his final, authoritative view, was free to either ignore or reject challenges to Church teaching. Consultation may have exposed the pope to more views, but it seemed to have little if any effect on his thinking.

The clear and direct line of command had been continued barely untouched, therefore, from pre-Council days. During the hundred years previous to Vatican II, the hierarchical model had been hardened and upwardly centered probably more than at any time in Church history. The revolutionary climate of nineteenth-century Europe had so threatened the Vatican that the popes had centralized power as a countermeasure. The arrangement had remained that way, resting on an old claim that Christ had left a "deposit of faith" with Peter, the first pope, who ruled over the Church together with his duly ordained bishops. Vatican I in 1869–70 had reinforced this conviction. The blueprint for the Church was top-down by Christ's own intention and for that reason it couldn't be changed. From that point, authority increasingly gravitated to Rome and it remained there. Vatican II did nothing essentially to change that, except to require bishops at most to go through the motions of "consulting" their people before delivering their decisions. They were not the subject of a Vatican Council document instructing them to undergo a searching analysis of their way or life or the nature of their offices. They weren't asked to update or renew or meet together to examine the nature of their authority. They were free to repeat their traditional formulas in describing their functions.

The power grid at Vatican II thus remained intact, which made Cardinal O'Connor's complaint about the sinfulness of nuns wanting power that wasn't rightfully theirs logically consistent if not ironic given the official rationale for hierarchical power. The Council, made up of the world's bishops, never required the hierarchy to investigate its long and difficult history on authority. Nuns were asked to recover their roots and immerse themselves in the Gospels, but bishops had not asked the same of themselves. It was like asking executives of an old-style, vertically structured American corporation to step into a modern team-oriented company without having undergone a thorough reeducation themselves.

The cardinal and his cohorts had been so marinated in the culture of the bishop as king of his diocese—the culture that upheld the claim of divinely instituted prerogatives and unilateral authority—that they had trouble understanding how a subgroup beneath them could aspire to decide things for themselves. Concern for their own authority made them especially sensitive to how others were obeying—or not. American Catholics were, on the whole, rejecting the Church's teachings on a variety of mostly sexual matters, starting with the ban on artificial birth control, so the bishops were under duress. Faced with a renewal climate they couldn't begin to understand, having not experienced anything similar, all they could see was sisters moving toward taking charge of more of their own lives and relying less on Church authorities. The bishops rightly identified obedience as the vow most in jeopardy in the renewal climate. On the other hand, most sisterhood congregations saw part of their mandate as abolishing the authoritarian model of the mother superior as arbiter of all things and rejected total submission as self-destructive. For them, obedience came to mean listening to God first, Church officials later. At their special chapters of renewal in the late 1960s, the governing structures of communities veered quickly toward representative democracy, with a strong council working with a "president," or even further toward a form of Quaker consensus that sometimes proved unworkable. Once Sisters of St. Joseph and Benedictines and Dominicans and scores of other orders had adopted systems of participation, as a salute to God's will, it became impossible to accept uncritically the unmediated authority of male clerics acting within the larger system and demanding unquestioned obedience.

A leading theologian of the time defined the abrupt turnabout. In the *St. Louis Review* in 1969, Father Gregory Baum wrote that those in authority needed to catch up with the changing role of leader. "Today we know that the leader does not have the answer beforehand," Father Baum wrote. "He does not know. He is in need of the cooperation and critical response of their entire community in order to discern the way in which to solve the problem at hand." At one time, he continued, it was assumed that leaders "had the answers." But in all fields of endeavor, he said, "no one has all the answers"; problems must be resolved "in a process in which all must participate."

The Vatican quickly took note of this hot-button issue. In a speech to the Assembly of the Italian Conference of Major Superiors of Women just months after the Council ended, Cardinal Ildebrando Antoniutti, head of the Sacred Congregation of Religious, emphasized the traditional exercise of authority, neither authoritarian nor shared, "service not dominion." The vocation of a nun was the "state of perfection," he said, using the phrase that had been rejected as an elitist anachronism by Council progressives. Major superiors must avoid coercion and "even the appearance of secret control, spying or any police-like methods," he said. But letting the community have its way was also wrong. "You must not permit yourself to be easygoing, tolerant, weak," the cardinal said. "Remember that when you fail to correct or punish, life itself will correct with merciless blows." Exercise "maternal correction," he advised; "radical feminism" had "smothered [women's] natural instincts toward humble and retiring self-growing." Cardinal Antoniutti had identified the problem. He would struggle with its implications for many years.

Shortly after the Council, most American nuns had moved far beyond the system of traditional control promulgated by bishops—and many bishops were mad as hell. The nuns, having been so confined and restricted, made decisions that sometimes bore the marks of anger and rebelliousness, further fueling the flames. For the sisters, the process of renewal was painstaking and painful, keeping one eye on the Church they loved, the other on what they had uncovered in the Scriptures and in their congregation's often forgotten origins. Though fired by a new vision, sisters still found it difficult to be bold on issues that counted, like dress and living conditions and work for the Church. Their behavior, on the whole, was still very deferential, nothing like the "rebellious" label often pinned on them by their scornful opponents.

Vatican officials and some American bishops, meanwhile, saw this clash as an uprising of uppity nuns not just against good order but also against the true faith. In the Church constitution that O'Connor had spoke about, everyone had a set place. The pushy nuns who had grasped some independence were seen as refusing to keep their place in this stepladder structure. That the servant class, nuns, would have the audacity to abandon their rightful positions to assert their right to self-determination was pure arrogance, however innocently misguided their efforts might be. They were mavericks trying to topple the established order. For pastoral reasons, as the bishops understood them, the nuns had to be put in their place for the good of Church order.

In Catholicism, a common refrain was that the "Church is not a democracy." The two systems by which hierarchy and nuns tended to operate were, therefore, worlds apart, the two sides were speaking different languages, on a collision course. One smacked of paternalism; the other smacked of revolution. While sisters had lived under the hierarchy's terms, the bishops often showed little sign of grasping the meaning of renewal. Tragically, the two camps confronted each other in an effort to be true to their calling. Neither side started the war out of animosity toward the other. Destiny simply steered them in directions with an almost inevitable outcome. No one in particular was to blame. The effects, however, were anguish and resentment and defeat on both sides.

Mary Jo Leddy, whose book, *Reweaving Religious Life: Beyond the Liberal Model,* offered a much-admired critique of both conservatives and liberals, believed that whatever the toll of internal, factional disputes, interference from Rome helped stifle crucial debate within congregations, which as a result found it necessary to close ranks. "Vatican meddling made it more difficult for us to set our agenda," she said in remarks to a Catholic audience. "If they'd left us alone we'd be far more self-critical."

Intrusion had already become the watchword, however. Before the curtain fell on the Second Vatican Council, officialdom had already tipped its hand by taming a major source of independent thinking among American nuns, the Sister Formation Conference. By uprooting it from its relatively autonomous situation within the National Catholic Educational Association and placing it under the Conference of Major Superiors of Women, where it would be required to report to Rome through the superiors, the Vatican had effectively restrained the group's maverick tendencies. The dramatic capstone to this episode was the heavy-handed ouster of Mother Piennett as superior of the Mt. Angel Benedictines in Oregon in light of the stand she took in favor of allowing Sister Formation to remain a semi-independent voice.

Piennett's order believes she was singled out as a troublemaker because at the climax of the struggle over the Sister Formation Conference's future, in 1964, she was the only superior to vote against subsuming Sister Formation under the Conference of Major Superiors of Women. Before she died, she confided to other sisters that she had been told that her vote would trigger repercussions. It wasn't possible to know for sure, of course, because, in keeping with Vatican secrecy, the charges against her were never made public, nor were reasons given for her summary removal as superior. The archbishop from Portland simply appeared one day, sisters were called to the chapel, and the verdict was pronounced.

Some sisters left the order in reaction to the ouster; others took time away to get some distance. But Mother Piennett didn't go anywhere; she stayed right there in Mt. St. Angel, fading back into the ranks to devote herself to the work left for her to do. Meanwhile, an undercurrent of confusion and bitterness remained.

Witnesses to the tense aftermath recall that at the time the community never discussed the traumatic events. It would be more than thirty years before the remaining sisters aired their feelings and thoughts with one another in an open meeting with the help of a psychologist. Looking back, Sister Alberta Dietrich remembered the shattering disillusion. "There was anger at the Church," she said. "You could not say Holy Mother Church because there was nothing holy or motherly about it."

What befell Mother Piennett was, in many ways, an ecclesiastical putsch of the old order when clerics typically assumed overall control of women religious. What made her case different was that her strife with Rome appeared to emerge from her enthusiasm for the self-development of nuns, both a major theme of the Sister Formation movement and a driving force in the incipient renewal movement that was to follow.

The act of deposing Mother Piennett appeared to be an early warning sign that Rome had seen in her an inkling of danger. In her defiance of Rome's wishes and in her loyalty to a Sister Formation vision of greater autonomy, she may have signaled a gathering storm. But that was just a prelude. Vatican II ended in 1965, having instructed nuns to renew, and the hierarchy and the sisterhoods soon found themselves having to figure out what renewal meant for their relationship.

The first big test, three years after Vatican II, in the midst of the required chapter meetings on renewal, was the calamity that pitted Cardinal James McIntyre of Los Angeles and his allies at the Vatican against the Immaculate Heart of Mary nuns. If the unusually progressive, socially activist nuns were pointed toward the twenty-first century, the cardinal looked back to the nineteenth. While they held congregational chapter meetings to endorse and advance the boundaries of renewal, he had tried in Inspector Javert fashion to subvert them at every turn, alarmed that they would wreck the traditional order of the Church. He persuaded Rome to send an investigator who demanded that the sisters return to their habits, teach in the Catholic schools, and obey the bishop's orders. Cardinal Antoniutti, head of the Sacred Congregation of Religious, denounced the IHM reforms as "falling into serious error" and "completely contrary to religious life" in a warning letter he sent to every religious superior in the United States. No change was to be made without Vatican approval.

In the end, of course, the IHMs refused to concede that the Vatican had any monopoly on the legitimate interpretation of renewal and would not back down. Most were ejected from archdiocesan schools. Pressure from the cardinal, who appeared to be sincere in his own effort to act for the good of the Church, forced 90 percent of the IHMs to surrender their status as members of an officially approved religious community.

As noted earlier, the highly visible nature of the drama drew sensational media attention across the country. It became a test case for renewal, both revealing and misleading. No community was more admired among progressive congregations than the Los Angeles IHMs. If lightning had struck there, it might reasonably be expected to land anywhere. Many other congregations noted that their own policies were no different from those followed by the IHMs. On the other hand, the case of the IHMs in L.A. was atypical inasmuch as the cardinal was at the extreme reactionary end of those bishops who resisted the whole of Vatican II. He was among the minority who saw no need for such widespread revision. To that extent, then, a battle of this kind was less likely to erupt elsewhere. Still, the prospect was scary to many nuns.

The heads of women's and men's superiors conferences complained in a letter to the pope's apostolic delegate to the United States, the Most Reverend Luigi Raimondi, that Rome had sought neither group's views before deciding to throw the IHMs out of the Sacred Congregation of Religious. They warned of "grave concern over the effects of the James Cardinal McIntyre–IHM dispute" because, they said, it was not simply a local matter. Archbishop Raimondi refused to discuss the matter with them. When the women's superiors considered a resolution of support for the IHM community in 1968, a representative of the Sacred Congregation of Religious advised them that such an action would display disloyalty. He insisted that the IHMs were not being disciplined for enacting renewal but for breaking certain monastic rules. "The fundamental complaint underlying the protests recently lodged on behalf of the Sisters of the Immaculate Heart of Mary is really groundless," read an official statement from the Sacred Congregation of Religious in an effort to quash support for a protest (the statement also accused the IHM nuns of trumping up outside support in their favor). Despite "excellent intentions," it continued, some IHMs and other American nuns "have been found wanting." The Sacred Congregation of Religious believed that the dispute had been blown way out of proportion by a few partisans, that it was, in effect, a tempest in a teapot. But the fact that the motion of support by the women's superiors for the IHMs was defeated by a single vote didn't quell the widespread resentment. For the moment the Vatican had saved face. The defeat of the motion also emboldened the small but resource-ful, energetic communities that sided with the Vatican.

By the time the IHM dispute hit the headlines, changes along similar lines were being implemented across the nation. Nuns were out of habits, starting to live in small groups, even twos and threes, outside the convent, making decisions as a group instead of waiting for a superior to render judg-ments, taking charge of their own work lives. The trends were very alarming to Vatican officials who sought to reverse the tide, but the sisters would re-sist. From the opening salvo in Los Angeles, the period of most intense struggle would span fifteen years until the mid-1980s. The first five years would largely define the struggle and sap much of the renewal energies of the sisters.

One early contest was largely symbolic; a second was more concrete in its effects. The first involved the decision to change the name of the organi-zation of U.S. major superiors of women from the Conference of Major Su-periors of Women to the Leadership Conference of Women Religious. It sounded like a mundane, pragmatic footnote to the weightier task of rewrit-ing the bylaws. While Rome grudgingly tolerated the revised bylaws, how-ever, the title switch stuck in its craw. "Leadership" in the hierarchs' view implied autonomy, as if nuns could take matters in their own hands and actu-ally "lead" rather than follow in the conventional presumption of "loyal docility." The apostolic delegate to the United States, Luigi Raimondi, noted in a letter to Sister Thomas Aquinas (Elizabeth Carroll), president of the con-ference, that such a name change was "prejudicial to the discussions that have been undertaken on the subject." A string of objections from Rome fol-lowed. The nuns' proposal was, well, uppity. So even after the major superi-ors conference approved the change in 1971, Rome fought it, refusing to use it. Well into the early 1970s, officials of the LCWR would receive commu-nications addressed under the old title. Faced with the sisters' persistence, however, the Vatican eventually gave in.

The second flash point, and a much more serious one, occurred when Rome threw its support behind forces trying to minimize or roll back re-newal. One group of nuns in particular, named Consortium Perfectae Cari-

tatis after the title of the Vatican Council Constitution on religious life, mobilized in reaction against the established conference of major superiors when
that group was still known as the Conference of Major Superiors of Women.
With each new foray into experimentation taken by the CMSW, the Consortium steeled its resolve to reverse this trend. Consortium leaders denounced the CMSW's new bylaws before they were sent to Rome. "The
Holy See, I am sure," wrote one of the Consortium's principal leaders,
Mother Claudia Honsberger of the Philadelphia IHMs, "has not authorized
the Conference of Major Superiors of Women to draft a document which
has *carefully removed every vestige of dependence on the Church's divinely established
hierarchy*" (italics mine). With encouragement and backing from many in the
hierarchy both in the United States and at the Vatican, the Consortium
gained strength under the banner of the traditional convent, the same one
that Cardinal O'Connor championed nearly thirty years later in Chicago. By
1971, Rome gave its blessing to the Consortium, stopping just short of
granting it official recognition. For the time being, the newly renamed Leadership Conference of Women Religious would remain the only official
voice of U.S. sisters. Still, an insurgent force committed to overturning much
of what the LCWR stood for—and eventually replacing it—had received
the Vatican's seal of approval. The Consortium's efforts might have been seen
as widening legitimate debate over renewal by granting stature to the dissenting minority. A more widespread interpretation was that it was a strategic effort to bolster the fight against the progressive majority. The Consortium
would act, in effect, as Rome's surrogate. By 1975, the Institute on Religious Life, the broader-based group of conservatives (the one later addressed
by Cardinal O'Connor in Chicago), had taken shape, also with Rome's ap-
probation, and with similar aims. Nuns who recoiled from what they saw as
the flouting of Church law by a growing number of congregations—particularly in questioning traditional authority from the Vatican on down—were
candidates for joining the embattled Consortium. In turn, the Consortium
sought hierarchical help. Sister Vincent Marie Finnegan, the Consortium's
director, said assistance was forthcoming. "We began because major superiors
saw deviation from Church teaching," she explained. "We felt we couldn't
reform within [the Leadership Conference]. We had to have heavy backing
from cardinals and bishops."

The same degree of muscle was not being flexed on behalf of the LCWR. Not only did the LCWR and many of its individual major superiors face tough going and outright resistance; they now had an adversarial organization on their doorstep. The Consortium had friends in high places and immediately began lobbying for full canonical recognition. If they got it, they would be on a par with the LCWR. The Vatican had already taken sides. Never had Rome given official status to two groups of women superiors in the same country, but the LCWR grew anxious that such a political move might be in the works, with the aim of undercutting its strength.

Increasing uncertainty and tension had prompted the LCWR to establish a joint liaison committee with the U.S. bishops in 1969. They also tried, with limited success, to iron out differences with the Sacred Congregation of Religious and the pope (it was during this wrangling that John Cardinal Krol told Sister Margaret Brennan that Rome might be more cooperative if the sisters did what the pope told them to do). These sessions, when they did take place, sometimes helped clarify confusion and clear the air. At other times, they were heated and nonproductive, with the two sides talking past each other.

U.S. bishops were in a bind. While they were expected to carry out the Vatican's commands regarding nuns, many felt solidarity with American sisters' efforts to renew their communities and had the highest regard for the sisters' intelligence and talents. The bishops were indebted to nuns for enormous service to the Church. Now that the sisters were dropping out of traditional Church roles and becoming less available, strains grew between bishops and women's communities. Other basic changes such as the discarding of habits had also caused some problems. But, on the whole, the relationships between bishops and sisterhoods in many dioceses remained constructive and might have evolved into new, creative partnerships. The stumbling block was the pressure from the Sacred Congregation of Religious to constrain the major directions taken by the sisters. Faced with choosing between loyalty to the Vatican and loyalty to the nuns, bishops tried to stay neutral or, like Cardinal O'Connor, joined the Vatican bandwagon. Missing was a group of bishops friendly to sisters who were willing to protest Rome's policies or to take steps to blunt them.

Instead, by example, the bishops in the liaison group with the LCWR delivered a list of complaints about the general course of American religious life at the committee's regular meeting on April 25, 1971. The makeup of the liaison committee spoke volumes about the rift that separated the two sides. Heading the bishops was Bishop James J. Hogan of Johnstown-Altoona, Pennsylvania, who would be of the principal founders of the Institute on Religious Life just four years later. The sisters present were all officers of the progressive LCWR.

Bishop Hogan had invited all U.S. bishops to describe what they liked and didn't like about the renewal of religious life. Of the fifty-five replies received, most likely the bulk came from those bishops who were most angry about what they saw the sisters doing. Not surprisingly, therefore, most of the responses were sharply critical. The bishops expressed alarm over the growing numbers of nuns living outside the convent; the trend toward discarding the habit altogether; the increasing departure of nuns from Catholic schools. Among the most caustic complaints was that sisters displayed "a negative attitude toward and inordinate criticism of the Holy See." Many bishops, the report added, "are persuaded that, in good faith, misinterpretation of Vatican II documents crept in." It was fairly standard fare: disapproval of what nuns had begun to decide for themselves. Bishops aligned themselves with the "correct" reading of Vatican II documents by indicting the nuns' interpretation as "faulty." According to this hierarchical understanding, the bishops as the higher authority had the final say. The repeated hammering away at these matters occupied the time and energies of sisters who felt it necessary to respond in one way or another.

The sisters who came to Detroit to attend the liaison committee meeting canvassed their own constituency in order to formulate replies to the major items in the bishops' bill of particulars. In most of their responses they made efforts to meet the bishops halfway without surrendering the sisters' distinctive views. A consistent demand of the sisters, often couched in polite terms, was that Rome must consult with the sisters about issues and decisions if peaceful coexistence was to be expected. Their point was that the two groups didn't understand each other and needed to talk. They had case after case to offer in proof of their argument that no consultation had taken place. Just arranging meetings with Vatican officials, let alone the pope, had been enormously difficult, seemingly because the American sisters were regarded as rebels. To many U.S. sisters, the Vatican was the problem. "A great deal of dialogue is necessary to improve Sisters' attitudes toward the Holy See," wrote one major superior to the liaison group, linking improvement to a change in Rome's behavior. "We have just begun this type of dialogue and I believe that as we continue to improve communications with the Holy See as it relates to religious communities and when justice and charity are more manifest, the negative attitudes will disappear."

The next winter, the Sacred Congregation of Religious fired off two more edicts aimed at the habit and the power of the major superior. The first, the demand that sisters return to the habit, was a thumb in the eye inasmuch as most communities by that time had made the traditional garb optional. To make matters worse, the orders had ignored consultation and had gone straight to Cardinal Krol, president of the U.S. Conference of Catholic Bishops, rather than to the Sacred Congregation of Religious. The incident exposed the utter contrast in styles: conventional top-down hierarchical versus emergent forms of collaborative decision-making.

The other instruction, a decree that was likewise a unilateral action by the Sacred Congregation of Religious, insisted that the new forms of governing adopted by communities must leave the superior's authority basically intact. The alternatives developed by many congregations gave the superior— increasingly called "president" or some other more democratic-sounding title—a variety of the "first among equals" status, the polar opposite of the mother-superior-as-God concept from the past. As early as 1967, the first landmark Sister Survey revealed that two-thirds of the gigantic sample (64 percent) believed that communities "must drastically revamp the decision-making processes to include all members." While an equal proportion believed that superiors did express God's will, 60 percent said they looked beyond the superior for guidance, and 55 percent thought decisions by superiors should be open to criticism.

The decree handed down by the Sacred Congregation of Religious, however, revived an image of that largely rejected past. "Superiors," the decree said, "must have personal authority, without prejudice to the practice of legitimate consultation and to the limits placed by common or particular law."

Sister Carroll, as president of the LCWR, had leveled a stinging rebuke to Archbishop Luigi Raimondi, the apostolic delegate, for routing the dress code command indirectly through Cardinal Krol. But beyond the specifics, her dismay was indicative of a broader sense of futility and weariness. The document handed down by the Sacred Congregation of Religious, and the way it was handled, she said, "leaves me in a state of utter discouragement." She questioned why the statement "was not channeled through our Conference" and reminded the archbishop that religious superiors had "pleaded for prior consultation in matters that pertain to religious life." The Vatican's drive to scale back the renewal process even at this early stage—just four years into renewal—made her wonder if the Sacred Congregation of Religious "is respecting the period of experimentation legitimately given to religious communities." The original plan called for a fifteen-year period of experimenting with religious life, beginning in 1967. Countermeasures such as the reinstatement of the habit raised doubts in the minds of Sister Carroll and many other progressives about whether Rome intended to keep its promise and, if so, how. Having voiced her protest, she forwarded the decree to U.S. superiors with her own letter of dissent.

By the mid-1970s, the LCWR was increasingly concerned about the influence of its traditionalist rival, Consortium Perfectae Caritatis, which had achieved the foreign policy equivalent of Rome's "client state." For strategic and theological reasons, of course, the LCWR was eager to remain the sole, official representative of American nuns. Jockeying for Rome's favor was part of the high-stakes competition of Church politics, however differently the competitors might regard the legitimacy of such favor or the value of seeking it. Playing the political game was the best available means of becoming a recognized part of the national and global Church forum. The impact of this struggle for effecting policy and climate at top levels differed greatly from one congregation to another, from one region to another. Most local communities never became directly engaged in the headline-grabbing debates, although they were usually somehow influenced by them. The overriding issue for the local community was the rewriting of its constitution and its acceptance by the Sacred Congregation of Religious. Some communities, of course, had taken renewal a long way, embracing concepts that the Vatican rejected. Other elements, such as a pledge of loyalty to the pope, were deliberately left out of constitutions. The rejected documents were shipped back to sisters to be corrected in conformity with Rome. Many convents balked; they sent a series of drafts without fully conforming. Sometimes the process went on for many years.

Though local convents didn't always pay much attention to the broader issues—and sometimes didn't care about them—the struggle over the shape of the American sisterhood was largely being waged by a highly talented group of nuns in conflict among themselves and with Rome. By the mid-1970s, the LCWR believed that it was suspect in the eyes of the Sacred Congregation of Religious. Rumors spread that the LCWR was under investigation by the Sacred Congregation of Religious, an allegation that body denied. At a joint meeting with Sacred Congregation for Religious officials in 1973, the LCWR condemned its rival group, the Consortium Perfectae Caritatis, as a source of friction and divisiveness. They also complained that the Consortium had received encouragement from the U.S. hierarchy and that the Sacred Congregation of Religious had made matters worse by giving aid and comfort to the conservative group. The climate had grown increasingly tense as a result.

No investigation into the LCWR was proved to exist, but members of that group felt dogged and challenged by the relatively small, favored group (the Consortium) while they themselves were considered renegades and outsiders. The shadowboxing continued for most of the next two decades. Finally, in 1992, the Consortium Perfectae Caritatis, reorganized as the Council of Major Superiors of Women, was promoted to official standing. The rumors and suspicions of the LCWR were borne out somewhat belatedly, perhaps, but forcefully nonetheless. The United States became the only country in the Catholic world with two officially recognized groups of women religious, the smaller group of Vatican loyalists touting a minimalist version of renewal versus the self-determinists who pursued the experiment in re-forming religious life beyond the narrow confines of tradition.

Two events underscore the widening rift between the two groups. One came from introductory remarks by the new apostolic delegate, Archbishop Jean Jadot, to the LCWR's 1973 annual meeting. The archbishop was a Belgian who had served as a chaplain to the colonial Belgian army in the Congo. When the Belgians were defeated in the war of liberation, the victorious nationalists paid him unusual tribute by asking him to stay to assist in nation building. In the United States he gained stature as an urbane, warm-hearted progressive with a penchant for helping pick liberal bishops, eventually known collectively as "the Jadot bishops," for major dioceses. But in his address to the LCWR, just six weeks after his arrival at his new assignment, before he had had a chance to visit a sampling of communities, Archbishop Jadot signaled that he'd been briefed to expect troublemakers. In the overall spectrum of Vatican II renewal, he ventured, sisters were "in the lead—sometimes far ahead—perhaps, at times even too far ahead." Moreover, "in their quest for relevancy, they are pushing and pulling all the People of God. It is only human that they may sometimes seem to be *going too far and too fast* [italics mine], at least too fast for some members of the Christian community." It was a gentle reproach, but it was a reproach from a potentially powerful friend. It mattered little at the time whether the thoughts were his or if he was carrying water for Rome.

The other contributor to the rift between the two organizations of nuns was a widely discussed article by a Marian priest and theologian, Thomas Dubay, in the May–June issue of *Review of Religious,* the respected journal covering trends and ideas. In his provocative analysis, "Religious Life: The Real Polarity," Father Dubay attempted to sort sheep from goats, sisters who had run amok with renewal as compared to those who had kept the faith. The types he defined weren't mutually exclusive, he cautioned, and a convent might include a mixture of the two. In his schema, the Trend A's were the outlaw banditos, the Trend B's the law-abiding sheriffs. The banditos were chiefly marked by a lack of sufficient rationale for religious life, wanting to cozy up to the laity, relying on psychology and other social sciences instead of the Bible and church theology, avoiding hierarchical control, shunning rules, and discarding the customs of the traditional, tight-knit community. The sheriffs, on the other hand, retained the ideal of religious vocation as set apart and consecrated, considered theirs a "higher" calling distinct from other laity, and looked to the Bible and Catholic doctrine for guidance rather than to the newfangled disciplines. Further, these upright individuals accepted authority from bishops and superiors, favored the stricter rules from the past, and believed in living together and sharing the load the way things had always been done.

Father Dubay's posing of the tension and conflict between the two groups, otherwise generally labeled progressive or liberal (the A's) and conservative (the B's), attracted considerable attention because it reflected a view that was common among the male, ordained leadership, including the top-shelf hierarchy in Rome. Although the numbers were unbalanced, with an estimated 90 percent of sisters in the progressive camp, the encouragement of the Vatican had inflated the strength of the minority. In that sense, Father Dubay's conviction that a crisis was at hand *between* religious communities and *within* them struck a nerve, apart from the issue of whether he had correctly summed up the conflict.

"The two visions that I have traced out are so radically different that they are incompatible," he wrote. Such ruptures tore communities apart. Members might be civil to one another on the outside, he said, "but the minority are often bleeding in their hearts." As attractive as many of the Trend A ideas might be, he added, their "weaknesses . . . are serious, even fatal."

Liberals predictably dismissed the article as a caricature of progressive renewal and for presenting a false dichotomy between the two camps. But they also saw Father Dubay's effort as an important element in the broader effort to press the hierarchy's cause against alleged radicalism. Every initiative required attention, energy, perhaps response. Meanwhile, the sisters on the progressive side had become adept at countermeasures.

Tensions between the competing visions of religious renewal grew in large measure in the 1970s from a series of actions by progressive sisters to bolster their cause and to respond more or less indirectly to Rome's badgering. One was the publication of a volume of reaction to the pope. In 1971 Pope Paul VI had issued an instruction to nuns entitled Evangelistica Testificato. In it, he urged sisters to devote themselves to a ministry of social justice, which sounded wonderful to progressives. But he also seemed to insist on a retreat from the more extreme forms of renewal. He warned of "an exaggerated distrust of the past" and of a "mentality excessively preoccupied with hostility conforming to the profound changes which disturb our times." As a result, he said, some have rejected "the specific forms of religious life." At these passages, the progressives stopped cheering and saw a roadblock, a version of the "hostility" raised among Church leaders toward women's rights in general and nuns' liberation in particular.

The LCWR was the national meeting ground for charting top-level progressive strategies. One decision the group made was to publish a small volume entitled *Widening the Dialogue* that would call for expanded discussion of the purpose and function of religious life. Completed in 1974, it was another implicit protest against the one-way communication typified by the pope's decree. The alternative, as the progressive sisters saw it, was to give them a voice in Vatican policies that affected them. The Consortium group saw things from an opposite standpoint. They regarded the authority of the pope as sufficient in itself, his definitions in no need of review. This wasn't a legislative process, the conservatives insisted, it was the word from on high, whence the truth flowed.

A fresh copy of the slender book was given to officials of the Sacred Congregation of Religious at a liaison meeting in Rome. It soon came under fire from several prelates, branded as an effort to undercut what they believed to be the divinely instituted teaching authority structure of the Church. Some of the book's defenders contended, as they had before, that while they upheld the authority of the Church itself, they questioned the hierarchical manner in which it was exercised. *Widening the Dialogue* resulted in no greater consultation, but it signaled to the Vatican that the question of how policy is assembled would not simply go away. The majority of nuns in the United States had found a new way and, although they saw the need for revisions, they weren't desirous of turning the clock back to the closed convent.

The extent to which attitudes had changed in the volatile area of Church authority became evident in the survey called Patterns in Authority and Obedience conducted by the LCWR in the early 1980s. In all, 256 congregations took part. In the guise of simply offering the facts, the LCWR's survey results sent a deft message to Rome that insinuated that the Vatican could no longer impose its will on nuns because nuns were completely unwilling to accept authority in that traditional manner. Among the findings of the survey: communities in general had switched from "pyramidal, hierarchical to circular, horizontal models" in their own governing; participation was highly rated; many congregations had ceased believing that any one person could be "representative and interpreter of God's will with the God-given right and duty to legislate for and judge subjects"; overall, there was "a rejection of dependence, submission, subjection, dominance of one over others"; there was rising sentiment for the "legitimate" independence of the religious congregation from bishops and Rome.

There it was, the gap sketched as starkly as it could be, with the progressive leadership in the position of simply displaying it. Rome couldn't "blame" anyone for merely reporting the facts. The LCWR insisted that it hadn't set out to be provocative. Yet the results had shrewdly dealt Rome a blow by documenting an increasing disconnect between the two worlds.

The emergence of the Women's Ordination Conference provided another occasion for subtle defiance. Nuns responded fervently to this call from many sectors of religious life. Members of twelve different congregations helped plan the first spectacular meeting in Detroit, November 28–30, 1975. The coordinator of the task force was a Dominican, Sister Nadine Foley, who presented a paper, "Women in the Future Priesthood Now: A Call to Action."

Archbishop Paul Augustine Mayer, then the secretary of the Sacred Congregation of Religious, demanded that the LCWR refuse to support the Detroit assembly. The LCWR executive committee turned down the appeal and sent a token $50 donation to the ordination group. The following year, the pope proclaimed that women could never be ordained because they lacked the male anatomical resemblance to Jesus Christ. The pope's effort to squelch the women's ordination movement was met by widespread rejection among progressives and glee among Consortium members. The issue would become a major sore spot in nuns' relationship with Church authority and helped forge bonds between the progressive sisters and the growing number of other laywomen who had begun to see priesthood as an issue of gender justice.

Sister Theresa Kane's stunning appeal for women's ordination directly to Pope John Paul II, in Washington in 1979, bore ample witness to the continuing passion for that concern. The underlying aim, the equality of the sexes throughout the Church, was not yet divided between those who sought ordination and those who believed that the barnacles of patriarchy needed to be scraped off the priesthood before women should consider becoming part of it. But the debate that was emerging on that point only underscored the awakening that had occurred among many nuns. Renewal had shocked many into conscious awareness of the huge disadvantages women religious had suffered because of their gender and the low status assigned to them because of that. Pope Paul VI's thin reasoning that women couldn't be ordained because they lacked male anatomy made it easier to subject the whole system to censure and ridicule. The fact that Rome was obliged to uphold a teaching that didn't convince many leading theologians gave some advantage to the nuns. Pope John Paul II subsequently forbade even discussing the ordination issue; at the same time, he endeavored to calm the waters by emphasizing his opposition to sexism without changing a dot or tittle of Church teaching. The cause has remained very much alive.

At the behest of Vatican officials Sister Kane paid a call to Rome to explain her remarks to the pope. None of the officials had much to say. She went to see all the U.S. cardinals and found them less critical of her comments than of her choice of setting in which to make them. At the time, she was president of the LCWR. Inadvertently, she had single-handedly placed the concerns of women in the forefront of the Catholic Church in America.

Rome surely misjudged the obstacles that stood in its way, but it still held the upper hand in many respects. In the early 1980s the Vatican issued a new code of canon law. The revision trimmed the Byzantine tangle of rules found in the 1917 code, but many sisters still considered it too thick with regulations in the old style and reflecting an outmoded view of vocation. More troubling were the provisions in Pope John Paul's 1983 letter entitled Essential Elements of Religious Life, which basically reiterated a traditional vision of the sisterhood, not on a par with other laity but once again above it and removed from it. Essential Elements was the most aggressive effort yet to restrain what the Vatican saw as renegade renewal. Nuns had ventured too far into the world, the pope thought, and it was time to head back to the convent. Little of the renewal experienced by the majority of nuns could be found in the nine elements that were being promoted as criteria for sister communities. In terms of dress, housing, work, and prayer, the document echoed the now familiar refrain that the Sacred Congregation of Religious wished renewal had never happened the way it did, or perhaps at all. But hadn't it been up to them? The question now up for grabs for many sisters was who would decide which elements, indeed, were essential to communities, and how so? One thing was for sure: Essential Elements gave conservative nuns some ballast and sent shudders through liberals, but it seemed far too late to alter the course of most communities. A Mercy sister said her community had "survival reactions—threatening our new life just born of renewal. Some of us felt worried, others angered, most of us fearful and hurt, because we might be separated from that which we now own as a deep value in ourselves, in one another and in the Church."

The pope's Essential Elements letter did provide a handy measuring stick for some bishops. Archbishop James Whelan of Hartford, Connecticut, stressed in a memorandum to religious leaders in 1984 that he saw "two sharply different approaches to religious life." One group followed "the Nine Essentials." The other group adhered to "some of the Nine Essentials, but has adopted a noticeably more democratic approach to authority, work, living arrangements and religious garb." The two ways were "irreconcilable," the archbishop wrote, creating a "painful division" not only between the two groups but within each community between progressive younger members (many of them especially bright and dedicated, he conceded) and conservative older ones. A solution he favored would be to call the strict observers the true "religious" nuns and find another name for the others.

On the heels of that effort to fix standards, Pope John Paul II ordered a major study of U.S. congregations. The news triggered alarm and suspicion that the premise of the study, to discover why the number of nuns was taking a nosedive, would be used as a pretext to undermine the gains that many nuns cherished. The study was called "a pastoral service," but it sounded like a Trojan horse to many nuns. The warning flags went up.

That the outcome, on the whole, was not dire was due mostly to the extraordinary perception and skill of Archbishop John R. Quinn of San Francisco, the bishop appointed to conduct the study. In announcing the study to his fellow bishops on November 15, 1983, Archbishop Quinn sought immediately to quiet fears. "The Pope," he said, "is not calling for an investigation of religious life in the United States." Despite widespread doubts, the archbishop calmly and respectfully invested credibility in those words. He engendered conversation between bishops and nuns that most on both sides considered helpful. He was respectful. He was, in the view of the late executive director of the LCWR, Sister Margaret Cafferty, "the best friend we could have had." In many other hands, the study could have produced disaster. The final report asserted that the bishops had learned a great deal about the enhanced status of the individual and the value of women in religious life. It noted both a weakening of identity in many congregations and "a decline in respect for the Pope and the Magisterium of the Church." There remained "certain tensions . . . between some religious and the Holy See," the report stated.

The conclusion of the report contained a ringing appeal for better treatment of women in both society and the Church. Many women, it said, were disturbed by being left out of "policy and decision-making roles in the church. In light of this potential candidates find other modes of service and hesitate to enter religious life."

The Quinn report came as close to a defense of American sisters as the bishops had ever achieved. It became an exercise in understanding, leaving women's congregations hoping that bishops had obtained a better grasp of the creative upheaval that had gripped their communities over the past twenty years.

In the midst of Quinn's study, the storm arose over the *New York Times* advertisement sponsored by Catholics for a Free Choice, an ad hoc group that claimed Catholics could, legitimately, hold more than the one view on abortion taught by the Church. There were a variety of valid stands, the ad said. The ad was a reaction to Cardinal O'Connor's attack on the pro-choice position of Geraldine Ferraro, the Democratic candidate for vice president, during the heat of the election campaign. Cardinals Krol of Philadelphia and Law of Boston had also blasted her, but O'Connor's hard line, coming only a few months after he had been installed in New York, had an edge of strident machismo right there in Ferraro's own backyard. O'Connor and Krol both crowed that no Catholic "in good conscience" could pull a lever for the likes of Ferraro. That assault, and a similar one later against Governor Mario Cuomo when he took a similar stand, stirred considerable ire. One result was the bold ad in the *New York Times*. Among the signers, twenty-four were later identified as nuns, although more had actually put their names to it.

At once, the Sacred Congregation of Religious ordered the sisters who had signed their names to the statement to retract and swear allegiance to the Vatican's teaching on abortion or face expulsion. Letters insisting on compliance were dispatched to superiors rather than to the signatories, presumably to reinforce the hierarchical character of the Church, much like school authorities communicating directly with parents, bypassing students. What the Sacred Congregation of Religious didn't count on was that the religious superiors of the signatories would balk at carrying out the orders of the Vatican. To the contrary, most superiors showed considerable sympathy and/or support for the signatories. It was clear that whether or not the superiors agreed with the signatories, their communities had adopted democratic and due process procedures that clashed with the Sacred Congregation of Religious's method of firing lightning bolts from the top. In the aftermath of the publishing of the ad there was a prolonged series of negotiations within congregations, among congregations, and between the LCWR and congregations, with Rome always in the picture. Some congregations closed ranks in defense of their sisters, while others were torn. It was at best a wrenching, time-consuming ordeal that once again set sister against sister. In the end, all but a couple of the cases were settled through artful compromise. Not a single sister recanted. Instead, the sisters, or their superiors, crafted nuanced statements alluding to the Church's right to its teaching on abortion and acknowledged the pope's jurisdiction over the whole Church without entirely surrendering the sisters' commitment to pluralism. The residue of the conflict was once again expenditure of energies that could have been devoted elsewhere.

Given its own ambitions and setbacks, the progressive foray into renewal would undoubtedly have lost much of its steam naturally. Many of the most passionate reformers had left by the mid-1980s, depleted communities were struggling with survival, and excessively collaborative styles of governing were producing decision-making gridlock in some congregations. But such impediments within weakened orders only made them more vulnerable to Vatican instrusion. Even though many congregations were never directly pressured by Rome, the wider squabble was inevitably felt and the signals were clear. Some congregations worked for many years to win approval of their new constitutions, for example. The sticking point often was obedience. To a renewed community, obedience had come to imply God rather than explicitly the pope. Without a direct promise to obey the pope, in one form or other, a constitution failed to meet the test. Some communities took a long time to iron this out. The effort continues. "Obviously there is a great deal of misunderstanding," said Sister Sharon Holland, a circumspect nun who works in the Sacred Congregation of Religious in Rome. "Some in Rome think 'we' are radical feminists who have gone off the deep end. Some here [in the United States] think no one there has moved into the twentieth century. I have to try to bridge those misconceptions."

While Rome ran into vats of molasses trying to discipline "disobedient" sisters through particular religious orders, it could resort to the direct hit, as it had with Mother Piennett. Reaching the twenty-four ad signers, on the other hand, entailed many obstacles and interference; for example, getting to Sister Agnes Mary Mansour was as easy as sending an agent of the Vatican to her doorstep with an ultimatum. Sister Mansour, a Mercy nun, was director of the Department of Human Services for the state of Michigan, appointed by the governor and approved by Archbishop Edmund Szoka of Detroit. Sister Mansour was well known in Michigan for her learning and her social concerns. As an educator, she had worked as a science professor and a college president. Before being chosen for the Human Services post, she had run unsuccessfully for the Democratic nomination in a race for U.S. Congress, with her congregation's permission. In taking the Human Services position, she stated openly that she opposed abortion but favored Medicaid funding for those poor recipients who chose to have the procedure. That mixed stand, on an issue that Sister Mansour understood to be a matter of conscience, and on which she chose to balance her own views with those of her poverty-stricken constituency, became a burr under the Vatican saddle.

The apostolic pro-nuncio, Archbishop Pio Laghi, demanded that Sister Theresa Kane, then head of the union of Mercy communities, force Sister Mansour to quit her job or quit her order. Sister Kane refused, as did Sister Emily George of the Mercy administrative team. Bishop Anthony Bevilacqua was deputized to bring Sister Mansour to heel. On May 9, 1983, he literally appeared at her door with a stark choice: either she quit her job or face forced dismissal. She was stunned. She later protested that she had not known ahead of time what message the bishop was bearing, had access to no sufficient counsel, and had had no chance to defend herself. But there was no redress. Before that fateful day, she had requested, and received, a leave of absence from her Mercy community—which was nullified by the bishop's action. Two days later she asked for a dispensation from her vows, citing her primary responsibility to the poor. "The directive I received . . . was not the result of a dialogic, objective process," she said in a statement, "but of a unilateral one where neither I nor my religious superiors were ever given the opportunity to appropriately present our case. I do not feel that I should or could witness to an obedience which, for me, would be irrational and blind." Bishop Bevilacqua, who would soon become Philadelphia's cardinal, attempted to reassure critics that his mission had "scrupulously attended to" canon law and Sister Mansour's rights.

The Mansour case was in many respects the most dramatic, but not the only, instance of a particular nun being singled out for punishment. Nuns in public office in Arizona and Rhode Island experienced similar fates. That these things could occur demonstrated that although the direct approach may have been blunted in many circumstances, it still remained a selective, and chilling, weapon.

Apart from ambushing a particular nun here and there (Sister Jeanine Gramick, a founder of a ministry to gays and lesbians was among those silenced later), Rome had done about all it could to straighten out these uppity nuns. The official time for experimenting was over. The Vatican's tactics of confrontation hadn't stopped renewal so much as helped wear it down. A crusade of attrition had killed nothing, but it had added substantially to the burdens that were overtaking religious communities. A gigantic problem was looming. Sisters were retiring in droves and congregations lacked the funds to provide for them. Survival took over as the paramount concern.

Chapter Eleven

Retirement Woes

The plain ten-story building on Chicago's North Side was originally meant to provide housing for nuns studying at Mundelein College just across the way. The place went by the classical moniker "scholasticate," and, when it was dedicated in 1959 by the Blessed Virgin Mary (BVM) sisters, it housed upward of one hundred young women earning degrees to strengthen their vocations.

Four decades later, the structure was occupied by a like number of retirees, most of them BVM sisters, a few from other congregations. The change in the use of that building was testimony to the radical shift in fortunes of the American sisterhood. The facility was a model of efficiency and care. Dining and meeting rooms were bright and cheerful, notices for excursions, events, and classes dotted the calendar, and resident art was on display. As sisters became more frail and infirm, assistance was provided for routines such as housecleaning. Most of them had known one another from the time they had worked as young nuns in Church schools, hospitals, and parishes. They were now spending their last years together, and the staff, headed by Sister Alice Caulfield, had not only retained the old-nun ties but had strengthened them. The word "community" in this instance was not a misnomer. There was vintage friendship and joy within the walls of this house.

Converting the building from one use to the other, and maintaining the $1.3 million operating budget, had required diligence and skill. Like most other orders, the BVMs of Dubuque had been caught in a vise: income from working sisters had fallen sharply as costs for retirees were skyrocketing. On the other hand, the congregation had resources. It had valuable unused properties to sell and sell them it did. With the proceeds, retirement funds became available and, with judicious use, could sustain sisters in their old age for many years.

The BVMs were among the more fortunate. Through good luck and wise planning, they had staved off the worst, a financial calamity, and created a climate in which their retired members could be comfortable and well cared for. Indeed, some communities had been blessed with similar assets that could be used to defray the flash flood of retiree expenses that deluged communities. But many others were not in such a good position and were left destitute. Nuns were responsible for themselves. Bishops, dioceses, and parishes did not step in to provide for congregations of sisters. They were on their own.

Signs of the crisis first appeared as nuns streamed out of communities in the late 1960s and early 1970s. With so many sisters disappearing from the workforce, it seemed only a matter of time before a minority of younger, employed nuns would be called upon to support the growing number of retirees. Over the decades since these first alarms, the median age of sisters has crept up beyond seventy, leaving a tiny group of under-sixties to foot the bill. Far in advance of the 1986 bombshell *Wall Street Journal* article that depicted retired nuns languishing in poverty and working as charwomen in motels to stay alive, sisters were aware that a potential disaster was engulfing them. Until the *Wall Street Journal* article dramatized the plight of sisters who had taught many of the readers of that newspaper, however, the crisis had remained in the background, due in part to the reluctance of congregations to admit their difficulties and in part to a system that left them in the lurch.

For decades, sisters had served as a rough equivalent of the Church's migrant labor force. Living on subsistence wages, moving from place to place at the behest of religious superiors, cultivating young sprouts and combating pests, returning each night to the company living quarters. While migrant laborers receive a pittance in wages, most nuns received a pittance in the form of a stipend. It was an amount reckoned to cover their bare living expenses, although it usually fell short of that. The stipend went straight to the community treasury for the collective outlays for food, clothing, shelter, and other necessities. This was all right, of course, when the convent was bulging with workers earning meager stipends. When the ranks thinned, however, so did the income. A few measly stipends simply wouldn't pay the bills. If one hundred nuns were making $100 a month for the convent by teaching school, nobody likely much felt the pinch. With ten earning even as much as $500 a month, the shortage became noticeable.

Even when the math looked good, communities often walked a knife-edge to keep from falling into hardship. The difference between keeping bread on the table and going without could be a matter of whether a variety of sudden needs and innocent mistakes tipped the tight budget out of balance. Sister Alice Lubin, a Sister of Charity at Convent Station, New Jersey, remembered a sister whose poor management of the books meant "we didn't get enough to live on." The humiliating alternative, Sister Lubin said, was "to try to charm the pastor to get enough." The pastor bailed them out, she said, but only after making known his disapproval of their plight. "It took years to get over that," Sister Lubin said.

In the midst of this severe reversal in fortune among the populations of communities, the stipend system became for some nuns a glaring symbol of subjugation. Unrest grew, and by the start of the 1980s many who served Church institutions had negotiated salaries. The willingness to sacrifice far more, materially, than priests or bishops was fading. Nuns were increasingly seeing themselves as feminists and professionals who deserved, for the sake of their own dignity and respect, something like the rewards that the market conferred for their skills, although the lion's share of their pay went right back to community coffers. Most refused to see themselves politically or ideologically as an exploited proletariat—though some did—but there was a widespread feeling that they had been treated unfairly.

Understandably, perhaps, dioceses were reluctant to give up the economic benefits of the old system. Running schools and health institutions had been possible with the huge, largely unacknowledged subsidy provided by nuns practicing their professions for wages far below market levels. The stipend system, with its uniformity, had been relatively easy to maintain. First as postulants, then as novices, nuns were prepared to be servants in tacit return for the reverence they received as practitioners of perfection. Any suggestion that they wanted more money and personal contracts could and was made to sound by male clerics and traditional Catholics like selfishness and renunciation of the vow of poverty. Allegations that they were becoming materialistic and egotistical, placing their own welfare ahead of the Church's, often stung. Conquering the self had long been held up as the ideal. In reaction to the charge that they were abandoning that ideal, many nuns retreated from the struggle to better themselves. Then suddenly, when elderly nuns were depicted in headlines as falling into abject poverty, things changed. The campaign to abolish stipends reignited.

Set against the enormous contribution of sisters to the vitality of the American Church, the stipend seemed more than ever a blatant insult, a symbol of the cheap labor with which a prosperous U.S. Church had been built. In a nation that equated income with worth and status, nuns increasingly understood themselves as having been taken advantage of. Sisters who had devoted a lifetime to their duties were living in conditions of poverty or near poverty. It wasn't only the lack of money, some sisters insisted, but the lack of respect that the lack of money signified. And the effort to shame them into not complaining only reinforced that disrespect. A Franciscan sister, for example, recalled the scolding she received from her parish pastor when she, as one of the three principal parish staff members, asked for a salary. Her congregation, like many others, needed the money and was asking sisters to become more assertive. The pastor first refused, then offered $8,000, the same salary as the associate pastor. But would he also include the same benefits (food, clothing, shelter, etc.) as the priest received? she asked. "He began to realize what the total cost would be," she remembered, "and wasn't willing to pay *that* for a *sister*."

The concreteness of the stipend debate raised the consciousness of some sisters in a manner that the more abstract aspects of renewal had not. Money *was* a measure many could easily grasp. A growing consensus was that nuns had been shortchanged because women were, by definition, left out of a male, hierarchical grid. Sisters increasingly agitated to get rid of the stipend and to increase salaries where they existed. "It was so hard for the Church when women got more vocal," noted Rita Hofbauer, executive director of Support Our Aging Religious (SOAR), a fund that assists religious retirees. "So much of the obedience was a way of keeping people in place." The difficulty for many sisters, however, was breaking the psychological barriers that had confined them to low expectations. But as the financial needs grew, many congregations pushed working sisters to seek the best possible rewards for their skills. This initiative quickly came back to vex them. Opponents of renewal saw this as a further sign of individual grasping and careerism at the expense of spiritual purposes. To a large number of congregations, asking to be paid fairly for their labor was seen as a matter of survival.

"Moving from stipend to pay put us in touch with reality," said Sister Carol Wester, former executive director of the National Association of Treasurers of Religious Institutes. "It put us in solidarity with other laypersons and enabled us to take the lead in improving church salaries. We also had independence and could stand in solidarity in a way that priests and bishops found offensive. We could pull out and go elsewhere, like our fellow employees." The downside, she added, was that parishes and dioceses preferred to hire ordinary Catholics "who won't rock the boat," rather than nuns.

The retirement crisis exploded publicly when the energies of religious communities had already been sapped by the huge exit of sisters and the backlash by Rome against the perceived excesses of experimentation. Renewal had been the first big shoe to drop; the plight of old nuns became the second. As has been noted, renewal may have been petering out anyway for a variety of reasons as Rome's designated period of experimentation drew to a close. But what life renewal still had had largely been snuffed out by the need to respond to the new emergency. No matter who was to blame, solving the problem would require a new way of thinking and acting for many congregations, some of which had ceded convent business to the mother superior who sometimes kept accounts in a glorified shoebox. Whether orders continued to exist depended largely on their ability to solve this problem. Perhaps a huge infusion of funds would have not only spared pain and suffering but restored vitality to renewal itself. As it was, congregations were left to fend for themselves.

Fortunately, communities obtained some relief when they gained Social Security benefits through an act of Congress. Nuns and religious brothers had never qualified because, among other things, they weren't classified as employees. That changed as the result of an agreement drawn up by the national organizations of men's and women's superiors, the United States Catholic Conference, and the Social Security Administration that made members of religious communities eligible. An amendment to the Social Security Act passed both the House and Senate in 1971 and was signed by President Richard Nixon. It went into effect the next year. Under the measure, sisters were defined as employees of the order, their "pay" rendered as the composite value of the benefits they received: housing, meals, and other necessities. If an order decided to take part, every sister was expected to participate at an equal level of income.

Further, Social Security checks could be collected retroactively for up to five years if congregations paid the retroactive tax that would have been contributed by employees and employers over that time. (The orders, of course, were required to pay both employee and employer costs because sisters lacked funds.) As of 1972, the fair market value of the total tax owed by the congregations was $83 million, roughly $772 for each sister for five years. Some congregations divested property and dipped into existing resources to pay up. Others strained to meet the obligation or simply could not do it right away. But nearly everyone wanted to join the program sooner or later. By the late 1990s, over 90 percent of nuns were covered.

It was, indeed, a floor, but hardly a solid or sufficient one. In 1972 the retired nun received, on average, a monthly check of $84.50, or $1,014 a year, which went to the community treasury. By 1998 the average benefit stood at $3,329, about a third of what other Americans received. Although the help was welcomed, it could do little to offset the skyrocketing costs of supporting a surge of aging sisters. Only a well-funded, comprehensive plan could ensure the well-being of senior sisters. Only a solid financial base could bring security. Those were exactly the assets and skills that, with a few exceptions, congregations had almost none of. It was like asking a family living on two minimum-wage jobs to develop a long-range investment portfolio. In addition, many nuns had been so inoculated against thinking in monetary terms—operating on the assumption that God would provide, and so forth— that they were averse to thinking in these concrete, seemingly grubby terms. Less appealing to some, even as funds dwindled to dangerous levels, was the suggestion that the way nuns had been treated by the Church's male authorities—the pay they had received for the work done—had anything to do with their current predicament. Unthinkable. They weren't in this for money, and so forth and so on. These aversions, among others, kept many sisters from dealing with the money crisis even as it moved into the disaster phase. The bleak situation was summed up in a letter from one superior of a major order to another in 1977. "I'm finding out," she wrote, "that religious, on the whole, have no retirement plans."

The *Wall Street Journal* report in 1985 showed how low the fortunes of many communities had sunk, both literally and figuratively. Already some efforts had begun to mobilize help for the retired nuns, but the newspaper article, by exposing a painful and embarrassing case of apparent neglect, projected the crisis onto a national screen and prodded quicker response. Catholics in parishes across the country were shocked. They may have told "mean nun" stories about their former Catholic school teachers and they may have made fun of life in the convent, but suddenly their tone became one of distress and gratitude for these dedicated and exemplary women. As word spread, so did the response of support and compassion. For all the kidding around and stereotyping that had made the rounds in the Catholic subculture, this was the moment of truth: these were *their* nuns who were in trouble.

The year before the newspaper's disclosures, a group of Catholic philanthropists called Foundations and Donors Interested in Catholic Activities (FADICA) met on Staten Island, New York, to consider the problem. By the end of the conference, they agreed to back a program of financial help. That became SOAR, the first ambitious public appeal.

With notable exceptions such as Archbishop Thomas Kelly of Louisville, Kentucky, bishops were less eager to get involved. As a group, they had other pressing concerns. They had collectively crafted a highly scrutinized pastoral letter on nuclear weapons, opposing them on nearly every front in the face of the Reagan arms buildup. It was a profoundly significant statement that attracted great attention in the media and among Washington's policy makers. The bishops were writing another major letter on the U.S. economy. Issued in 1987, it boldly appealed for economic justice on several fronts. The level of poverty in the United States was scandalous, the bishops asserted, and the causes of it included greed and widespread willingness to tolerate damaging income disparities. Underlying their arguments, which were harshly criticized by Catholic conservatives such as former treasury secretary William E.

Simon, was the traditional Catholic ideal that saw society as a network of mutual responsibility for providing everyone with basic needs.

By comparison, the specter of old nuns living on the edge was not unimportant to them but neither was it central. On the one hand, one of the central concepts in the drafts of the pastoral letter on the economy was that the Church should practice the economic justice that it preached in its relationships with its employees (though technically nuns were not normally considered employees of the Church). On the other, bishops weren't officially responsible for the financial welfare of the sisters. They may have used their services and, until recently, meddled in convent affairs, but fiscally the communities were, by definition, on their own. Some dioceses made contributions to them; others did not. Complicating matters was the climate of tension and distrust that had grown between nuns and bishops over the course of renewal. Many bishops were in no hurry to assist "radical feminists"—a term often used loosely to encompass a wide range of sisters—but quietly blamed the sisters for largely bringing the financial crunch on themselves by being rebellious. If communities hadn't rejected authority and tradition, the reasoning went, the great exodus would not have taken place (more sisters would have stayed, more recruits would have been attracted to the convent), coherence wouldn't have been undermined, and disaster would have been averted. Why should they help nuns who had spurned their authority?

In turn, the sisters viewed the bishops with suspicion and resistance. A prevalent feeling among nuns was that if they put the habit back on and returned to living under the convent roof, abundant help would flow from the hierarchy and everything would be all right. As it was, the strife between the two sides stymied progress on retirement relief.

"Response from the bishops was mixed," said Hofbauer. "There were those who felt a moral responsibility and those who didn't. One provincial sister I know went to her bishop, talked to him about when her community came here and the cumulative service they had given, and asked him what he thought would happen 'if we went bankrupt.' The bishop sat up and said, 'Gee, I don't know.'"

That was before the *Wall Street Journal* publicity made involvement more than optional. Before then, a committee of bishops had explored the scope of the crisis but had done nothing concrete. Within a year of the article, in 1986, the bishops had established an office to oversee a drive to give relief. The strategy was to conduct an annual Retirement Fund for Religious appeal during Masses at all U.S. parishes. The first, in 1988, raised $27.2 million, the biggest single collection of the year. Each year since it has generated more than twice the amount of the next largest single appeal. Since 1998, donations have totaled more than $460 million; impressive but still far short of the $800 million yearly expense for caring for retired nuns, priests, and brothers of American religious orders. As dispersed to the needy congregations of sisters, that amounted to a little more than $700 a year toward the $16,000 to $20,000 (depending on region and method of computing expenses) each retiree required. Meanwhile, the lay-led SOAR drive, ably coordinated by Frank Butler, head of the original sponsoring group, FADICA, and Hofbauer, continued to show enthusiasm, creativity, and dedication. Enlisting the help of such notables as television host Phil Donahue, baseball announcer Tim McCarver, and Senator Pete Dominici, the project built a broad network of thousands of contributors, many of whom were not regular churchgoers but were eager to find a way to lend support to women for whom they were grateful. Annual totals regularly reached nearly a quarter of a million dollars. For each recipient, that meant about $350 toward yearly maintenance.

These were by all means generous outpourings of support and appreciation from lay Catholics across the land, but hardly enough to keep pace with the galloping gap between income and expenses. The estimated gulf exceeded $6 billion, collectively. The sizable donations, though gratefully received, were obviously a proverbial drop in the bucket. A survey done in 1990 by the Arthur Anderson company showed that more than a third of religious communities, 37 percent, had less than a tenth of the retirement funds they needed, while half had less than half.

Nothing can measure the amount of time and effort that this looming threat sapped from the creative energies of communities, but it was surely huge. The diversion of resources and focus on increasingly frantic efforts to repair a leaking ship did incalculable damage to the psyche and mission of many communities. Opponents of renewal, meanwhile, saw their cause gain success although they regretted the reason for it: the growing peril facing old nuns had effectively shifted attention away from changes in religious life to matters of survival. Recruitment was hampered, too. Now every woman who considered entering religious life had to been willing to work to support an average of 2.5 senior nuns in addition to pledging herself to a life of service. The lopsided age distribution produced its own brand of gallows humor. One sister, who was the sole member of her order in her thirties and a decade younger than two in their forties, gazed over an expanse of the Great Plains while driving down a county road one summer day. Her order owned the tract of land but its members were dwindling rapidly. "Someday," she said with a mischievous grin, "this will all be mine."

In the rising turmoil, the first need was to make sense out of fiscal records. Many communities had retained the old ways of keeping accounts. In the past, the mother superior knew where the money was and shared that knowledge with a treasurer, if one existed. Nobody else knew. At chapter meetings, financial information was scarce and passed over as unimportant. Nothing was set aside. Every sister's stipend went into the pot and that was that.

When the crisis emerged, many communities had no treasurer or financial plan. Each group kept its records to itself. Suddenly communities were appointing chief financial officers from the outside or from other congregations. Sisters were going to the Wharton School and other temples of financial management to learn about development and budget allocations. More and more congregations were urging sisters to find jobs with full salaries to help defray expenses. "They began to take the picture more seriously," Sister Wester of the religious treasurers office said. "You still run into a community that doesn't have a balance sheet. But there is much more understanding and sophistication about these things. The trend is to look at health care and care of the elderly. How can we economize, take advantage of government programs, cooperative programs, collaborate with other communities, move members into nursing homes open to the public?" Increasing resources, Sister Wester said, often entailed both belt tightening, fund-raising, and benefits like Medicaid. Despite the experts and the positive responses, Sister Wester saw a lot of communities in dire straits, on the brink of extinction within a decade or so. "By the actuarial charts," she said, "few even come close to having sufficient funds."

The overwhelming nature of the problem shook all but a relative hand-ful of the larger communities that had resources including lucrative, dispos-able properties. For the rest of the four hundred communities, the alarm altered the face of the convent. The mother house became, in effect, the grandmother house. What had once been a spacious building bustling with generations of sisters increasingly resembled an office complex. Across the spectrum of orders, nursing home facilities and health care units became defining traits of communities that took on the aspect of holding areas where old nuns, perhaps a solid majority of the membership, said the rosary, await-ing their final reward. Meanwhile, many communities had their hands full just keeping themselves from going under. Motives were intertwined: a drop in numbers obviously precipitated both a retirement crisis and the possibility of the community's death.

The Ursulines in Paola, Kansas, offer an example of a community that tried to coordinate a response to both problems. Major decisions reached in 1996 put them on a different course. The most visible evidence of this turn was the refashioning of the elegant old three-story community center to re-flect the new realities. The first floor was remodeled and made available for rent-paying community service groups that needed office space and a Baptist church that brought a kind of rousing singing and preaching the old stone walls have never known before. The second floor was redone to house the whole community of sisters, older and younger. Elevators were installed to prevent older nuns from falling on the stairs. The first-floor kitchen and dining area were revamped to make them user-friendly. The third floor was marked as an assisted living facility. In addition, a new kitchen took shape. A health care unit was also on the grounds. The project, which would cost at least $3 million, was the heart of the plan to ensure retirees a decent life and to begin salting funds away for future needs. There were forty-five members at the time. Half were still able to work, mostly as high school principals and parish associates; the rest were at the mother house. The Ursulines were the sole remaining order working in the Archdiocese of Kansas City.

The Ursulines had never sought outside funds before, said Sister Pat Lynch, the able president of the community, but she was pleased to find much support among people "who love the Ursulines." The community had sold a large plot of land to a developer of a shopping plaza and had the unusual good fortune to pump a small amount of low-grade oil from drilling rigs on its property. But the community was at a new bend in the road. The plan adopted by the sisters indicated, Sister Lynch said, "that they continue to say that we have life, there is a future, we want to stay the course, be faithful to our vows, and keep our commitment to the archdiocese." Part of that future plan included attracting tourists to the site at which, by the order's claim, the habit was first modified in this country.

While the Ursulines took a new tack, the Sisters of St. Joseph of Springfield, Massachusetts, were using more of their spacious buildings atop Mont Marie in nearby Holyoke for programs such as retreats and seminars that produced badly needed revenue. The community was much larger than the Paola Ursulines, numbering 425 members. Sixty were retired and living there; another fifty-five were in the health care center on the grounds. In ten years, said Sister Carol Quinn, assistant to the president, the retired would outnumber working sisters. The community "never had resources," Sister Quinn said. Low pay in Church jobs over the years had not made establishing a retirement fund possible. With a deluge of obligations just over the horizon, she added, the underfunded portion of the retirement tab stood at a staggering 87 percent.

The St. Joseph story was a graphic documentary of the drama of American congregations over three decades. From its beginnings in the area in 1880, when seven sisters arrived from Flushing, New York, to teach in St. Patrick's school in nearby Chicopee Falls, the sisters repeatedly outgrew their facilities. In 1960, the most ambitious expansion program by far resulted in an impressive array of new and renovated buildings. When finished in 1966, it included spacious housing for novices and postulates, with a chapel; classrooms, library, and gymnasium, with top-flight swimming pool, for those preparing to take vows and other members of the community; an administrative building with chapel; and an infirmary. The striking campus vista was an outward expression of robust confidence in the community's future, an optimism generally shared throughout the American sisterhood.

Hardly had the paint dried on these new walls, however, before the bottom began to drop out of the consensus that had fostered the surge of sisters during previous decades. Vatican II and the debates began. The Sisters of St. Joseph were, as has been shown, in the throes of the tensions and turmoil no less than other communities. Sisters left during the exodus in approximately the same proportions as they did in other orders. Recruits dried up. The big new spaces built to house and educate them were empty. New uses had to be found to help pay for the upkeep. The one growth area was providing health care. The infirmary became inadequate for the demands placed on it, so in 1993 it was expanded into a comprehensive health care center. At the outset, it was intended for nuns and priests, but it now accepts patients from the general public. A day-care center, which predates the most recent retirement crisis, accommodates ninety children each day. Two other sisters operate a center for women who are making the transition from mental illness or prison to life on the outside. All three of these centers form an independent corporation.

Mont Marie had become a multipurpose center, far from pursuing the univocal mission of its past. But a reversal of sorts seemed in the works. This magnificent center could fill up again as the influx of retirees picks up momentum. The Fund for Religious and SOAR would do what they could, but finally, Sister Quinn's observation came back to haunt the community: "We were never able to build a retirement fund."

Chapter Twelve

Will Sisters Survive?

Tell the Sisters of America to be faithful to their commitment to community life and to their Gospel direction. *Pius XII once told me that the Sisters of the United States are the strength of the Church. And I know it is true.* Tell them I esteem them and that I pray for them. I pray for them very much [emphasis added].

Pope Paul VI to Sister Angelita Myerscough, A.S.C.,
president of the Conference of Major Superiors of Women, 1971

Nothing better captured official ambivalence toward late-twentieth-century U.S. nuns than the anguished message of Paul VI to Sister Myerscough. His repetition of Pius XII's tribute to the sisters as the heart and soul of the American Church was surely as sincere as it was extraordinary. "Strength of the Church," no less. But the high praise came with caution and a note of implied discomfort. Tell the sisters also, Paul said, to stay within the boundaries of community life that were, at that very time, being stretched and redrawn against Rome's desires. The sisters were loved but, since breaking loose from old constraints, not terribly trustworthy, admired but less willing to salute Rome.

For all of Pope Paul's sincerity, therefore, he was extolling a bygone company of supine, regimented workers that would never exit and yearning for a highly regulated convent that most American sisters had long since rejected.

In Church theology, the Holy Spirit coaxes the Church to read the "signs of the times" that indicate where God is stirring in the world. With the Spirit as wind at its back, the Church then moves toward that future.

Many American nuns believed they clearly saw the signs of the times in Vatican II. They felt swept along by the sometimes turbulent Holy Spirit that created disruption and change, both welcome and unwelcome. They felt responsible for defining and understanding this new calling and mission. Their boldness ran into a powerful headwind from male authorities, however; it was an impeding force fueled by both the Church leaders' antipathy toward the sisters' growing independence and their frustration at losing control over the nuns' affairs.

The result was tough slogging for America's sisterhoods and a loss of momentum that translated into shrinking numbers. The hierarchy seemed willing to sacrifice a host of consecrated women whom two popes had described as the American Church's most valuable strength, rather than grant them the freedom and encouragement that could have helped them grow. What else but a mixture of pride and resentment could cause Church leaders to squander the treasure described by two popes as the "strength of the [U.S.] Church?"

The ingrained loyalty of most sisters to Church authority made it difficult for them to lay blame for the malaise on the hierarchy, much as it disinclined them to identify openly with feminism. To that extent, the sisters may have contributed to their own demise, although if they had engaged in a more forceful rebellion greater harm might have been caused to existing communities.

Occasionally, a voice would warn them against servility toward Rome. Back in 1970, for example, the Reverend John C. Haughey, a distinguished Jesuit ethicist, implored the annual assembly of major superiors to "add up the ways you've been ignored by Bishops and the Sacred Congregation of Religious even in the recent past.

"To put it bluntly," he continued, "you are being made fools of."

Father Haughey, then the associate editor of *America* (the national

Catholic weekly), urged the sisters to embrace women's liberation, to insist on being consulted about any decision made by Rome concerning religious life ("legislation without representation is intolerable"), and to disband the conference of major superiors because it had been created by the Vatican and was beholden to it.

He went on to suggest that any Church authority that treats nuns with disrespect (without "pagan courtesy" at the least) should have their directives "treated by you as if they do not exist." He added, wryly, "Many of you have had pupils who are now bishops—you still have some lessons to teach them."

Finally, he cautioned them against caution. "It's too late to go slowly and you've just begun to go fast," Father Haughey said. "Don't get timid now. God reward your efforts."

Decades later, the record of advance and retreat was decidedly mixed. Thirty years after Vatican II sparked the greatest revolution among sisters in their nearly two-thousand-year history—an upheaval countered at every step by Rome—several once proud, strong congregations were close to death and others were staving off the end only by dint of size and resources. The stereotypical image of a yardstick-wielding dynamo was giving way to that of an old, stooped nun dozing in a wheelchair. Neither picture was terribly fair, yet each reflected a considerable slice of reality.

The numbers told it all. Every day the totals fell as the steady cadence of departed souls depleted the rolls. During the eight years spent researching and writing this book, more than 25,000 sisters died, leaving fewer than 70,000. Old nuns, once the valiant missionaries of Catholic tradition to Catholic people who would otherwise have remained unaware of what their Church stood for, had, for the most part, ceased debating the causes of the breakdown or strategies for keeping their communities alive. They were more aware of their fragility. Scarce funds and resources had placed their final days and years in jeopardy. They quietly hoped that they would have enough to die with a modicum of comfort and peace.

From the other end of the age spectrum—sparse as it was—came a different view. Sister Julie had entered the Daughters of Charity at age thirty-seven after putting in twenty years as an administrator at the University of California at Santa Barbara. "I didn't really know about the dying," she said one morning at the Daughters center in Los Altos. "But as I watched sisters age and die—their bodies deteriorate—that was the frightening part, and it hit home. I had to let go of it. Our life will be drastically different.

"My life in this community will be transitional and I don't know what it will be. I trust that my time won't be to maintain something that will die. We bring our culture to this commitment. There is a richness of our charism [special mission and gift] that is the heart of who we are. How do we translate that into today's need?

"I know sisters who have been here under ten years who are really struggling. They see things around them dying. I think it has really hit. I've been in eleven years; during the last five there have been the shocks of deaths and missions closing. The first six years we were hitting our heads against the wall of denial. Still, there isn't total acceptance and still there is some fear of change.

"So long as we don't just keep saying, 'Something is going to happen [to rescue us] but we don't know what it is.' "

A researcher's comments echoed that sentiment. Sister Miriam Ukeritis, a Sister of St. Joseph and co-conductor with the Reverend David Nygren of the major study "The Future of Religious Orders in the U.S.," observed from her office at DePaul University in Chicago that many communities "were convinced that God's going to come through. There's massive denial going on." But she saw hopeful signs. "People are taking the downturn seriously. There are chinks in the denial." But the wall is thick. Many old nuns felt "a sense of betrayal or failure," she said, believing their lifelong commitment had gone for naught. "They said they did their best and look at where things are," Sister Ukeritis said. As for the particular frictions that had stemmed from failures of renewal, Sister Ukeritis said many orders "don't know how to talk about them," thereby prolonging the paralysis.

Failure to look squarely at the demise stifled efforts to sort out the causes. That, in turn, hampered the development of strategies for survival. For Sister Ukeritis and other analysts, that was the paralysis that threatened many communities.

At a 1993 FADICA-sponsored conference on the future of religious life, Sister Ukeritis cited three scenarios set down keenly by Brother Lawrence Cada and his Marianist group of researchers. One was flat-out extinction. A second was bare survival. The third was rebirth through recapturing the spirit and purpose from which the community had sprung. The third, of course, was a restatement of the mandate nuns had received from Vatican II.

The death of orders was nothing new, she reminded them; two-thirds of the men's orders founded before 1800 had folded. Other communities would comply with renewal by doing an external face-lift, she said, but "fail to renew themselves" or "fail to capture religious life's prophetic character," not standing for anything much but scraping by.

The obviously preferred option, refounding, required, in Sister Ukeritis's view, such intangibles as "a transforming response to the signs of the time," rediscovery of the inspiration that gave birth to the order and renewed faith in Christ.

In their joint study of future possibilities, Sister Ukeritis and Father Nygren, a priest of the Vincentian order, were, on the whole, issuing a call for nuns to retreat from personal pursuits and destructive pluralism and move toward a form of community life that emphasized solidarity and singleness of purpose. To underscore this need, the two researchers, both psychologists, pointed out that nearly a third of the respondents said they had only a "fuzzy" sense of their purpose as nuns. Others had drifted to the fringes of their communities. The growing number of sisters joining the staffs of parishes and diocesan offices was, in their view, blunting the community's call to urgent needs in the world, including that of social justice, by constricting them within institutional limitations.

The key to achieving inspiration, meaning, and communal harmony, they felt, was finding leaders who could point the way without being restrained by endless searches for consensus. Leadership was the pivotal factor in deciding whether an order found new strength and resolve, thus making it attractive to those seeking a religious vocation, or collapsed into itself. To live, a congregation needed to combine adept leaders with the rebirth in the themes of its founding and a ministry to the unmet needs of the world.

The Nygren-Ukeritis report was widely applauded for its scope and comprehensiveness. Of the 9,999 hefty surveys mailed out to sisters, priests, and brothers, nearly two out of three (6,359) were returned, a remarkable percentage. A variety of other methods drew further information from hundreds of nuns. Leaders of communities would presumably find such material helpful in revivifying their congregations. It also exposed barriers that could keep social activists and non-white women from entering orders.

Most shocking, yet most understandable, was the finding that a third of the sisters sampled were fuzzy about what it meant to be a nun. Lots of Catholics had wondered something similar about what it meant to be a layperson in an evolving Church that had changed the definition of the laity.

Despite the papal appeals to exercise a "preferential option for the poor," the survey found only slightly more than half (55 percent) were willing to do so. But it was unclear what that meant. Sister Neal, for example, was quick to assert that roughly the same results would likely have been obtained in the past. While sisters had long espoused support for helping the poor, she said, a much smaller percentage had actually done so for a variety of reasons not necessarily tied to opposition to those ministries. Racism had also revealed itself in the study. Asked whether minority group members would feel "uneasy in my congregation," more than a third (36 percent) said they would, two-fifths (42 percent) said they wouldn't, and the rest were undecided. Not surprisingly, 96 percent of communities were white. The need to attract Hispanic women was growing and presented ethnic obstacles. "The research indicates," Nygren and Ukeritis wrote, "that a complex dynamic of unconscious racism makes penetration by minority populations very difficult."

Overall, the study's conclusions and prescriptions were conventional and backward looking. The key to revival was linked to a recovery of much that had been discarded, such as the obligation of living and working together. Nuns had dwelled so intently on reforming their congregations that they'd become harmfully self-centered, the report implied. Rome believed that the same alleged nemeses had combined with "radical feminism" to plunge the American sisters into crisis. Not so subtly, sisters were accused of selling out to the secular culture. Nygren and Ukeritis weren't spurning renewal or Vatican II but they were suggesting that U.S. orders could survive only by clipping their wings and pulling back from the frontiers where three decades of exploration had taken them. Doing so hinged on restoring authority where it had collapsed into stalemates among contending groups of nuns, producing endless wrangling.

To Sister Ukeritis, no factor had caused more mischief to religious communities than individualism. She joked that some sisters in her community would go to their grave to the strains of "I'll Do It My Way" pealing from the community bell tower. Individualism as a destroyer of community was in the eye of the beholder, however. What to some was a scourge was to others a sign of maturity, a sign that nuns were gaining a healthier sense of themselves than sister predecessors who were told repeatedly that, in effect, they had no selves. If self-centeredness sometimes did take hold of some sisters now, it was often considered an acceptable price to pay for the freedom to develop the gift of the self.

Though Nygren and Ukeritis were by no means arguing for a return to strict monastic existence, their advice tilted in that direction. Theirs was an approach nearer to convention built on sociology and psychology than conservatism bolstered by medieval theology. For Mother Vincent Marie Finnegan, on the other hand, the path to a faithful future led decidedly through the past. The stalwart head of the Council of Major Superiors of Women—the traditionalist organization that succeeded Consortium Perfectae Caritatis, made up of a tenth of U.S. nuns—hailed the accomplishments of Vatican II but insisted that the dominant style of American renewal was far from what the Council fathers had had in mind. Feminism had wreaked havoc on American communities, she believed, as had the indulgence of sisters in social and political causes. Authority had been wrecked on the shoals of "consensus." The answer she posed was straightforward, drawn mostly from the pope's reactive letter, Essential Elements of Religious Life, intended as a means of getting American sisters back into line and re-invoking the image of the nun as otherworldly. As promoted by Mother Finnegan, moving into the future meant, among other things, donning the habit (some modifications acceptable), living in community instead of singly or in pairs, adhering to a set schedule of daily prayer, and serving missions defined by the rightful authorities of the order. Such coordination could usher in "springtime" for those communities that adhered to it, she said.

It was a viewpoint dedicated to recovering the sense of higher calling that Vatican II had, perhaps inadvertently, flattened into the appeal for "universal" holiness encompassing all Catholics. Mother Finnegan and Cardinal O'Connor wanted to retrieve enough of the past to restore sisters to a place that was different and special. One of the clearest advocates of this cause was the Reverent Albert Diianni, a Marist priest, provincial superior of his order, and author of a book, *Religious Life as Adventure*. At a symposium on religious life in 1995, Father Diianni attacked "individualism, pluralism [and] egalitarianism" as the chief corrupters of congregations. Sisters had abandoned their proper roles as "spouse of Christ" to become "prophets," activists in worldly causes, he believed. "Can we survive if we dwell on social and political issues?" he asked rhetorically. Nuns must "follow a different way," he said, bearing witness to otherworldliness rather than crusading against racism, sexism, and patriarchy.

Others who had contributed to bolder forms of renewal had second thoughts. For example, Mary Jo Leddy, an activist, writer, and sister for many years, came to the conclusion that many orders had lost their way by falling captive to a Western, liberal culture that placed personal well-being over group welfare and promoted differences instead of unity and common convictions. Communities had splintered, losing their vital center. Dusting off old ways wouldn't fix anything, she hastened to add, but it was time to envision new methods for developing communities with a core set of beliefs and goals. The outstanding sociologist of religious orders, Sister Patricia Wittberg, had similar reservations. During renewal, she stressed, factors that encouraged the care and growth of religious orders had faded or disappeared altogether both in the Church (e.g., families were no longer likely to cheer their daughters becoming sisters) and in secular culture (more career opportunities opened to young women). Those forces were so powerful, she said, that the traumatic exodus of nuns starting in the late 1960s was well nigh inevitable. Without a strong sense of purpose and enough sameness in lifestyle to impart adequate bonding, Sister Wittberg predicted religious communities would probably flounder. She was careful to avoid endorsing a "put 'em back in the convent" pitch or be identified as a traditionalist, but there were elements in her analysis that conjured images of the new communities that she had studied that, indeed, resembled the old days in several key respects.

Advocates of readopting key practices that had been widely set aside argued that recruitment trends supported their case. Young people who showed any interest in religious life were inclined more toward an older, contemplative model of community than the post–Vatican II concept of worldly involvement. The most conservative communities where the old ways had been kept claimed to be showing the most growth. In a nation that bows before the gods of growth and the gross national product, such claims command great attention and respect. They constitute, in many minds, proof of what works. To religious communities, of course, success was far more than an imitation of America's obsession with increasing sales figures and portfolio returns. It was a case of do or die. And, as Mother Finnegan put it squarely one day on the peaceful grounds of her Carmelite community in Alhambra, "Clearly the vitality is in our communities."

The numbers, however, were ambiguous. First, counting heads had always been difficult, owing to many factors including the tendency of orders to guard their privacy. Many new communities had cropped up (Dominicans in Nashville, Franciscans in Boston, and so forth) that were hard to track. Most represented themselves as orthodox and relatively cloistered. Sister Wittberg's research found these groups to be full of vigor and rigor, bearing the traits of clear purpose and concerted mission that Nygren and Ukeritis had identified as essential to a viable future.

While the new centers had attracted younger, committed Catholics, Sister Wittberg discovered, they also lost many, creating a revolving door effect that often made it difficult to tell whether vitality was, indeed, producing growth. On the more established side, some contemplative congregations such as the Poor Clares and the Carmelites were experiencing small gains. True, they were more nearly holding their own compared to less traditional communities, and the line of applicants was nowhere near the flood that swamped congregations in the 1950s. Mother Finnegan's Carmelites, for example, had eleven novices at the time of our visit in 1995, squarely within the range of nine to twelve that the community had sustained in recent years. It was a relatively large group for a community of 125 fully vowed sisters. The previous year, four young women entered, age twenty-four on average. As communities fared, this was impressive. The picture was more mixed than initial optimism might warrant, however. Half or more of the newcomers had come from foreign countries: Nigeria, Haiti, Mexico, the Philippines, and elsewhere. Vocations were more plentiful in the poorer countries of the world and many of these candidates, having been shaped by conservative Catholicism at home, joined the more traditional American communities. Though they kept the orders' fires alive, they didn't answer the problem of U.S. recruitment. The Alhambra Carmelites, like other communities, also experienced attrition. Five sisters had been lost recently for a variety of reasons. So growth, where it appeared to exist, seemed to be fleeting and illusory. Traditional orders might flourish, after a fashion, loyal to the directives of nostalgic bishops, but the membership of such communities would likely be skewed in the direction of Catholic conservatism rather than, as in days past, representative of a cross section of the Church. Most American Catholics had long since moved beyond those older, perfectionist conceptions of Church and vocation.

For the majority of dwindling orders, returning to the customs of yore was simply out of the question. Though they struggled to find their way through the difficulties that accompanied decay, the Essential Elements prescription lacked much appeal. What was past was past. Better to disappear than to grasp at a "panacea" that seemed to them inauthentic. Lay Catholics other than nuns were rapidly taking over jobs and ministries once monopolized by the orders. There might be no such thing as reviving an expression of Catholicism that had served well but had ceased to be needed. Few sisters outside the traditionalists wanted anything to do with turning back the clock. Even the recent practice of working on a parish staff, which had become one of the most available employment options, was sharply criticized as diverting sisters from more legitimate ministries. In their report, for example, Nygren and Ukeritis took a dim view of this increasing involvement in parishes, arguing that sisters who worked in such establishment settings risked losing a grasp of their critical role as prophets.

From another direction, the nontraditionalist mainstream faced disapproval from bishops and Vatican prelates who saw "radical feminists" behind rampant deviations from the strict norms the pope had tried to impose. A test question posed at a meeting of an order's province was "Who wants us to die?" Increasingly, sisters included "bishops" in their responses. The sisters, once at the beck and call of the clergy, had become a thorn in its side. A sister who was president of a Catholic college confided, "On the whole, they would much rather be rid of us." How much different would the outcome have been, asked some sisters, if the bishops had at the least gotten out of their way?

"Religious life as we've known it is passing away," Sister Wester, head of the national treasurers' office, told a gathering of the Leadership Conference of Women Religious. "For all practical purposes it has passed. You have an enormous responsibility to help it die well. God with it in death brings new life in unimagined ways."

Nuns across the country voiced a similar forecast, surprisingly free of gloom or dismay. It was a version of Jesus' mustard-seed parable. In order for the plant to bloom, the seed must enter the ground and die. Whether every order died was beside the point. Most probably would, but even those that remained seemed sure to find a distinct new way of being a community of committed women carrying out a Catholic mission. No one had a very clear idea what might be in store, but many believed they would involve, within a framework of reinterpreted vows, the enduring quests for knowing God, serving human needs, and assuring justice for women.

Perhaps the most miraculous aspect of the dying process was that so many communities remained buoyant even as the roof was falling in upon them. As Sister Sandra Schneiders has observed, their behavior was contrary to what would be expected. Failing organizations were prone to become fearful, miserly, and intensely inward looking. Not so nuns. Through the travail, many had maintained a counterintuitively joyful attitude of acceptance. They had not centralized power or shut themselves off or become frozen with anxiety the way they might be expected to. They had carried on with enthusiasm though less energy. Perhaps some of it was denial or faith that God would rescue them. Maybe God *would* rescue them. In any event, they were refusing to grasp formulas out of the past to help them recruit. They appeared ready to let the mustard seed take its course. Meanwhile, as Sister Schneiders indicated, they weren't *acting* like dying institutions.

A strategy that brought some relief was the cultivation of groups of associates that took part in a community's life and work. Dozens of orders opened the doors to this part-time participation by women (sometimes men) who lived as married and single women in the world and visited the community regularly. The influx of concerned women, some of whom had left convents long before, bolstered morale and contributed to the mission of the order. Some analysts saw the associate model as the springboard to a new kind of revitalized community made up of a small number of full-time vowed sisters and a large number of associates. But there were strong objections to this arrangement. As welcome as support was, said the critics, the associate concept tended to blur the distinct value of vowed sisterhood. Why be a fully committed sister when you could achieve about the same thing part-time? The other strong complaint was that associates often anchored the community in the past by preferring religious life as it was rather than helping to create something new. Associates tended to like the status quo when what was needed, the critics said, was a vastly different approach, even one that ran counter to what Rome might find to its liking. For all its value as a temporary boon, the trend toward associates was generally dismissed as a long-term solution.

Having been cultivated so long, the garden of religious life seemed certain to yield new species. Even with all the distractions and opportunities open to twenty-first-century Catholic women, it seemed reasonable to assume that divine auspices would call enough women to a compelling way of life. A remaining question was whether Rome had stifled new life by trying to blunt renewal or had helped bring it about by making sure the mustard seed died. At this remove, the guess is that U.S. sisters would have already experienced new life if the Vatican had refrained from obstruction and harassment. That may sound too simple, but the course of events from Vatican II to the turn of the century demonstrates, it seems, that the sisters were taking the Council's instructions seriously and evolving their own answers. Those answers weren't perfect, as the sisters readily concede, but communities were often hampered from carrying out the revisions and shaping their missions to meet new needs. They would, of course, have found the process tough and messy under any conditions. With the stream of hectoring from Rome on the side of traditionalists, however, the deliberations often took on a particularly acrimonious tone. Nuns had been given a job they weren't allowed to finish. Had they finished it on their own terms, in a climate that would have been more self-critical in the absence of interference from the hierarchy, the outcome would certainly have been different, probably preparing for new life. As matters stood, that possibility had been at least forestalled by angry popes who, like the medieval King Canute raging from the shoreline against an encroaching sea, commanded the tides to cease.

Worse than Rome's constant reprisals against U.S. progressives was the manner in which the backlash was conducted. "Truth" was something formulated by Pope John Paul and the Curia alone, not by underlings, especially those who claimed a different "truth." U.S. nuns were, by definition, allowed no part in defining what was what. They had sought collaboration on the nature and function of religious life and had had the door slammed in their faces. Government was from the top, giving barely a nod to the concept of shared authority (being non-ordained women effectively disqualified them right away) or to the recently resurrected principle of subsidiarity. That principle, which emerged somewhat ironically in a Church that had theoretically pledged itself to soften the hard lines of vertical hierarchy, stated that problems were best solved at the most local possible levels by appropriate Church leadership. Had this strategy been applied to the dilemmas of American nuns, they would have been responsible for their own destiny without meddling from the top. Meanwhile, the cadre of traditionalists that defended Rome continued to place blame on the progressives themselves for creating their own troubles by their headstrong attitudes. Obsessed with a quest for power, the conservatives argued, the progressives created a hostile relationship with the Vatican.

Rome had pushed back in an effort to contain the many elements of renewal in the United States that it found most frightful, but succeeded only marginally. The evolution of new forms and experiments was slowed, sometimes blunted, but never reversed. The Church's highest officials had been on the wrong side of an historical force called feminism and could only score minor and temporary victories. On the other side, Rome's prolonged badgering may have prevented communities from resolving their differences and finding a vital, viable center.

Nobody won and everyone lost a great deal.

Mary Daniel Turner, the thoughtful, liberal former president of the Leadership Conference of Women Religious who devoted herself to caring for AIDS-stricken homeless men in their final days, advanced one version of what might yet be. "If we could get the hunger and thirst for God with the hunger and thirst for justice," she told a meeting of colleagues, "then we'd understand what a new paradigm is all about."

Meanwhile, even as some communities prepare to die as gracefully as they can, the Ursulines of Paola and other groups rich in memory continue not only to shrink but to plan and to hope for a future they cannot yet see. From a further remove, however, the great body of older, Mass-going American Catholics wonder what happened to that huge cohort of remarkable, black-swathed women who appeared then disappeared from their vulnerable lives.

Acknowledgments

I SET OUT to explore why Catholic sisters in America were disappearing so rapidly. It seemed to me that an irreplaceable component of the Catholic heritage in this country was passing out of existence with relatively little notice. That was the "why" I wanted to know about.

For many sisters, this is understandably a painful topic. The last half-century has been wrenching for most of them. They might have been excused for keeping to themselves when asked to talk about that experience, but I found them, almost without exception, to be open and honest about those aspects of their lives that had meant so much to their work and their daily purpose.

My gratitude goes out to the scores of sisters from dozens of communities who tried to tutor me in the complexities and realities of the world within religious communities. Three communities in particular—the Ursulines of Paola, Kansas; the Daughters of Charity of Los Altos, California; and the Benedictines of Grove City, Indiana—each provided hospitality to me for several days of research and interviews. Along with kindness and good humor, these sisters and the many others whom I had the good fortune to meet over three years of travel and conversation imparted above all a treasure of wisdom and insight. My guides were invaluable and true.

What I valued most in them was their vivid personalities that defy all the hideous stereotypes of nuns either as objects of fear or subjects of sentimentality. In part, these extreme images had been fostered by the uniformity that prevailed before Vatican II when individual expression was squelched. Their history as exceptional women on the American landscape has yet to be given its due.

Obviously, any perspectives or interpretations that I draw from what they told me or gave me to read are mine alone, not the responsibility or fault of my guides.

The list of sisters to whom I am indebted is much too long to run in its entirety here, but I will take the liberty of naming a few whose contributions were particularly significant in moving my train of thought along. My use of their last names—their original family names—on second reference through-out the book is intended as respect for the emphasis by Vatican II as the "people of God" who seek holiness as equals. Sisters were once referred to almost exclusively by their first names, a practice that often reflected warmth and affection, but also, it seems to me, signaled either a higher status (which Vatican II opposed) or a girlish one. A return to the birth name was also approved and even though it may sound stark to some sisters and other Catholics, I think it places nuns in the mainstream of the Church in a symbolic manner. In rare instances, that was not possible, owing to very special circumstances.

Because the nature of my project was distinctly analytical, my attention most naturally focuses on those intellectual leaders who offer conceptual options for considering the shifts in religious life through their writing and teaching: Margaret Susan Thompson, not a sister but a superb historian of sisters at Syracuse University; Sister Elizabeth Johnson, a gifted theologian at Fordham; Sister Sandra Schneiders, a New Testament scholar and supreme analyst of religious life; Sister Ellen Joyce, a historian at St. Elizabeth's College in New Jersey; Sister Mary Margaret Funk, a Benedictine who has at-tempted to strike a proper balance between renewal and tradition; Sister Patricia Wittberg, a first-rate sociologist at Indiana University at Indianapolis who has devoted much of her career to understanding trends in religious communities; Sister Joan Chittister, the indefatigable scholar/activist/con-templative who has produced a steady stream of creative options for recon-sidering sisterhood; Sister Margaret Brennan, who taught theology at the University of Toronto and was a fount of ideas about women religious; Sister

Elizabeth Carroll, whose reminiscences of her years as a national leader for American sisters were scintillating; and Sister Theresa Kane, the Mercy sister who gained national attention for calling directly on the pope to ordain women but whose soft-spoken, sagacious reflections on the lives of sisters today were profound in quite a different manner.

Many sisters took time from busy schedules to give me guidance, including Mother Vincent Marie Finnegan, head of a conservative alternative to progressive trends in renewal; Sister Miriam Ukeritis, who helped compile a broad study of women and men religious in the United States; and Sister Mary Johnson of Emmanuel College in Boston, who is studying recent entrants into religious orders. The Loretto Sisters in Denver welcomed me on short notice. Sister Mary Luke Tobin, who holds a special place in American religious history, was among the Loretto sisters who were generous with their time and insights.

Inevitably, with so many sisters at an advanced age when my research began, some of the most memorable and helpful have since died. They include the remarkable Marie Augusta Neal, who sat with me for most of two days discussing her research; Agnes Mary Mansour, who could discuss her dismissal by the Vatican without bitterness; and Margaret Cafferty, a younger sister who met an untimely death while serving as the executive director of the Leadership Conference of Women Religious. On several occasions, she delivered to me the fruits of her keen mind on the subject of the plight of sisters.

The University of Notre Dame houses the archives of the Leadership Conference of Women Religious. Its staff, principally William Kevin Crawley, were most helpful in assisting me identify key materials. Likewise, Sister Elizabeth McLoughlin, keeper of the archives at the Sister of Charity center in Convent Station, New Jersey, was generous and patient in allowing me to search, in particular, the Sister Survey.

In preparing the book, I want especially to thank both Mary Beckman and Matthew Briggs for their willingness to review and comment upon the manuscript. I also extend salutes to Trace Murphy, my editor at Doubleday, for his encouragement and discernment, and to Bob Markel, my agent and friend, for sharing me with Gilbert and Sullivan.

Outcomes aside, it was a journey worth taking just for the blessing of those met along the way.

Notes

ABBREVIATIONS

CLCW Leadership Conference of Women Religious Archives.
UNDA University of Notre Dame Archives.
SCR Sacred Congregation for Religious.

CHAPTER ONE
MAKING WAVES IN KANSAS

17   "I spent a lot of time": Sister Raymond Dieckman interview by author at Ursuline convent, Paola, Kans., June 3, 1995.

18   "If it's in the plan": Sister Karen Klaffenbach interview by author at the University of Kansas in Lawrence, Kansas, June 2, 1995.

CHAPTER TWO
LIVING BY THE RULE

24   "The day was momentous": A Sister of St. Joseph who requested anonymity, interview by author in Gardner, Mass., June 1997.

26   Will Herberg, *Protestant, Catholic, Jew* (Chicago: University of Chicago Press, 1955, 1960, 1983). Herberg's book remains the best lens through which to view the social and religious forces of the 1950s.

26   "If you cannot find": Maria Del Rey, *Bernie Becomes a Nun* (New York: Farrar, 1956), p. 117.

26   A promotional pamphlet from that time: "Brides of Christ" (Washington, D.C.: Conference of Major Superiors of Women).

29   Sister Ann Patrick Ware: Ann Patrick Ware, ed., *Midwives of the Future: American Sisters Tell Their Story* (Kansas City: Leaven Press, 1985), p.1; out of print.

31   There were exceptions: Sister Mary Agnes O'Donnell interview by author at the Blessed Virgin Mary retirement house, Chicago, October 30, 1996.

33   there are real-life parallels: Sister Thomas Roach interview by author at "Earth Turners" conference in Monroe, Mich., April 18, 1996.

35   refusing to call themselves a religious community: Patricia Wittberg, S.C., *The Rise and Fall of Catholic Religious Orders: A Social Movement Perspective* (Albany: State University of New York Press, 1994), p. 37.

36   When the Jesuit president of Fordham University: Sister Anne Munley, then superior of the Immaculate Heart of Mary Sisters in Scranton, Pa., discussed the history of the community in her Scranton office with author on October 19, 1996.

36   Of the 261 religious communities: Wittberg, *The Rise and Decline of Catholic Religious Orders,* p. 84.

37   Professor Margaret Susan Thompson: Professor Thompson reflected on the role of nuns in American Catholicism in an interview with the author at the Women's Ordination Conference in McClean, Va., November 11, 1996.

38   Sister Patricia Curran's study: Patricia Curran, *Grace Before Meals* (Urbana: University of Illinois Press, 1989), p. 135.

CHAPTER THREE
IMPROVING BY DEGREES

42   In her 1994 essay: Mary Lea Schneider, "Educating an Elite: Sister Formation, Higher Education and Images of Women." In *A Leaf from the Great Tree of God: Essays in Honour of Ritamary Bradley,* ed. Margot H. King, pp. 23–37 (Toronto: Peregrina Publishing House, 1994).

43   Sister Penet, a college professor at Marygrove College: Marjorie Noterman Beane, *From Framework to Freedom* (Lanham, Md.: University Press of America, 1993), p. 29.

44   Sister Ritamary Bradley remembered: Ibid., p. 37.

45   "Sisters are afraid": Ibid., p. 21.

46   "A high quality of spiritual and intellectual reading": Ibid., p. 42.

47   Sister Penet, a woman of exacting standards: Ibid., p. 41.

48   A drumbeat for the educational upgrading: Bertrande Myers, *The Education of Sisters* (New York: Sheed & Ward, 1941).

48   Before that friction arose: M. Madeleva, "The Education of Our Young Religious Teachers," *National Catholic Educational Association Bulletin, Proceedings and Addresses, Forty-Fifth Annual Meeting*, pp. 253–56 (Philadelphia, April 20, 1949).

52   The committee soon sent questionnaires: Beane, *From Framework to Freedom*, pp. 12–20.

55   Looking back at her decade at the helm: Ritamary Bradley, "A Survey of a Decade Past," *Sister Formation Bulletin* 10, no. 4 (1964): 32–36.

55   None proved more provocative: Annette Walters, "The Local Superior as Spiritual Leader," *Sister Formation Bulletin* 9, no. 3 (1963): 53–60.

58   Sister Bradley recalled: The author spoke with Sister Bradley about her leadership in the Sister Formation movement, including her meeting with Cardinal McIntyre, at her home in Davenport, Iowa, in late October 1995.

58   a small, broad-based group called the Better World Movement: CLCW 23/09, UNDA.

59   "It seems to me": Beane, *From Framework to Freedom*, p. 118.

60   Sister Walters, who had been elected executive director: Ibid., p. 126.

60   wrote to the Sacred Congregation of Religious in 1962: Beane, *From Framework to Freedom* pp. 121–22; from Sister Walters's letter to the Reverend Elio Gambini, September 12, 1962, Sister Formation Conference Archives, Milwaukee, Wisc.

60   Sister Bradley remembered that night in Cincinnati: From Sister Bradley interviews with author, October 1995.

63   In the aftermath of the move: Memo by the Reverend Luis Dolan regarding his telephone conversation with Bishop Philip Hannan, March 6, 1994. Copy provided by Sister Ritamary Bradley.

65   The impact of Sister Formation: Beane, *From Framework to Freedom*, p. 131.

65   Sister Schneider of Cardinal Stritch College: Karen M. Kennelly, "Women Religious, the Intellectual Life, and Anti-Intellectualism" in *Women Religious and the Intellectual Life: The North American Achievement*, ed. Bridget Puzon (San Francisco: International Scholars Publications, 1996), p. 63.

66   But by another token: Beane, *From Framework to Freedom*, p. 131.

CHAPTER FOUR
VATICAN II:
UNFORESEEN CONSEQUENCES

69   Cardinal Suenens wrote: Leon Joseph Cardinal Suenens, *The Nun in the World* (Westminster, Md.: Newman Press, 1963), pp. 33, 45, 49.

79   Those sisters attending Vatican II: Carmel McEnroy, *Guests in Their Own House: The Women of Vatican II* (New York: Crossroad, 1996), p. 195.

80   In a July 1993 issue of the *Catholic Historical Review:* Angelyn Dries, "Living in Ambiguity," *Catholic Historical Review* 79, no. 3 (1993): 482–86.

81   The need for the Church: Sister Mary Luke Tobin interview by author in her home in Denver, August 11–12, 1995.

81   The challenge, the pope said: "Pope John's Opening Speech to the Council," in *The Documents of Vatican II,* ed. Walter M. Abbott, S.J. (New York: The America Press, 1966), pp. 714–15.

CHAPTER FIVE
OLD HABITS SOMETIMES DIE HARD

84   The only restriction: Ann Patrick Ware, ed., *Midwives of the Future: American Sisters Tell Their Story* (Kansas City: Leaven Press, 1985), p. 190.

84   Aware of the significance of that moment: M. Charles McGrath, *Yes Heard Round the World: A History of the Ursuline Sisters of Paola, Kansas, 1895–1975* (Paola, Kans.: Ursuline Sisters, [1975]), p. 253.

85   "When they saw the habit": Ibid., p. 257.

86   Mother McGrath, the last superior: Ibid., p. 259.

89   Only six months after the Vatican Council: Mary Bonaventure, "The Religious Habit," *Review for Religious* 25, no. 3 (1966): 505.

90   The reviews from onlookers: Mary Wilma, "Sisters and Change," *Review for Religious* 23, no. 2 (1964): 185–96.

94   A year before Vatican II fired up the debate: M. Claudelle Miller, "Attitudes Toward Religious Garb," *Review for Religious* 25, no. 3 (1966): 438–46.

95   Her first shock: McGrath, *Yes Heard Round the World*, p. 257.

96   The group of Sisters of Charity: Seven Sisters of Charity of Convent Station were interviewed by the author, at Convent Station, N.J., in October 1996.

98   None was more articulate: Mother Vincent Marie Finnegan, superior of the Carmelite monastery, interview by author in Alhambra, Calif., July 1995.

CHAPTER SIX
BREAKING THE CONVENT MOLD

103   The story of one group of Benedictines: For a complete account see the volume by Joan Chittister, O.S.B., et al. *Climb Along the Cutting Edge: An Analysis of Change in Religious Life* (New York: Paulist Press, 1977).

104 All of this was achieved: Ibid., p. 59.

105 Asked to describe religious life: Ibid., p. 205

108 The awareness buoyed them: Benedictine 1967 opinion survey. Ibid., pp. 131–44.

109 But the path ahead was rocky: Ibid., p. 241.

110 Sisters of St. Joseph of Springfield, Massachusetts: Sisters Maxyne Schneider and Mary Hennon interview by author at their residence in Gardner, Mass., June 1995.

114 "The cardinal was always very critical of us": Anita Caspary of the Immaculate Heart Community of Los Angeles, phone interview by author, August 1995.

CHAPTER SEVEN
STORMING THE EXITS

119 Sister Mary Jeremy Daigler: Sister Daigler interview by author near College of Notre Dame in Maryland, December 1998.

119 Sister Mary Margaret Funk: Sister Funk interview by author during a visit to the Beech Grove Benedictine Monastery in Indianapolis, February 28–March 3, 1995.

120 For Sister Patricia Lynch: Sister Lynch phone interview by author, September 1998.

120 When religious superiors were asked in 1966: Marie Augusta Neal, *Catholic Sisters in Transition* (Wilmington, Del.: Michael Glazier, 1984), pp. 21–24.

122 Their report went to the 1971 meeting: "Points Submitted by Various Bishops for the Consideration of the CMSW. Presented to the Representatives of the CMSW by the NCCB [National Conference of Catholic Bishops] Liaison Committee, April 24, 1971, in Detroit": CLCW 6/18, UNDA.

123 Sister Jeanne Knoerle: Sister Knoerle interview by author at the Sisters of Providence center in St. Mary-of-the-Woods, Ind., November 1994.

126 The survey allowed sisters to hear one another: Sister Marie Augusta Neal interview by author at her home in Boston, October 1995.

129 Lillanna Kopp, an accomplished sociologist: Ann Patrick Ware, ed., *Midwives of the Future: American Sisters Tell Their Story* (Kansas City: Leaven Press, 1985), p. 212.

130 Sister Margaret Brennan, a leading intellectual: Sister Brennan interview by author at the Immaculate Heart of Mary mother house, Monroe, Mich., August 1995.

132 Sometimes the mending took a long time: Sister Carita interview by author, at Sisters of Charity center in Convent Station, N.J., February 1999.

CHAPTER EIGHT
SEEKING JUSTICE

137   Sister Mary Luke Tobin, the esteemed: Sister Tobin interview by author at the Sisters of Loretto home in Denver, Colo., August 1995.

138   This was shockingly true: Dorothy A. Vidulich, *Peace Pays a Price: A Study of Margaret Anna Cusack, the Nun of Kenmore*, rev. ed. (Washington, D.C.: Sisters of St. Joseph of Peace, 1990).

139   In her 1874 book, *Women's Work*: quoted in Ibid., p. 15.

139   During her exile as a virtual nonperson: Ann Patrick Ware, ed., *Midwives of the Future: American Sisters Tell Their Story* (Kansas City: Leaven Press, 1985), p. 163.

140   By 1974, they had made peace: Sister Dorothy Vidulich phone interview by author at her office in Washington, D.C., December 1999.

142   Ten years after its founding: Nancy Sylvester, "Looking Back, Looking Forward," *Network* 20, no. 3 (1992): 11–12.

146   In her book based on the second survey: Marie Augusta Neal, *Catholic Sisters in Transition: From the 1960s to the 1980s* (Wilmington, Del.: Michael Glazier, 1984), p. 27.

147   The fact that "some clergy and religious": Ibid., p. 72.

148   She recalled the experience two decades later: Sister Margaret Brennan interview by author at the Immaculate Heart of Mary mother house, Monroe, Mich., August 1995.

149   A decade before, she had helped write: Sister Jeanne Knoerle, "Reflections on a Variety of Things . . . But Mostly on Community" (unpublished paper circulated among members of Sisters of Providence, St. Mary-of-the-Woods, Ind., 1984), pp. 19–20.

150   It was a moment of transformation: Sister Florence Deacon e-mail to author, March 28, 1996.

151   For every action, there was a reaction: Lora Ann Quinonez and Mary Daniel Turner, *The Transformation of American Sisters* (Philadelphia: Temple University Press, 1992), p. 131.

CHAPTER NINE
SISTER SISTERHOOD

152   The total of doctorates awarded to sisters: Bridget Puzon, ed., *Women Religious and the Intellectual Life: The North American Achievement* (San Francisco: International Scholars Publications, 1996), p. 37.

154   painted the aftermath in stark, progressive terms: Lillianna Kopp phone interview by author, December 1998.

155   Some nuns recoiled: Sister Miriam Ukeritis interview by author at DePaul University, Chicago, October 1995.

156   Sister Theresa Kane, the Sister of Mercy: Sister Kane phone interview by author at her Sister of Mercy residence in upstate New York, October 1995.

157   "I'm not sure you can be a Christian and an ideologue": Sister Ellen Joyce interview by author at the Sister of Charity mother house, Convent Station, N.J., September 1995.

157   Mother Finnegan was a spirited: Mother Vincent Marie Finnegan interview by author at the Carmelite monastery in Alhambra, Calif., July 1995.

159   To cite Cardinal Josef Ratzinger: Patricia Wittberg, *The Rise and Fall of Catholic Religious Orders: A Social Movement Perspective* (Albany: State University of New York Press, 1994), p. 264.

159   In her landmark 1991 book: Sandra Schneiders, *Beyond Patching: Faith and Feminism in the Catholic Church* (New York: Paulist Press, 1991), pp. 1–31.

162   In the spring issue: Mary E. Hunt and Frances Kissling, "The *New York Times* Ad: A Case Study in Religious Feminism," *The Journal of Feminist Studies in Religion* 3, no. 1 (1987): 115–27.

163   Most advocates of ordination: Dr. Margaret Susan Thompson, "Pressures by and on a Marginal Group—Or, Are Catholic Feminists Either" (paper delivered at the meeting of the American Political Science Association, Washington, D.C., 1986), p. 8.

164   She blasted clericalism: Dr. Rosemary Radford Reuther as quoted in Ibid., p. 9.

165   The air of rebelliousness: Marie Augusta Neal, "Pathology of the Men's Church," *Concilium* vol. 15, no. 4 (1980): 53–62.

165   Therefore, a year after the Detroit uprising: Pope Paul VI, *Inter Insignores: A Declaration on the Question of Admission of Women to the Ministerial Priesthood* (October 15, 1976). Section 2, "The Attitude of Christ," contains the Pontifical Biblical Commission's conclusion that the Bible cannot by itself settle the ordination issue: "questions that the Word of God brings before us go beyond the obvious. In order to reach the ultimate meaning of the mission of Jesus, a purely historical exegesis of the texts cannot suffice."

166   Rome had reason to worry: Sister Elizabeth Johnson, interview by author at Fordham University, Bronx, N.Y., September 1995.

168   "I never really knew it was all boys": Sister Elizabeth Johnson phone interview by author, October 1995.

168   As the drama has usually played out: Sister Mary Luke Tobin, interview by author at the Sister of Loretto mother house, Denver, Colo., August 1995.

169   the explanation was subtle but sure: Dr. Mary Jo Weaver, *New Catholic Women: A Contemporary Challenge to Traditional Religious Authority* (New York: Harper & Row, 1985), p. 133.

170   One bone of contention: Sister Joyce Weller, D.C., interview by author at the Daughters of Charity mother house in Los Altos, Calif., September 1995.

171   The story begins when Sister Kane: Sister Theresa Kane, Sister of Mercy, recounted the process of addressing Pope John Paul II during a telephone interview with the author, October 1995.

CHAPTER TEN
BACKLASH

182   A leading theologian of the time: Gregory Baum, *The St. Louis Review*, November 27, 1970, p. 7.

182   The Vatican quickly took note: Cardinal Antoniutti's speech, "The Exercise of Authority," to the 14th Assembly of the Italian Conference of Major Superiors of Women, May 15, 1966: CLCW 1/21, UNDA.

183   Mary Jo Leddy, whose book: Mary Jo Leddy, "Leadership for Tranformation," videotape (1990; LCWR annual meeting, Spokane, Wa.).

185   Looking back, Sister Alberta Dietrich: Sister Alberta Dietrich interview by author at Queen of Angels monastery in Mt. Angel, Ore., December 1999.

186   "The fundamental complaint": Archbishop Luigi Raimondi to Mother Mary Omer, April 9, 1968: CLCW 1/8, UNDA.

187   The apostolic delegate to the United States: The Most Reverend Luigi Raimondi to Sister Thomas Aquinas Carroll, March 2, 1972: CLCW 8/1, UNDA.

187   Faced with the sisters' persistence: For more background on the debate over adoption of the word "leadership," see letter from Archbishop Luigi Raimondi to Sister Elizabeth Carroll, April 14, 1972: CLCW 1/8, UNDA.

188   Consortium leaders denounced the CMSW's new bylaws: Mother Claudia Honsberger to Sister Angelita Myerscough, July 8, 1971: CLCW 10/21, UNDA.

188   assistance was forthcoming. "We began": Mother Vincent Marie Finnegan interview by author at the Carmelite monastery in Alhambra, Calif., July 1995.

189   Instead, by example, the bishops: minutes of the meeting of the Bishops' Liaison Committee and CMSW Committee for Liaison with the Bishops, April 25, 1971: CLCW 6/18, UNDA.

192   But beyond the specifics, her dismay: Sister Elizabeth Carroll to Archbishop Luigi Raimondi, March 2, 1972: CLCW 8/1, UNDA.

193   At a joint meeting with Sacred Congregation for Religious: Sister Mary Daniel Turner report to LCWR executive committee, November 15, 1973: CLCW 6/20–21, UNDA.

194   The other contributor to the rift: The Reverend Thomas Dubay, "Religious Life: The Real Polarity," *Review for Religious* 32, no. 3 (1973): 578–86.

196   The extent to which attitudes had changed: LCWR, Patterns in Authority and Obedience (Washington, D.C.: LCWR, 1974), pp. 3, 4, 5.

197   Archbishop Paul Augustine Mayer: minutes of LCWR board meeting, August 23, 1975: CLCW 2/17, UNDA.

199   Archbishop James Whelan: memo to provincials of religious communities, November 7, 1984: CLCW 85/10, UNDA.

199   That the outcome, on the whole: "Religious Life and the Decline of Vocations," *Origins* 16, no. 25 (1986): 467, 469.

201   The effort continues: Sister Sharon Holland interview by author at LCWR assembly, Anaheim, Calif., August 1996.

202   The apostolic pro-nuncio: record of Archbishop Pio Laghi's ultimatum to Sister Theresa Kane, March 23, 1983: CLCW 45/52, UNDA.

CHAPTER ELEVEN
RETIREMENT WOES

205   Far in advance of the 1986 bombshell: John J. Fialka, "Sisters in Need: U.S. Nuns Face Crisis as More Grow Older with Meager Benefits," *Wall Street Journal*, May 19, 1986, front page.

206   Sister Alice Lubin: Sister Lubin interview by author at the Sisters of Charity mother house at Convent Station, N.J., September 1996.

207   The concreteness of the stipend debate: Sister Carol Wester phone interview by author, September 1995.

207   "It was so hard for the Church when": Rita Hofbauer interview by author in the office of Support Our Aging Religious in Washington, D.C., July 1995.

209   Further, Social Security checks: Records and statistics relevant to obtaining Social Security benefits for nuns, CLCW 9/18–20, UNDA.

211   "Response from the bishops' was mixed": Hofbauer interview, July 1996.

213   One sister, who was the sole member: Wester interview, September 1995.

214   The Ursulines had never sought outside funds: Sister Pat Lynch phone interview by author, September 1998.

215   While the Ursulines took a new tack: Sister Carol Quinn interview by author at Mont Marie, mother house of the Sisters of St. Joseph of Springfield, Mass., June 1995.

CHAPTER TWELVE
WILL SISTERS SURVIVE?

218   Occasionally, a voice would warn them: The Reverend John C. Haughey's address ("Where Has Our Search Led Us?") to the Assembly of the LCWR, February 23–25, 1970, St. Louis, Missouri: CLCW, ALCW, 1970, C3290, UNDA.

219   Sister Julie had entered the Daughters of Charity: Sister Julie interview by author at the Daughters of Charity mother house in Los Altos, Calif., September 1995.

220   A researcher's comments echoed that sentiment: Sister Miriam Ukeritis, co-author of the study of religious orders, interview by author at DePaul University, Chicago, October 1995.

220   At a 1993 FADICA-sponsored conference: Sister Miriam Ukeritis's analysis is included in proceedings of a national FADICA symposium, "The Future of Religious Life," held in Palm Beach, Florida, January 29–30, 1993 (Washington, D.C.: FADICA, 1993, pp. 18–26).

221   In their joint study of future possibilities: Miriam Ukeritis and David Nygren, "Future of Religious Orders in the United States," *Origins* 22, no. 15 (1992), pp. 257–72.

223   One of the clearest advocates: The Reverend Albert Diianni, contributor, "Religious Life 30 Years Later: Is This What Vatican II Intended?" (Jesuit Center for Spiritual Growth, Wernersville, Pa., October 26–29, 1995).

224   Others who had contributed: Mary Jo Leddy, *Reweaving Religious Life: Beyond the Liberal Model* (Mystic, Conn.: Twenty-Third Publications, 1990), pp. 33–39.

224   The outstanding sociologist of religious orders: Sister Patricia Wittberg interview by author in Indianapolis, March 1995.

225   It was a case of do or die: Mother Vincent Marie Finnegan interview by author at the Carmelite monastery in Alhambra, Calif., July 1995.

226   "Religious life as we've known it": from the address of Sister Carol Wester to the plenary session of the Assembly of the LCWR, Anaheim, Calif., August 24, 1995.

227   Perhaps the most miraculous aspect: Sister Sandra Schneiders interview by author at the Immaculate Heart of Mary mother house, Monroe, Mich., August 1995.

Selected Bibliography

Arbuckle, Gerald A. *Out of Chaos: Refounding Religious Congregations*. New York: Paulist Press, 2000.

Beane, Marjorie Noterman. *From Framework to Freedom*. Lanham, Md.: University Press of America, 1993.

Chittister, Joan, et al. *Climb Along the Cutting Edge: An Analysis of Change in Religious Life*. New York: Paulist Press, 1977.

Chittister, Joan. *The Fire in These Ashes: A Spirituality of Contemporary Religious Life*. Kansas City: Sheed and Ward, 1995.

Curran, Patricia. *Grace Before Meals*. Urbana: University of Illinois Press, 1989.

Del Rey, Maria. *Bernie Becomes a Nun*. New York: Farrar, 1956.

Dolan, Jay P. *The American Catholic Experience: A History from Colonial Times to the Present*. Notre Dame, Ind.: University of Notre Dame Press, 1978.

Ebaugh, Helen R. *Women in the Vanishing Cloister: Organizational Decline in Catholic Religious Orders in the United States*. New Brunswick, N.J.: Rutgers University Press, 1993.

Ferraro, Barbara, and Patricia Hussey. *No Turning Back: Two Nuns' Battle with the Vatican over Women's Right to Choose*. New York: Poseidon Press, 1990.

Fialka, John. *Sisters: Catholic Nuns and the Making of America*. New York: St. Martin's Press, 1993.

Foley, Nadine, ed. *Claiming Our Truth: Reflections on Identity as U.S. Catholic Women Religious*. Washington, D.C.: Leadership Conference of Women Religious, 1988.

Herberg, Will. *Protestant, Catholic, Jew*. Chicago: University of Chicago Press, 1955, 1960, 1983.

Johnson, Elizabeth A. *She Who Is: The Mystery of God in Feminist Theological Discourse.* New York: Crossroad, 1992.

King, Margot H., ed. *A Leaf from the Great Tree of God: Essays in Honour of Ritamary Bradley.* Toronto: Peregrina Publishing Company, 1994.

Leddy, Mary Jo. *Reweaving Religious Life: Beyond the Liberal Model.* Mystic, Conn.: Twenty-Third Publications, 1990.

Lerner, Gerda. *The Creation of Feminist Consciousness.* New York: Oxford University Press, 1993.

McEnroy, Carmel. *Guests in Their Own House: The Women of Vatican II.* New York: Crossroad, 1996.

McGrath, M. Charles. *The Yes Heard Round the World: A History of the Ursuline Sisters of Paola, Kansas, 1895–1975.* Paola, Kansas: Ursuline Sisters, 1975.

McNamara, Jo Ann. *Sisters in Arms: Catholic Nuns Through Two Millennia.* Cambridge, Mass.: Harvard University Press, 1996.

Myers, Bertrande. *The Education of Sisters.* New York: Sheed and Ward, 1941.

Neal, Marie Augusta. *Catholic Sisters in Transition: From the 1960s to the 1980s.* Wilmington, Del.: Michael Glazier, 1984.

———. *From Nuns to Sisters: An Expanding Vocation.* Mystic, Conn.: Twenty-Third Publications, 1990.

———. "The Sisters' Survey, 1980: A Report." *Probe* 10 no. 5 (1981): 1–7.

Nygren, David, and Miriam Ukeritis. *The Future of Religious Orders in the United States: Transformation and Commitment.* Westport, Conn.: Praeger, 1993.

Oates, Mary J. *The Catholic Philanthropic Tradition in America.* Bloomington: Indiana University Press, 1995.

Puzon, Bridget, ed. *Women Religious and the Intellectual Life: The North American Achievement.* San Francisco: International Scholars Publications, 1996.

Quinonez, Lora Ann, and Mary Daniel Turner. *The Transformation of American Sisters.* Philadelphia: Temple University Press, 1992.

Reuther, Rosemary Radford. *Women-Church: Theology and Practice.* San Francisco: Harper & Row, 1985.

Schneiders, Sandra Marie. *Beyond Patching: Faith and Feminism in the Catholic Church.* New York: Paulist Press, 1991.

———. *New Wineskins: Re-imagining Religious Life Today.* New York: Paulist Press, 1986.

Suenens, Cardinal Leon Joseph. *The Nun in the World.* Westminster, Md.: The Newman Press, 1963.

Thompson, Margaret Susan. "Pressures by and on a Marginal Group—Or, Are Catholic Feminists Either?" A paper delivered at the meeting of the American Political Science Association, Washington, D.C., 1986.

Vidulich, Dorothy A. *Peace Pays a Price: A Study of Margaret Anna Cusick, the Nun of Kenmore*. Washington, D.C.: Sisters of St. Joseph of Peace, 1990.

Ware, Ann Patrick, ed. *Midwives of the Future: American Sisters Tell Their Story*. Kansas City: Leaven Press, 1985.

Weaver, Mary Jo. *New Catholic Women: A Contemporary Challenge to Traditional Religious Authority*. New York: Harper & Row, 1985.

Wittberg, Patricia. *Creating a Future for Religious Life: A Sociological Perspective*. New York: Paulist Press, 1991.

————. *The Rise and Fall of Catholic Religious Orders: A Social Movement Perspective*. Albany: State University of New York Press, 1994.

Index